New England

BED & BREAKFAST

Cookbook

Featuring Recipes from the
finest B&Bs in Connecticut,
New Hampshire, Maine,
Vermont, Massachusetts, and
Rhode Island

T0306496

trails books

AN IMPRINT OF BOWER HOUSE

DENVER

Composition: D. Kari Luraas
Editor: Linda Doyle
Assistant Editor: Loren Szenina

Front cover photos: The Inn at Stockbridge; fruit by Byron Cain of Brewster
by the Sea B&B and Captain Freeman Inn
Back cover photos: by Byron Cain of Brewster by the Sea B&B and
Captain Freeman Inn

The Bed & Breakfast Cookbook Series was originated by Carol Faino and Doreen Hazledine of Peppermint Press in Denver, CO in 1999.

Library of Congress Cataloging-in-Publication Data Available Upon Request

ISBN 978-1-889593-31-9

10 9 8 7 6 5 4 3 2

Contents

U.S. Measurement Equivalents

pinch/dash	$1/16$ teaspoon
½ teaspoon	30 drops
1 teaspoon	$1/3$ tablespoon
3 teaspoons	1 tablespoon
½ tablespoon	1½ teaspoons
1 tablespoon	3 teaspoons; ½ fluid ounce
2 tablespoons	$1/8$ cup; 1 fluid ounce
3 tablespoons	1½ fluid ounces; 1 jigger
jigger	1½ fluid ounces; 3 tablespoons
4 tablespoons	¼ cup; 2 fluid ounces
$5^1/3$ tablespoons	$1/3$ cup; 5 tablespoons + 1 teaspoon
8 tablespoons	½ cup; 4 fluid ounces
$10^2/3$ tablespoons	$2/3$ cup; 10 tablespoons + 2 teaspoons
12 tablespoons	¾ cup; 6 fluid ounces
16 tablespoons	1 cup; 8 fluid ounces; ½ pint
$1/8$ cup	2 tablespoons; 1 fluid ounce
¼ cup	4 tablespoons; 2 fluid ounces
$1/3$ cup	5 tablespoons + 1 teaspoon
$3/8$ cup	¼ cup + 2 tablespoons
½ cup	8 tablespoons; 4 fluid ounces
$2/3$ cup	10 tablespoons + 2 teaspoons
$5/8$ cup	½ cup + 2 tablespoons
¾ cup	12 tablespoons; 6 fluid ounces
$7/8$ cup	¾ cup + 2 tablespoons
1 cup	16 tablespoons; ½ pint; 8 fluid ounces
2 cups	1 pint; 16 fluid ounces
3 cups	1½ pints; 24 fluid ounces
4 cups	1 quart; 32 fluid ounces
8 cups	2 quarts; 64 fluid ounces
1 pint	2 cups; 16 fluid ounces
2 pints	1 quart; 32 fluid ounces
1 quart	2 pints; 4 cups; 32 fluid ounces
4 quarts	1 gallon; 8 pints
1 gallon	4 quarts; 8 pints; 16 cups; 128 fluid ounces
8 quarts	1 peck
4 pecks	1 bushel

The Cuisine of New England

The early cuisine of the New England states—Maine, Vermont, New Hampshire, Massachusetts, Connecticut, and Rhode Island—mirrored the cuisine of the mother country, England. The earliest transplants from the old world, the Puritans, brought with them baked pies and biscuits, and boiled vegetables and meats. The first Native Americans introduced the early settlers to parsley and sage, pumpkins and corn, and the process of frying.

Prominent characteristic foodstuffs native to New England are maple syrup, cranberries, blueberries, and diary products. New Hampshire and Vermont vie for first place in the maple syrup category; while Massachusetts ranks as the second largest U.S. commercial producer of cranberries. Vermont's Ben and Jerry's ice cream is an American icon, and the blueberries of Maine inspired Robert McCloskey to write the 1949 classic Caldecott Honor winner, *Blueberries for Sal.* The extensive dairy farming operations produce cheeses to rival even the premier cheeses of Wisconsin.

The present day cuisine of New England is characterized by an extensive use of seafood, with its historical reliance on its seaports and fishing industry. Maine lobster and Massachusetts's soft-shell blue crab are staples in the Northeast, and are served in fine restaurants throughout the U.S.

The recipes in this book will give you an opportunity to put some of these wonderful foods on your table in a new and creative way.

Listing of Inns by State

Connecticut

1	An Innkeeper's Place	Stafford Springs
2	Butternut Farm	Glastonbury
3	Chimney Crest Manor	Bristol
4	Deacon Timothy Pratt B&B	Old Saybrook
5	Manor House	Norfolk
6	Roger Sherman Inn	New Canaan
7	Scranton Seahorse Inn	Madison
8	Thimble Islands B&B	Thimble Islands
9	Westbrook Inn B&B	Westbrook

Rhode Island

10	Francis Malbone House	Newport
11	Marshall Slocum Inn	Newport
12	Shelter Harbor Inn	Westerley

Massachusetts

13	Addison Choate Inn	Rockport
14	Beach Plum Inn & Restaurant	Menemsha
15	Birchwood Inn	Lenox
16	Brewster by the Sea	Brewster
17	Brook Farm Inn	Lenox
18	Captain Freeman Inn	Brewster
19	Chatham Gables Inn	Chatham
20	Gateways Inn	Lenox
21	Golden Slipper	Boston
22	Harborside House	Marblehead
23	Honeysuckle Hill Inn	West Barnstable
24	Inn at Cape Cod	Yarmouth Port
25	Inn at Stockbridge	Stockbridge
26	Inn on Cove Hill	Rockport
27	Morrison House B&B	Somerville
28	One Centre Street Inn B&B	Yarmouth Port
29	Parsonage Inn B&B	East Orleans
30	Seagull Inn B&B	Marblehead
31	Sherburne Inn	Nantucket
32	The Wauwinet	Nantucket
33	Yankee Clipper Inn	Rockport

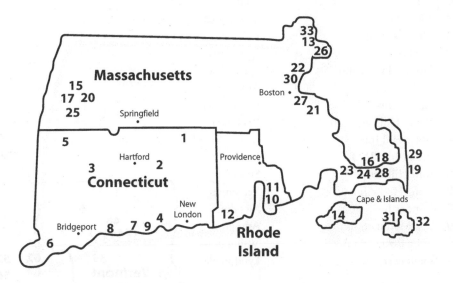

Massachusetts

15

17 20

25

Springfield

5 1

Hartford

3 2

Connecticut

Bridgeport 8 7 9 4

6

New
London

12

33

13

26

22

30

Boston

27

21

Providence

11

10

**Rhode
Island**

16 18

23 24 28

Cape & Islands

14

29

19

31 32

Listing of Inns by State

Vermont

34	Brass Lantern Inn B&B	Stowe
35	Casa Bella Inn & Restaurant	Pittsfield
36	Combes Family Inn B&B	Ludlow
37	Deer Brook Inn	Woodstock
38	Echo Lake Inn	Ludlow
39	Grünberg Haus	Waterbury
40	Hartness House Inn	Springfield
41	Hill Farm Inn	Arlington
42	Inn at Ormsby Hill	Manchester Cer
43	Liberty Hill Farm Inn	Rochester
44	Rabbit Hill Inn	Lower Waterfor
45	Sinclair Inn B&B	Jericho
46	Stone Hill Inn	Stowe
47	Strong House Inn	Vergennes
48	Vermont Inn	Mendon
49	West Mountain Inn	Arlington
50	White Rocks Inn B&B	Wallingford
51	Wildflower Inn	Lyndonville

New Hampshire

52	1785 Inn & Restaurant	North Conway
53	Adair Country Inn & Restaurant	Bethlehem
54	Benjamin Prescott Inn	Jaffrey
55	Colby Hill Inn	Henniker
56	Inn at Crystal Lake	Eaton Center
57	Inn on Golden Pond	Holderness
58	Lake House at Ferry Point	Sanbornton
59	Lazy Dog Inn	Chocorua
60	Mt. Washington B&B	Shelburne
61	Rosewood Country Inn	Bradford
62	Sugar Hill Inn	Sugar Hill
63	Sunset Hill House	Sugar Hill

Maine

64	1802 House B&B	Kennebunkport
65	Bear Mountain Inn	Waterford
66	Blue Harbor House	Camden

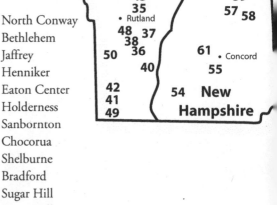

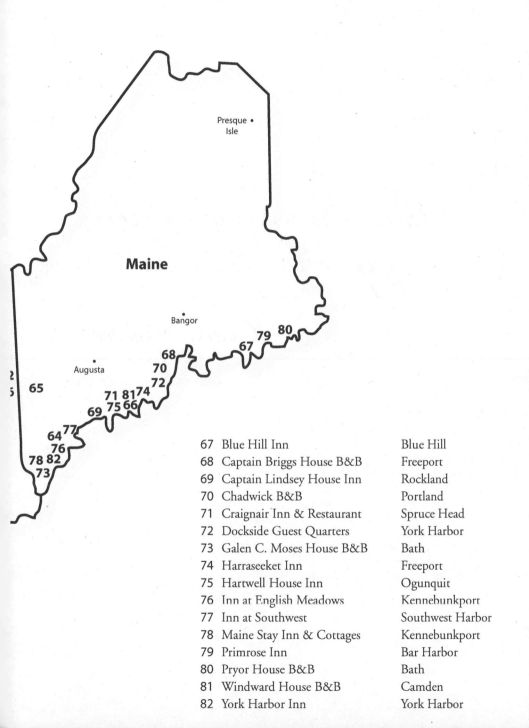

67	Blue Hill Inn	Blue Hill
68	Captain Briggs House B&B	Freeport
69	Captain Lindsey House Inn	Rockland
70	Chadwick B&B	Portland
71	Craignair Inn & Restaurant	Spruce Head
72	Dockside Guest Quarters	York Harbor
73	Galen C. Moses House B&B	Bath
74	Harraseeket Inn	Freeport
75	Hartwell House Inn	Ogunquit
76	Inn at English Meadows	Kennebunkport
77	Inn at Southwest	Southwest Harbor
78	Maine Stay Inn & Cottages	Kennebunkport
79	Primrose Inn	Bar Harbor
80	Pryor House B&B	Bath
81	Windward House B&B	Camden
82	York Harbor Inn	York Harbor

"There is hardship in everything except eating pancakes."

— Charles Spurgeon

Connecticut and Rhode Island B&Bs

AND THEIR SIGNATURE RECIPES

AN INNKEEPER'S PLACE

INNKEEPERS	Danele & Christopher Rhoads
ADDRESS	111 Stafford Street, Stafford Springs, CT 06076
TELEPHONE	860-481-2181
CONTACT	innkeepersplace@gmail.com | www.innkeepersplace.com
FEATURES	2 Rooms, 1 Suite; Private and shared bath | Children welcome | Pets: call ahead

Full of American history, this home was built in 1778 and holds the history of Stafford Springs' earlier years. From the wide plank floors, along with hand-carved molding and chair rails, to the barreled ceilings and mullion window, the history of the place is still evident today.

Stafford is a quiet little place with all the makings of New England at its best. There are antique shops, country stores, a wonderful Historical Society, and the best of *pure* country settings. Neighbors are right out of a Norman Rockwell portrait and everyone knows each other. Friends from town often stop by the inn and visit with the innkeepers and guests.

An Innkeeper's Place isn't your norm for a B&B. You will find an extra effort goes into making this B&B feel like it is a home-away-from-home. Guests will enter as strangers and leave as friends.

"We are a traditional European B&B in that we live in and raise our three children in our nearly 250-year-old home. Our children are well behaved (as children go). They are very friendly and when in the common areas of our home you will likely meet them. They have separate quarters, of course, but you may encounter them as you relax on the deck, walk in the yard or have a seated breakfast. Since everyone has a different tolerance for children, we do want our guests to know that we accept children as guests."—Innkeepers

Blueberry Cottage Cheese Pancakes

Yield: 18 pancakes (4″)

- 1¼ cups all-purpose flour
- ⅓ cup sugar
- 1 tsp baking soda
- ½ tsp salt
- 1 cup sour cream
- 1 cup cottage cheese
- 2 eggs
- 1 tsp vanilla
- 2 cups blueberries
- butter or cooking spray for griddle
- berries, to garnish

In a medium bowl, whisk together flour, sugar, baking soda, and salt. In a large bowl, stir together sour cream, cottage cheese, eggs and vanilla. Add flour mixture, stir until just combined. Gently stir in blueberries.

Heat a griddle over medium heat. Butter griddle lightly. Spoon level ¼ cup batter onto griddle for each pancake. Cook until lightly brown and bubbles begin to form, 3–4 minutes. Turn and cook other side. Keep in warm oven on baking sheet until ready to serve. Garnish with berries and citrus wedges.

Tip: Use only Bradway Sugar House Maple Syrup for best quality and taste.

BUTTERNUT FARM

INNKEEPER	Don Reid
ADDRESS	1654 Main Street, Glastonbury, CT 06033
TELEPHONE	860-633-7197 | 860-659-1758 fax
CONTACT	www.butternutfarmbandb.com
FEATURES	3 Rooms, 2 Suites; Private baths | Children: inquire | Pets not allowed

Overnight accommodations are in rooms furnished in keeping with the Colonial period. The only modern touches are the 20th-century bathrooms, decorated in Colonial style. Each room includes a private bath, wireless Internet, telephone, alarm clock radio, and complimentary sherry and chocolates. Two parlors, a "keeping room," and a sitting room are available for guests. A full breakfast with fresh eggs, milk, cheese, and homemade jams is served in the original dining room or in the intimate breakfast room.

Modest as Don Reid is about his wealth of cooking talents, he is noted for some of his popular New England dishes. He has been featured in *Yankee Magazine*, and has created several original recipes for Campbell's Soup and Jones Sausages.

> *"Wine, dine or slumber, Butternut Farm is a place out of time."*
> —The Glastonbury Citizen

> *"Beyond the secret garden is the entrance to the suite in the barn. These rooms are reserved for Reid's very special guests. A canopy bed commands a view of the secret garden and there is a private kitchen and bath. It's hard to imagine there is a working barn on the other side of the wall.*—The Hartford Monthly

Veal Collops* in Mushroom and Marsala Sauce

Yield: 4 servings

1½ lbs. veal stew pieces, trimmed and flattened
2 Tbsp olive oil, divided
2 Tbsp butter, divided
1 large onion, quartered lengthwise and thinly sliced
½ lb. mushrooms, sliced (mushrooms are optional)
1 can Campbell's Condensed Cream of Mushroom Soup
²/₃ cup Marsala
1 Tbsp paprika
¹/₈ tsp salt
½ tsp freshly ground black pepper
1 tsp thyme

Brown half the veal in a large heavy pan over high heat, using half of the oil and butter. Stir and turn constantly, cooking only enough to sear the meat. Transfer to a large bowl, and repeat with remaining veal; adding oil and butter as needed. Remove meat. In the same pan, sauté sliced onion over medium heat until well softened. Add optional mushrooms. Continue cooking for several minutes until liquid is mostly evaporated.

In a small bowl, blend the mushroom soup with Marsala, paprika, salt, pepper, and thyme. Stir until smooth. Add veal to cooked onions and pour sauce over all. Bring to a simmer, stirring to mix evenly. Cover pan loosely to permit slow evaporation. Turn heat down to very low and let mixture bubble gently for at least an hour, turning collops once or twice. Veal should be tender and the liquid reduced to a finished sauce. Serve with fluffy white rice and a green vegetable.

Collop means a small slice or piece of something—especially of meat. It is a very old word first used in the 14ᵗʰ century.

CHIMNEY CREST MANOR

INNKEEPERS	Cynthia and Dante Cimadamore
ADDRESS	5 Founders Drive Bristol, CT 06010
TELEPHONE	860-582-4219
CONTACT	innkeeper@chimneycrestmanor.com | www.chimneycrest.com
FEATURES	2 Rooms, 3 Suites; Private baths | Children 10 and older welcome | Pets not allowed; Resident dog

Chimney Crest Manor is housed in a splendid Tudor mansion that possesses an unusual castle-like atmosphere and overlooks Connecticut's Farmington Hills. The inn was built in 1930 in what is now the Federal Hill Historic District of Bristol. The inn's ornate plasterwork, beamed ceilings, framed artwork, and stately fireplaces express a grandeur unparalleled in the area.

Activities abound within a 30-mile radius of the inn. State parks and many of the state's finest restaurants, vineyards and museums are within a few miles. Antique hunters will be entranced by the dozens of nearby shops. Your stay includes a sumptuous, homemade breakfast served in the spacious, formal dining room overlooking the panoramic view of the hills.

"Stunning mansion with a comfortable feel—beautiful stone and woodwork. Friendly owners, nicely maintained, and the yogurt pancakes were beyond words!"—Guest

Yogurt Pancakes

Yield: 3 servings

"Makes a light, tasty pancake your guests will love!"

1½ cups unbleached, all-purpose flour, sifted
1 tsp salt
1 tsp sugar
1 tsp baking powder
½ tsp baking soda
1 cup milk
1 (8-oz.) carton flavored yogurt (vanilla is good)
   Club soda, as needed to thin batter
   Maple syrup, for serving (optional)

Combine flour, salt, sugar, baking powder, and baking soda. Add milk and yogurt; mix until batter is smooth. Add club soda, as needed, to lighten batter. Cook pancakes on a preheated, greased griddle or skillet until golden brown on both sides. Serve with maple syrup, if desired.

DEACON TIMOTHY PRATT B&B

INNKEEPER	Patricia McGregor
ADDRESS	325 Main Street, Old Saybrook, CT 06475
TELEPHONE	860-395-1229
CONTACT	stay@pratthouse.net | www.pratthouse.net
FEATURES	6 Rooms, 3 Suites; Private baths | Children age 10 and older welcome
	Sunday through Thursday nights only | Pets not allowed

Step back in time in this magnificent, circa 1746, center chimney, Colonial B&B listed on the National Register of Historic Places. The Deacon Timothy Pratt is located in the charming, quintessential New England village of Old Saybrook, on a pretty, gas-lit main street in the heart of the historic and shopping districts. An ice skating pond and great canoe/kayak launch are not far away. This B&B is also part of a walking tour and scenic bicycle loop.

The romantic guest rooms feature award-winning décor that combines the historical charm of yesteryear with the relaxing luxuries of today. Each room has a four-poster or canopy bed, Jacuzzi tub, and fireplace.

"Breakfast was a highlight of our stay. Imagine a candle-lit breakfast by the fire on fine china, with softly playing music in the background."—Guest

Cappuccino Chocolate Chip Muffins

Yield: 12 muffins

"A great, tasty way to complement your coffee."

1½ sticks butter, softened
1⅓ cups sugar
2 large eggs
2 tsp vanilla extract
¼ cup instant coffee
¼ cup coffee-flavored liqueur (optional)
3½ cups unsifted all-purpose flour
1 Tbsp baking powder
1 tsp salt
½ cup milk
1½ cups chocolate chips

Preheat oven to 350°F. Grease muffin cups. In a large bowl, beat butter and sugar with an electric mixer at medium speed until light and fluffy. Beat in eggs, vanilla, instant coffee, and coffee liqueur until instant coffee is dissolved and coffee liquor is blended in.

In a medium bowl, combine flour, baking powder and salt. Add flour mixture and milk alternately to butter mixture, beating just until combined. Fold in chocolate chips. Divide batter among muffin cups. Bake for 25–30 minutes or until centers spring back when lightly pressed. Serve warm.

MANOR HOUSE

INNKEEPERS	Chef Kurt and Kathy Doerflinger
ADDRESS	69 Maple Avenue Norfolk, CT 06058
TELEPHONE	866-542-5690
CONTACT	innkeeper@manorhouse-norfolk.com | www.manorhouse-norfolk.com
FEATURES	8 Rooms, 1 Suite; Private baths | Children age 10 and older welcome | Pets not allowed

In the heart of the Green Woods lies the quintessential New England Village of Norfolk. This little center of culture is part of the distinct charms of Connecticut's Litchfield County, and is in close proximity to the Berkshires and New York's Columbia and Dutchess Counties.

When staying at the Manor House in Norfolk, travelers can enjoy an array of antique and craft shops, music festivals, theatre, auto racing, vineyards, museums, and fine dining. For the outdoor enthusiast, the preserved land trust and state parks offer miles of hiking trails. There is also downhill and cross-country skiing, tennis, golf, boating, horseback riding, and fishing.

For the romantic, there are horse-drawn carriage and sleigh rides, gourmet picnic baskets, and luxurious spa services. Manor House is one of the best B&Bs in Connecticut.

"The Manor House was fantastic! Just the perfect spot to relax and enjoy. Chef Kurt and Kathy are so sweet and attentive. The location of this estate is perfect and away from any distractions so being relaxed is an understatement!! We enjoyed it so much and are looking forward to a longer stay perhaps in the fall/winter. The rooms were cozy and clean and we also enjoyed wine by a fire in the common area/living room. Breakfast was great!"—Guest

Orange Waffles

Yield: 8 servings

1 cup all-purpose flour
1 Tbsp sugar
¼ tsp salt
1½ tsp baking powder
1/8 tsp nutmeg
2 eggs
½ cup milk
   grated zest of 1 orange
2 Tbsp butter, melted
   powdered sugar, for garnish

Combine flour, sugar, salt, baking powder, nutmeg, eggs, milk, and orange zest; beat until smooth. Add butter and mix to combine. Pour into hot waffle iron and bake until golden brown. Sprinkle with powdered sugar to serve.

Tip: These waffles are delicious with fruit syrup, such as cherry or raspberry, or serve them with whipped cream or chantilly cream with a little grated orange zest for a "Creamsicle" waffle.

ROGER SHERMAN INN

INNKEEPERS	Joseph and Nes Jaffre
ADDRESS	195 Oenoke Ridge, New Canaan, CT 06840
TELEPHONE	203-966-4541
CONTACT	info@rogershermaninn.com | www.rogershermaninn.com
FEATURES	16 Rooms, 1 Suite; Private baths | Children welcome | Pets not allowed

The circa-1740 Roger Sherman Inn is a restored Colonial landmark located near the center of New Canaan and its fashionable shops and historic sites. The inn is named for Roger Sherman, a lawyer and delegate to the Continental Congress who was a signer of the Declaration of Independence and the United States Constitution.

The inn offers quiet surroundings, seasonal outdoor dining, a well-stocked wine cellar, and award-winning, contemporary Continental cuisine. The menu features daily seasonal offerings, fresh seafood, and Swiss specialties. The inn is fortunate to have on staff Executive Chef Christophe Cadou, whose skill and artistry is respected and appreciated by all the guests to the inn.

"It's been a long time since I have seen a menu so appealing that I've wanted to order every single dish. This one can best be defined as modern American with a French accent and a number of specifically New England ingredients. Not only was almost every dish expertly prepared and very fresh-tasting, but the plate presentations were uniformly lovely and appetite-inspiring."—The New York Times

New England Lobster Bisque

Yield: 4 servings

4 (1½-lb.) lobster culls*
¼ cup soy oil (vegetable oil will work as well—do not use olive oil)
2 oz. carrots, peeled and diced into small cubes
2 oz. celery root, peeled and diced into small cubes
4 oz. shallots, diced into small cubes
2 oz. leeks, cleaned and diced into small cubes

2 oz. potatoes, peeled and diced into small cubes
¼ cup tomato purée
¼ cup cognac
1 cup white wine
6 cups clam juice
½ bunch tarragon
2 bay leaves
3 juniper berries
2 cups heavy cream
salt, to taste

Separate lobster tails and claws from heads and thoroughly clean inner parts. Keep all lobster parts. In a large pot, heat oil over medium-high heat; add lobster parts and cook just until they begin to turn red. Add carrots, celery root and shallots; cook until tender. Add leeks and potatoes; cook for 5–10 minutes, or until golden brown.

Add tomato purée, stirring constantly (do not let tomato purée turn brown—it will make the bisque bitter). Add cognac and white wine; reduce heat to low and simmer. Once most of the alcohol is cooked off, add clam juice and simmer for about 5 minutes. Add tarragon, bay leaves and juniper berries.

Remove all lobster shell parts from soup. Separate lobster meat from shell; set lobster meat aside and keep warm. Slowly simmer soup over medium heat for about 20 minutes. Add heavy cream. Purée soup in blender. Strain through a fine sieve. Season with salt, if needed. Pour soup into bowls and top with some lobster meat to serve.

*Lobster culls are lobsters missing a claw, often sold at a lower price.

SCRANTON SEAHORSE INN

INNKEEPER	Michael Hafford
ADDRESS	818 Boston Post Road, Madison, CT 06443
TELEPHONE	203-245-0550
CONTACT	info@scrantonseahorseinn.com | www.scrantonseahorseinn.com
FEATURES	7 rooms; Private baths | Children 12 years and older welcome; call to inquire | Limited pet-friendly; call to inquire

The Scranton Seahorse Inn is located in the heart of the village of Madison on the Connecticut shoreline. This wonderful inn, opened January 2006, is close to spectacular beaches, charming boutiques, elegant restaurants and outlet shopping. Housed in the 1833 Greek revival home of Sereno Scranton, the inn offers its guests the convenience of luxurious newly appointed accommodations along with the charm and ambiance of a historic New England homestead.

The inn was selected as a winner in the 2007 *Shoreline Newspaper* Comfiest Bed & Breakfast category and Best B&B by the *New Haven Advocate* 2008 Readers Poll.

Michael, the innkeeper, is also a professionally trained pastry chef. Guests can count on a delicious breakfast each morning that includes ingredients from his own gardens or from the shoreline's many farm markets.

"One thing for certain—we love food at the Scranton Seahorse Inn. Periodically we open our kitchen to share ideas and recipes, teach basic skills and techniques and most important, we get to sit down and eat good food together. Unless noted otherwise, all of our classes are hands-on and are kept small, which will enhance your learning experience. Printed recipes are always provided for you. Customized classes for group events are also available. See you in the kitchen!"—Innkeeper

Rhubarb Sour Cream Coffee Cake

Yield: 10–12 servings

"I was delighted to see how great the rhubarb in our garden was looking this morning. It means two things—springtime and tasty, tart, breakfast treats."

3½ cups finely chopped rhubarb (about 1 lb.)
2   Tbsp all-purpose flour
1½ cups packed dark brown sugar
5   Tbsp unsalted butter at room temperature
2   large eggs
1   cup sour cream
    zest of one medium orange
2   tsp good quality vanilla extract
1½ cups all-purpose flour

1   cup whole-wheat flour
1   tsp baking soda
1   tsp ground cinnamon
½   tsp kosher salt

Topping:
¼   cup Turbinado sugar
½   tsp ground cinnamon
2   Tbsp unsalted butter, chilled, cut into small pieces
¼   cup walnuts, toasted, chopped

Preheat oven to 375°F. Grease a 9-inch square baking pan.

In a medium bowl, combine rhubarb and flour; toss well to coat.

Using a stand mixer, combine brown sugar and butter and beat at medium speed until light and fluffy. Add eggs, one at a time, beating well after each addition. Add sour cream, zest, and vanilla. Beat until well combined.

In a separate bowl, combine flours, baking soda, cinnamon, and salt, stirring with a whisk. Gradually add flour mixture to butter mixture, beating at low speed just until combined. Fold in the rhubarb mixture. Spread the batter into the prepared baking pan.

Topping: Combine sugar and cinnamon in a small bowl. Cut in the butter with a pastry blender or 2 forks until mixture is crumbly. Stir in the nuts. Sprinkle streusel evenly over batter. Bake for 50 minutes or until a wooden pick inserted in the center comes out clean.

THIMBLE ISLANDS B&B

INNKEEPERS	Tony and Julie Broom
ADDRESS	28 West Point Road, Stony Creek, Branford, CT 06405
TELEPHONE	203-488-3693 | 203-927-5167
CONTACT	julie@ThimbleIslandsBB.com | www.thimbleislandsbb.com
FEATURES	2 Rooms; Private baths | Children: inquire | Pets not allowed

Located in Branford's picturesque village of Stony Creek, this secluded luxury B&B features magnificent views of the Thimble Islands and Long Island Sound for an elegant and tranquil getaway—ideal for pleasure and business travelers.

Innkeepers Tony and Julie Broom warmly welcome their guests. Enjoy teacakes and a beverage shortly after your arrival. Relax with a glass of wine and cheese before your departure for dinner. In the morning, enjoy your coffee (or beverage of choice) and a delicious home-cooked breakfast while looking out on sparkling harbor views.

"The village of Stony Creek, settled by the quarry workers who came to work in the famous granite quarries that give the town its name, is today one of the most popular residential communities on the Connecticut shoreline. Its informal yet sophisticated character and premier coastal setting make it a magnet for summer visitors. We hope you come visit us and our town."—Innkeeper

Tony's Special Omelet with Caramelized Onions, Shiitake Mushrooms, and Gorgonzola

Yield: 2 servings

Filling

1 Tbsp olive oil
1 Tbsp butter
2 medium or 1 very large onion, chopped
2 oz. (or more) shiitake mushrooms, roughly chopped

Omelets

4 extra-large eggs, divided
¼ tsp salt, divided
  dash Worcestershire sauce
1 Tbsp butter, divided
⅓ cup grumbled Gorgonzola, divided
  fresh chive, chopped (optional)
  paprika (optional)

Prepare filling: heat olive oil and butter in a nonstick frying pan over moderate heat until bubbly; add chopped onion and shiitake mushrooms; toss. Cook over low heat for approximately 45 minutes, tossing every 15 minutes, until the onion-mushroom mixture is greatly reduced and turns a deep rich caramel color. The filling may be made ahead and refrigerated overnight.

Prepare omelets: whisk 2 eggs thoroughly in small mixing bowl with touches of salt and Worcestershire sauce. Add ½ tablespoon of butter to omelet pan over medium heat. Pour in egg mixture, reduce heat to low and let set for 1 minute until egg is slightly cooked. With a spoon, put a line of half of the onion mixture down the center of the pan. Top with half of the Gorgonzola. Cover. As egg mixture cooks, run rubber spatula around edge of pan, tilting it to let runny mixture resettle at edges. When egg is almost cooked, flip one half of the egg over the onion/cheese center, then flip the other half over. Carefully turn omelet over, seam-side down. For moister interior, cook 1 more minute on low heat, for firmer interior, cook another 1–2 minutes. Sprinkle with chopped chive or paprika. Keep warm while preparing the second omelet.

Westbrook Inn B&B

INNKEEPERS	**Glenn and Chris Monroe**
ADDRESS	**976 Boston Post Road, Westbrook, CT 06498**
TELEPHONE	**860-399-4777	800-342-3162**
CONTACT	**info@westbrookinn.com	www.westbrookinn.com**
FEATURES	**9 Rooms, 1 Cottage; Private baths	Children under 12 welcome in cottage only	Pets not allowed**

Westbrook Inn B&B was built in 1876 by a local sea captain. Extra rooms were used to house travelers and seamen who passed through the town of Westbrook. Over the years it became popular with actors vacationing from New York. Today, this beautifully restored, four-season inn has nine charming rooms plus a two-bedroom cottage complete with a full kitchen.

Breakfast starts off with fresh coffee cakes or muffins all made in-house. The main entrée includes pancakes, French toast, and egg dishes. The inn grinds its own organic wheat and uses only the freshest ingredients possible.

After breakfast, the town of Westbrook has plenty to keep you busy going from one historic site to another. If that isn't enough, Mystic Seaport is only 15 minutes away; Essex is a 10-minute drive; and East Haddam boasts of Devil's Hopyard with its hiking and biking trails and 60-foot cascading falls.

"We certainly did enjoy our stay at your lovely B&B! We are still talking about it and we will be back soon for another stay. I have been telling everyone about the lovely yard, the delicious breakfasts and the proximity to the beach. Your B&B had everything that we needed to help rejuvenate us—so relaxing and close to everything that we could possibly need. Thank you for your hospitality."—Guest

Spinach Bread

Yield: 12 servings

"Especially good reheated the next day—too bad there is never any left!"

¼ cup olive oil
1 Tbsp butter
½ green or red bell pepper, diced small
1 medium onion, chopped
½ (7-oz.) can sliced mushrooms or 6 oz. fresh mushrooms, sliced
1 clove garlic, chopped
1 (10-oz.) pkg. frozen spinach, thawed in microwave
pinch of cayenne pepper
freshly ground pepper, to taste

pinch of parsley
pinch of basil
pinch of oregano
1 tsp garlic powder
pinch of crushed red pepper
pinch of salt
1 lb. pizza dough
4 slices provolone cheese
1½ cups grated mozzarella cheese
2 Tbsp Romano cheese
cornmeal

Preheat oven to 350°F. Heat olive oil and butter in a skillet over medium heat. Add bell peppers and onions and cook until soft. Add mushrooms and chopped garlic; cook until mushrooms are soft. Add spinach and spices; cook for 1–2 minutes. Add more olive oil if mixture looks too dry.

Roll dough to a thin oval shape. Spread bell pepper mixture over dough. Sprinkle with cheeses. Roll up jellyroll style; seal ends and seams well. Place on a baking sheet brushed with a light coat of oil and sprinkled with cornmeal. Bake for 30 minutes, or until lightly browned on top.

FRANCIS MALBONE HOUSE

INNKEEPERS	Will Dewey and Mark & Jasminka Eads
ADDRESS	392 Thames Street, Newport, RI 02840
TELEPHONE	401-846-0392 | 800-846-0392
CONTACT	francismalbone@yahoo.com | www.malbone.com
FEATURES	17 Rooms, 3 Suites; Private baths | Children age 12 and older welcome | Pets not allowed

The Francis Malbone House estate was built in 1760 for Colonel Francis Malbone, who made his fortune as a shipping merchant. Apparently, the Colonel was not above smuggling dutiable merchandise into the house to avoid the King's custom taxes. Subterranean passages found in the cellar have been traced to a subway leading to the pier where Colonel Malbone moored his fleet.

The mansion has been lovingly maintained and restored through the years. Each luxurious guest room is tastefully decorated with Colonial antiques and period reproductions. With its downtown harbor front location, the inn is within walking distance of nearly all of Newport's attractions.

Each morning the culinary team prepares a different multi-course breakfast which is served fireside in the dining room or by the fountain in the lush courtyard. Afternoon tea, served daily from 3–6 p.m., is a reason to stop what you are doing and return to the inn for a treat. The chef prepares savory and sweet items baked fresh daily.

"We hope you think of us for those important times in your life when you need a special place to celebrate with your significant others, family and friends—birthdays, anniversaries, even elopements. And for the business traveler, think of suggesting us for small business meetings, retreats, etc."—Innkeeper

Chocolate Walnut Bars

Yield: 24 bars

Crust:
- 1½ cups all-purpose flour
- 1 stick butter or margarine, softened
- ¼ cup packed brown sugar

Filling:
- 3 large eggs
- ¾ cup light corn syrup
- ¾ cup sugar
- 2 Tbsp butter or margarine, melted
- 1 tsp vanilla extract
- 1 (12-oz.) pkg. semi-sweet chocolate chips
- 1½ cups coarsely chopped walnuts

Preheat oven to 350°F. Grease a 9x13-inch baking pan.

In a mixing bowl, beat together flour, butter, and brown sugar until crumbly; press into the bottom of the baking pan. Bake for 12–15 minutes, or until lightly browned.

For the filling: In a mixing bowl, beat together eggs, corn syrup, sugar, butter, and vanilla. Stir in chocolate chips and walnuts. Pour filling over hot crust.

Bake for 25–30 minutes, or until center is set. Cool completely in pan on a wire rack, then cut into bars.

MARSHALL SLOCUM INN

INNKEEPERS	**Mark and Dana Spring**
ADDRESS	**29 Kay Street, Newport, RI 02840**
TELEPHONE	**401-841-5120	800-372-5120**
CONTACT	**info@marshallslocuminn.com	www.marshallslocuminn.com**
FEATURES	**6 Rooms; Private baths	Children age 12 and older welcome	Pets not allowed**

The Marshall Slocum Inn has been meticulously restored to reflect the charm and beauty of its Victorian heritage while offering today's comforts. The Newport mansions, harbor, and beaches are only steps away from the inn. All rooms include fluffy down comforters, robes, Greenwich Bay Trading Company toiletries, and a chocolate treat at night.

A three-course breakfast is served each morning. Entrées may include fluffy Belgian waffles with fresh strawberries, crêpes with asparagus, ham, and cheddar cheese sauce, or peaches and cream French toast.

Chef Mark Spring and staff aim to create a warm environment combined with top-notch service and sumptuous food. Educated at Johnson & Wales University and trained at the AAA rated 5-star Cliffside Inn, Chef Spring presents an innovative menu for guests.

Named in Yankee Magazine's *"Best of New England—Editors' Choice" as the 2011 Best Rhode Island Bed and Breakfast*

America's Cup Lemon Sugar Cake

Yield: 10—12 slices

1   cup butter, softened
3   cups sugar
5   eggs
1   Tbsp vanilla extract
3   cups all-purpose flour
1   tsp baking soda
⅛   tsp salt
1   cup vanilla yogurt
¼   cup lemon juice

Topping:
1   cup powdered sugar
1   egg white
    strawberries, chopped, for garnish

Preheat oven to 350°F. Grease and flour a standard Bundt pan.

In a mixing bowl, cream together butter and sugar. Add eggs one at a time and blend well. Add vanilla extract, and mix well, scraping sides of the bowl. In a separate bowl, combine flour, baking soda, and salt. Add the dry mixture to the wet mixture, alternating with the yogurt and lemon juice. Pour batter into the prepared Bundt pan, and bake for 45 minutes, or until a cake tester comes out clean. Cool the cake and remove from the pan.

For the topping: mix powdered sugar and egg white to form an icing. Drizzle icing over the cake and top with strawberries.

SHELTER HARBOR INN

INNKEEPER	Jim Dey
ADDRESS	10 Wagner Road, Westerly, RI 02891
TELEPHONE	401-322-8883	800-468-8883
CONTACT	reservations@shelterharborinn.com	www.shelterharborinn.com
FEATURES	24 Rooms; Private baths	Children welcome	Pets: inquire

B uilt in the early 1800s, the Shelter Harbor Inn has been transformed into a comfortable, unpretentious country inn where the emphasis is on relaxation, good food, and a warm, friendly atmosphere. The inn sits at the entrance to Shelter Harbor and is near one of the most beautiful sections of Rhode Island's shoreline. The inn's private beach stretches for two miles along the shores of Quonochontaug Pond and the ocean.

Each day, the inn's chef prepares creative American cuisine using only the freshest of ingredients and seafood from local waters. Guests come from around the world to enjoy exquisite dining and to indulge in some of the best wines from the extensive wine list. The Shelter Harbor Inn has a long tradition of hosting monthly Gourmet Dinners and Wine Tastings. Wine dinner guests may take advantage of a special room rate if they choose to stay the night, which also includes a sumptuous full breakfast.

"If you should choose to join us for one of these Gourmet Dinners, the menus are posted on our website. But to whet your appetite, here is the menu from our Summer by the Sea buffet:

Grilled Swordfish with Tarragon Mustard Marinade; Grilled Chicken with Fresh Herbs and Sautéed Lemon Slices; Olives and Feta Sweet Corn; Pancetta Bread Pudding; Inn Baked Breads ... oh, and, of course, wine."—Innkeeper

Indian Pudding

Yield: 6–8 servings

4 cups milk
2 cups heavy cream
1 cup molasses
¾ cup white cornmeal
½ cup packed brown sugar
1 Tbsp butter
1 Tbsp cinnamon
1 Tbsp ground ginger
1½ tsp salt
   Ice cream, for serving

Preheat oven to 350°F. Grease a 9x13-inch baking dish.

In a heavy saucepan over medium-high heat, bring milk, cream, and molasses to a boil. Stir in cornmeal, brown sugar, butter, cinnamon, ginger, and salt. Lower heat and simmer, stirring frequently, for 5 minutes. Pour pudding into the baking dish. Put baking dish in a 12x18-inch baking pan. Add enough hot water to come halfway up the sides of baking dish. Bake for 60 minutes, stirring with a whisk or a wooden spoon for 1 minute every 15 minutes, until firm to the touch. Remove from oven. Cool for 15–20 minutes. Serve warm with ice cream.

"More and more clearly as the scones disappeared into his interior he saw that what the sensible man wanted was a wife and a home with scones like these always at his disposal."

— P.G. Wodehouse
Bachelors Anonymous

Massachusetts B&Bs

AND THEIR SIGNATURE RECIPES

ADDISON CHOATE INN

INNKEEPER	Jan Duffy
ADDRESS	49 Broadway, Rockport, MA 01966
TELEPHONE	978-546-7543 | 800-245-7543
CONTACT	reservations@addisonchoateinn.com | www.addisonchoateinn.com
FEATURES	5 Rooms, 1 Suite, 2 Cottages; Private baths | Children: inquire | Pets not allowed

The Addison Choate Inn is an elegant, late Greek Revival home that has served as a B&B for almost 40 years. If you appreciate traditional décor and modern comforts, you will feel totally at home in the Addison Choate. Guests may relax with a book in the library or sip a cup of herbal tea in front of a roasting fire in the living room. The inn provides the perfect retreat from the hectic pace of everyday life.

Breakfast is served near the fireplace in the dining room during cool seasons and on the awning-shaded veranda in warm weather. Afternoon refreshments include home-baked cookies and a choice of seasonal beverages.

"We've had such a lovely stay. We had just the right amount of privacy and friendly conversation; the room and house were very comfortable; and the breakfasts bear replicating! The Addison Choate Inn will always have a special spot in our hearts, and we'll be sure to bring friends and family next time."—Guest

Goat Cheese, Asparagus & Spring Onion Frittata

Yield: 6–8 servings

"This recipe can be adapted to use whatever vegetables you have on hand."

- 1   Tbsp olive oil
- 1   cup diced asparagus, zucchini or summer squash
- 1   medium shallot, diced
- 8   large eggs, beaten
- ½   tsp sea salt
- ½   tsp freshly ground pepper
- ½   cup crumbled goat cheese
- 2   Tbsp thinly sliced spring onion (green onion)

Preheat oven to 400°F. Heat oil in an ovenproof 10- to 12-inch skillet over medium-high heat. Add asparagus and shallots; cook until asparagus is crisp-tender and shallots are soft.

Combine eggs, salt and pepper; add to asparagus mixture and cook for about 2 minutes. Sprinkle goat cheese and spring onions over ingredients in skillet. Place skillet in oven and bake for 25 minutes. Cool slightly, then invert onto a serving platter. Slice and serve.

BEACH PLUM INN & RESTAURANT

INNKEEPERS	**Bob and Sarah Nixon**
ADDRESS	**50 Beach Plum Lane, Menemsha, MA 02535**
TELEPHONE	**508-645-9454	877-645-7398**
CONTACT	**thefrontdesk@innsatmenemsha.com	www.beachpluminn.com**
FEATURES	**5 Rooms, 6 Cottages; Private baths	Children welcome	Pets not allowed**

The Beach Plum Inn is a romantic hideaway perched above scenic Menemsha Harbor and surrounded by colorful gardens and lush pastures. With its picture-perfect ocean views and spectacular sunsets, the Beach Plum Inn is an enchanting setting for a relaxing getaway. Praised for its outstanding cuisine and panoramic sunset views, the Beach Plum Inn Restaurant provides a dining experience that tantalizes all the senses and is a favorite of island residents and visitors alike.

The Beach Plum Inn began its life as a private home built from wood salvaged from shipwrecks caused by a vicious storm in 1898. In 1958, the property was converted into an inn and quickly took its place as one of Martha's Vineyard's premiere destinations.

"Located just down the hill in Menemsha Village, is one of our sister restaurants—the Home Port—an island tradition. Renowned for their lobster dinners, sunset views and famous clam chowder, the Home Port is a must-visit for island visitors. As a guest of Beach Plum Inn, the Front Desk can assist you in making a preferred reservation. Or order a delicious take-out meal at the back door to enjoy at a picnic table on our deck."—Innkeeper

Corn & Wild Rice Cakes with Smoked Salmon

Yield: 6 servings

1¾ cups all-purpose flour
2 Tbsp sugar
2 tsp baking powder
½ tsp salt
3 eggs
1¼ buttermilk
½ stick butter, melted
½ cup cooked, drained wild rice
½ cup raw corn, from the cob or frozen
6 Tbsp crème fraîche
½ lb. high quality Norwegian smoked salmon, thinly sliced

In a medium bowl, sift flour, sugar, baking powder, and salt. Add eggs, buttermilk, and melted butter; beat until smooth and creamy. Fold in wild rice and corn.

Heat skillet over medium heat until a few drops of water dance across the surface. Add batter to pan using about 2 tablespoons of batter per cake. Cook first side until bubbles form and edges look dry. Turn and cook until second side is a rich, golden brown. Serve immediately or cool (may be held for 1 day) and reheat in a 350°F oven for 2–3 minutes.

To serve: Place 1 corn and wild rice cake in center of each plate. Coat each cake with 1 tsp of crème fraîche. Criss-cross 2 slices of smoked salmon over each cake. Repeat layers 2 more times until you have a 3-layer-tall tower. Beautiful and delicious!

BIRCHWOOD INN

INNKEEPER	Ellen Gutman Chenaux
ADDRESS	7 Hubbard Street, Lenox, MA 01240
TELEPHONE	413-637-2600 | 800-524-1646
CONTACT	innkeeper@birchwood-inn.com | www.birchwood-inn.com
FEATURES	10 Rooms, 2 carriage houses; Private baths | Children age 12 and older welcome | Pets: inquire

Birchwood Inn has been welcoming guests with warmth and hospitality since 1767. Antiques, collectibles, featherbeds, quilts, and down comforters are very much at home in this Colonial Revival B&B mansion, the only Lenox inn listed on the National Register of Historic Places.

Secluded among white birch, stately oaks, and towering pines, the inn has the pastoral stillness of a country morning, yet is only a short walk from the celebrated restaurants, shops, and galleries of historic Lenox village.

The Berkshires abound not only with world-class cultural events, but also with a plethora of extraordinary culinary experiences with chefs, bakers, wine aficionados, and a chocolatier as maestros of their own kitchens and wine cellars, orchestrating decadent and intoxicating creations.

Imagine … awakening to the aroma of freshly brewed coffee and homemade breads baking in the oven … savoring memorable soufflés and pancakes, crisps and fruitinis. Guests have voted Birchwood Inn "Best Breakfast in New England." Ellen uses only the freshest ingredients and strives to meet and exceed her guest's expectations.

"If a country inn exists in heaven, it's the Birchwood Inn."—Guest

Carolina Plantation Bake

Yield: 8 servings

*"People say they don't eat grits—and I was one of them.
I tried the incredible combination of yellow stone-ground grits,
sausage, eggs, and cheese—and I am, now, a believer! Just don't
tell anyone it's grits until after they've cleaned their plates."*

4½	cups water
1	cup yellow, stone-ground grits (www.carolinaplantationrice.com)
2	Tbsp unsalted butter
1	lb. Italian turkey sausage (½ sweet and ½ hot)
1	large onion, chopped
4	Tbsp unsalted butter
2	eggs, slightly beaten
2	cups cheddar or Parmesan cheese, grated
¼	cup parsley, minced

Mix the water, grits, and butter in a large saucepan or pot. Bring to boil over medium heat. Reduce the heat to low, cover, and simmer 45 minutes or until thick. If the grits become too thick, add more water.

Preheat oven to 350°F. Grease a 9x13-inch pan. (You can also use individual baking dishes.) Sauté the sausage, breaking it into small pieces. Set aside. Sauté the onion in the fat from the sausage. Drain. Add the onion to the sausage. Add the butter, eggs, and cheese to the grits. Add the sausage and onions. Pour the mixture into the prepared pan.

At this point you can refrigerate the casserole for up to 2 days before baking. It also freezes well. Bake for 1 hour (30 minutes if you are using individual baking dishes).

BREWSTER BY THE SEA

INNKEEPERS	Donna and Byron Cain
ADDRESS	716 Main Street, Brewster, MA 02631
TELEPHONE	508-896-3910 | 800-892-3910
CONTACT	stay@brewsterbythesea.com | www.brewsterbythesea.com
FEATURES	6 Rooms, 2 Suites; Private baths | Children age 14 and older welcome | Pets not allowed; Resident dog

As you approach Brewster by the Sea B&B, a sense of graciousness and gentility abounds. This award-winning, romantic country inn is one of Cape Cod's finest B&Bs. Situated in the heart of Brewster's historic district, the inn's convenient Main Street location belies the peaceful solitude of this expansive property, replete with outdoor pool, whirlpool spa, gardens, and orchard.

Breakfast is a feast for the eye and the palate, made fresh each day from the finest ingredients, including herbs from the inn's garden.

Brewster by the Sea is a highly sought after destination during shoulder and quiet seasons as people find they relax here, enjoying exquisite breakfasts and romantic fireplaces.

"Several organizations on Cape Cod are heavily supporting the Slow Food, Farm-to-Table movement and various other Fresh Food movements on Cape Cod. We support them and try to do our part to help our B&B guests discover a healthier experience. Our eggs are cage free fresh and are often only a day or two old versus store bought eggs which can be weeks old."—Innkeeper

Plum Torte

Yield: 8 servings

"Italian plums make this a delicious fall treat.
Peaches or apples may also be substituted."

 1 stick unsalted butter
 1 cup sugar, plus extra for topping
 1 cup all-purpose flour, sifted
 1 tsp baking powder
    pinch of salt
 2 eggs
12 Italian plums, halved and pitted
    lemon juice, to taste
 1 tsp cinnamon
    Whipped cream and/or ice cream, for serving

Preheat oven to 350°F. Grease a 9-inch springform pan. In a large bowl, cream together butter and sugar. Add flour, baking powder, salt, and eggs; beat well. Spoon batter into the prepared springform pan. Place plums, skin-side-up, on top of batter. Sprinkle lightly with sugar and lemon juice, to taste. Sprinkle with cinnamon. Bake for 1 hour. Serve with whipped cream and/or ice cream.

BROOK FARM INN

INNKEEPERS Linda and Phil Halpern

ADDRESS 15 Hawthorne Street, Lenox, MA 01240

TELEPHONE 413-637-3013 | 800-285-7638

CONTACT innkeeper@brookfarm.com | www.brookfarm.com

FEATURES 14 Rooms, 1 Suite; Private baths | Children age 13 and older welcome | Pets not allowed

Located just down the hill and around the bend from the center of historic Lenox, Brook Farm Inn welcomes guests to the grace of its Victorian past and the comforts of the present. Tastefully furnished, this 130-year-old home offers comfort and tranquility surrounded by the beauty of the Berkshires and a tradition of poetry and literature.

Start your day with a sumptuous breakfast. You'll wake to the aroma of one of Linda or Phil's legendary dishes … perhaps apple baked French toast, sun dried tomato strata, or vegetable frittata. The hot entrée, which changes daily, is always accompanied by home baked muffins, coffee cakes, and fresh breads, along with cereals, yogurt, and a fresh fruit platter.

Then take the short walk into town, where you can find charming boutiques, discover antique treasures, view fine art in many galleries, and dine in splendid restaurants. The innkeepers carry on a tradition of inviting poets for readings and telling stories at teatime.

TripAdvisor 2012 Certificate of Excellence Winner

Blueberry Morning Glory

Yield: 12 servings

"This rich breakfast/brunch casserole can be made with fresh blueberries or frozen. It's spectacular when served with hot blueberry sauce. It can be prepared the day before and refrigerated overnight."

- 1 loaf challah bread or unsliced white bread, crusts removed
- 1 (8-oz.) pkg. cream cheese, cut into small pieces
- 2 cups fresh or frozen blueberries
- 8 large eggs
- ⅓ cup maple syrup
- ½ cup sugar
- 2 cups half & half

Blueberry sauce:
- 1 cup sugar
- 1 cup water
- 2 Tbsp cornstarch
- 1 cup fresh or frozen blueberries

Preheat oven to 350°F. Grease a 9x13-inch glass baking dish with non-stick cooking spray. Tear bread into small pieces and arrange half of the bread pieces over bottom of dish. Scatter cream cheese over bread. Scatter blueberries over cream cheese. Arrange remaining bread on top.

In a bowl, beat eggs, then mix in maple syrup, sugar, and half & half. Pour carefully and evenly over bread (at this point, you can cover and refrigerate overnight). Bake for 50 minutes. Serve with warm blueberry sauce.

For the blueberry sauce: In a saucepan over medium heat, combine sugar, water and cornstarch. Cook for about 5 minutes, stirring constantly, until thickened. Add blueberries; simmer for 10 minutes, stirring occasionally.

CAPTAIN FREEMAN INN

INNKEEPERS	Donna and Byron Cain
ADDRESS	15 Breakwater Road, Brewster, MA 02631
TELEPHONE	508-896-7481
CONTACT	info@captainfreemaninn.com | www.captainfreemaninn.com
FEATURES	7 Rooms, 4 Queen Boutique Rooms; Private baths | Children age 14 and over welcome | Pets not allowed

A truly magnificent sea captain's home on Cape Cod, this B&B has a perfect location with easy strolls to Breakwater Beach, the Brewster General Store and Ice Cream Scoop, an upscale restaurant, and a family-style Chowder House.

A wraparound porch with a screened-in breakfast area overlooking the pool makes for a perfect start to the day. Relaxing in wicker lounge chairs and rocking chairs on the front porch defines the perfect vacation.

Breakfast is both gourmet and farm-to-table and is accomplished in a commercial kitchen. An indoor dining room makes breakfast and afternoon teas a year-round pleasure.

"Our chef, Carol Edmondson, has been combining the simple, healthy preparations of Mediterranean cuisine with fresh local ingredients in the kitchen of the Captain Freeman Inn for many years. Her professional training, world travel, love of food, and sharing her cooking knowledge with others, was the inspiration for our cooking classes. Classes are held in our welcoming kitchen, built by master shipbuilders in the mid-nineteenth century, with an eye for light and air."— Innkeeper

Apricot Scones

Yield: 6 servings

"We are always trying new recipes at the inn, but always come back to this one as it is so flavorful and moist—certainly a guest favorite."

- 8 oz. chilled unsalted butter, cut into small cubes
- 1¾ cups all-purpose flour
- 4 Tbsp sugar
- 2½ tsp baking powder
- ¼ tsp salt
- ¼ tsp baking soda
- 1 egg, beaten
- ½ cup dried apricots, chopped (can substitute cranberries, raisins, etc.)
- 4–6 Tbsp half & half

Preheat oven to 400°F. Cut butter into flour, sugar, baking powder, salt, and baking soda until mixture resembles fine crumbs. Stir in egg, apricots, and just enough half & half so dough leaves side of bowl. Turn dough onto lightly floured surface and knead 10 times. Form into biscuit-sized pieces or cut into diamond shapes.

Place on ungreased cookie sheet. Brush dough with egg wash. Bake 10–12 minutes or until golden brown.

CHATHAM GABLES INN

INNKEEPERS	David and Andrea Smith
ADDRESS	364 Old Harbor Road, Chatham, MA 02633
TELEPHONE	508-945-5859 | 800-628-6972
CONTACT	tmnhi@comcast.net | www.chathamgablesinn.com
FEATURES	8 Rooms; Private baths | Children age 10 and over welcome | Pets not allowed

Quiet, luxurious and leisurely, the historic Chatham Gables Inn offers guests the quintessential Cape Cod B&B experience. Few Chatham B&Bs can compare to this 170-year-old inn, rich in New England coastal history and hospitality. Whether you visit for a cozy fall weekend, a winter escape, or a long leisurely week in summer, everything you want from your Cape Cod B&B getaway you'll find here at the Chatham Gables.

Spacious common areas include the reception parlor, the chart room and the breakfast gallery featuring fine works from local artists. The Chatham Gables Inn provides the classic Cape Cod inn experience within a short stroll to all of Chatham's world-class offerings, including great beaches and the many shops, galleries and restaurants found on Main Street.

"When you choose Chatham for your escape, you choose a very special place, and we are here to make sure your stay with us will become a wonderful 'forever' memory, and that you will be sure to return again and again. We are here for you, and whatever it is you could possibly need, just ask. You can count on our warm welcome and our kind and knowledgeable staff to help make Chatham Gables Inn your one and only Chatham destination."—Innkeeper

Breakfast Sandwich

Yield: 1 serving

2 eggs
2 Tbsp sour cream
¼ cup sharp cheddar cheese, shredded
2 slices whole grain, hearty, hand-cut bread, toasted
1 slice proscuitto
2 Tbsp baby spinach, wilted
¼ cup fresh Parmesan, shaved
3 Tbsp hollandaise sauce
   salt and pepper, to taste
   seasonal fruit
   asparagus spears, cooked

Whisk the eggs in a small bowl and add the sour cream and cheese. Blend together well and cook until soft, yet firm.

Place two slices of toast on an individual serving plate. On one slice of toast layer the proscuitto, scrambled eggs, spinach, and Parmesan. Drizzle hollandaise sauce over this. Top with the second slice of toast. Serve with fruit and asparagus spears.

GATEWAYS INN

INNKEEPERS	Michele and Eiran Gazit
ADDRESS	51 Walker Street, Lenox, MA 01240
TELEPHONE	413-637-2532 | 888-492-9466
CONTACT	innkeeper@gatewaysinn.com | www.gatewaysinn.com
FEATURES	11 Rooms, 1 Suite; Private baths | Children welcome with restrictions | Pets not allowed

L et the Gateways Inn take you to another time and place. The incomparable elegance of the Procter mansion, infused with the charm and hospitality of the innkeepers, will surely enchant you.

Located in the heart of Lenox, Massachusetts, in the Berkshire Hills, the Gateways Inn offers a perfect getaway for any occasion. The inn's twelve guest rooms are each uniquely inviting. Choose from rooms with queen or king-sized beds, brass or sleigh beds and fireplaces.

The on-site Restaurant and Piano Bar offer a distinctive mixture of ambiance and taste for the discerning. The Restaurant at the Gateways Inn is among the finest in Lenox, with our seasonal a la carte menu that is sure to delight. The Piano Bar offers late-night fare in a relaxed atmosphere, so come unwind after a show, or plan your entire evening around live entertainment and a delicious menu.

"From the moment we arrived, it was a pleasure. We felt as though we had traveled back to a quieter time. The rooms were beautiful. Our host and hostess did their best to make our stay one of the most memorable. The food was top of the line. We loved it and hope to have this experience again soon."—Guest

Creamy Crimini
Mushroom Soup with Brie

Yield: 4 servings

1   Tbsp butter
½   small onion, diced
1   clove garlic, minced
6   cups crimini mushrooms, sliced, divided
4   Tbsp Wondra (very fine flour for sauces, or use 2 Tbsp flour mixed
    with 2 Tbsp water, but Wondra is best)
2   cups vegetable stock
1   cup water
2   tsp thyme, minced, plus sprigs for garnish
½   cup half & half
1   cup crème di Brie

Heat saucepan over medium heat. Add butter, and sauté onion and garlic for 3 minutes. Add mushrooms and sauté another 3 minutes. Set aside about ½ cup mushrooms for garnish. Whisk in the flour until smooth. Add the stock, water, and thyme. Gently boil until mushrooms are very tender. Reduce heat to medium-low, and stir constantly until mixture comes to a boil, and thickens to soup consistency. Using an immersion blender, or just a blender, purée soup until it is still slightly chunky. Turn off heat and add half & half. Garnish with Brie, reserved sliced mushrooms, and thyme sprig.

Golden Slipper

INNKEEPERS	Gretchen and Jack Stephenson
ADDRESS	PO Box 251 Minot, MA 02055 | Lewis Wharf, Boston, MA 02190
TELEPHONE	781-545-2845
CONTACT	bnbafloat@gmail.com | www.bostonbedandbreakfastafloat.com
FEATURES	40' Chris Craft (sleeps up to 6); Shared bath | Children welcome | Pets not allowed

The *Golden Slipper*, Boston's B&B "Afloat" is a traditional Catalina Chris Craft. The 40-foot yacht is docked at Lewis Wharf, in the heart of Boston's historic North End. The boat stays moored at the slip and you come and go as you please. This is a private party yacht accommodating up to six guests, with a continental breakfast left for you. Cruises of Boston Harbor and dinners are available upon request during your stay. The *Golden Slipper* offers a unique B&B experience with the opportunity to cruise Boston Harbor for a day or sunset cruise.

The yacht has two private state rooms and a comfortable main salon that offers a roomy galley and a spacious sofa that converts to a double bed. A continental breakfast is left for the guests.

"Gretchen's hospitality and service is top notch. She is professional and you immediately feel at ease and relaxed as soon as you step aboard the boat. We've been going to Boston for many years and if we ever book a hotel again it'll be because the Golden Slipper *was booked. Location can't be beat and the city skyline from the boat at night is fabulous. Loved our stay and we can't wait until springtime to book a weekend away!"*—Guest

Rum Cake

Yield: 10 servings

"This is a favorite dessert of our charter guests."

1 (18¼-oz.) pkg. yellow cake mix
1 (4½-oz.) pkg. instant vanilla pudding
½ cup water
½ cup vegetable oil
½ cup rum
4 large eggs

Rum sauce:
1 stick butter
½ cup sugar
¾ cup rum
¼ cup water

Preheat oven to 350°F. Grease a standard Bundt pan.

In a large bowl, combine cake mix, pudding mix, water, oil, and rum. Beat in eggs, 1 at a time. Pour batter into Bundt pan. Bake for 1 hour, or until a toothpick inserted in center comes out clean. Remove cake from oven and poke holes in it with a toothpick. Pour rum sauce slowly over cake. Let cake cool about 30 minutes before slicing and serving.

For the rum sauce: Just before cake is done baking, combine butter, sugar, rum, and water in a small saucepan over low heat. Cook, stirring, until butter is melted and combined and sugar is dissolved.

HARBORSIDE HOUSE

INNKEEPER	Susan Livingston
ADDRESS	23 Gregory Street, Marblehead, MA 01945
TELEPHONE	781-631-1032
CONTACT	stay@harborsidehouse.com | www.harborsidehouse.com
FEATURES	2 Rooms; Shared baths | Children age 8 and older welcome | Pets not allowed

The Harborside House offers gracious accommodations and warm hospitality in an ideal location. This handsome, circa-1850 home in Marblehead's historic district overlooks picturesque Marblehead Harbor. Guests enjoy water views from the wood-paneled parlor, dining room, and summer breakfast porch. Guest rooms feature antique furnishings and period wallpaper.

Only a short walk from the inn are antique shops, art galleries, and shops of local craftsmen, as well as dining choices to suit every taste and budget.

A generous continental breakfast is included with each stay, as well as afternoon tea on request. Additional treats may include homemade cookies, chocolates, or house specialty Muesli bread.

"Great little B&B in a beautiful setting! Enjoyed visiting with Susan and also appreciated the alone time my wife and I had while sitting in the great room and reading books. I would highly recommend this inn to any couple who wants a quiet and relaxing holiday away from it all."—Guest

Chocolate Walnut Espresso Biscotti

Yield: 30 biscotti

- 2 cups unbleached all-purpose flour
- 1 cup sugar
- ½ tsp baking powder
- ½ tsp baking soda
- ½ tsp salt
- ½ tsp cinnamon
- ¼ tsp ground cloves
- ¼ cup plus 1 Tbsp strong brewed coffee, cooled
- 1 Tbsp plus 1 tsp milk
- 1 large egg
- 1 tsp vanilla extract
- 1¼ cups chocolate chips
- ¾ cup chopped walnuts (or almonds or pistachios)
- ¾ cup dried cranberries

Preheat oven to 350°F. Grease and lightly flour a baking sheet.

In a large bowl, combine flour, sugar, baking powder, baking soda, salt, cinnamon, and cloves. In a small bowl, combine coffee, milk, egg, and vanilla; add to dry ingredients, mixing until flour is moistened (add a few more drops of coffee if needed). Stir in chocolate chips, walnuts, and dried cranberries.

On a well-floured surface, form dough into 3½-inch-long, ½-inch-thick flat logs. Transfer logs to the baking sheet. Bake for about 20 minutes. Remove from oven and cool. Cut logs into ½-inch-thick slices. Lay slices cut-side-down on baking sheet. Lower oven temperature to 300°F. Bake for 6–8 minutes (for crisper biscotti, turn and bake for 6–8 minutes longer).

HONEYSUCKLE HILL INN

INNKEEPERS	Nancy Hunter-Young and Rick Kowarek
ADDRESS	591 Main Street, Route 6A, West Barnstable, MA 02668
TELEPHONE	508-362-8418 | 855-211-0509
CONTACT	stay@honeysucklehill.com | www.honeysucklehill.com
FEATURES	4 Rooms, 1 Suite; Private baths | Children welcome | Pets not allowed

Step back in time and relax at this traditional Cape Cod B&B, circa 1810, on the edge of the small village of West Barnstable. Stroll through the lovely gardens, curl up on the peaceful screened-in front porch, stretch out on a sun-lounger or luxuriate in the hot tub amid a symphony of perennial blossoms. Select a book from the extensive library—or simply enjoy the welcoming charm and romance of this historical inn.

You will delight in the inn's casual Cape Cod ambiance and your hosts' gracious New England hospitality. Honeysuckle Hill has all the warmth of its heritage: wide-planked floors, ship captain's staircase, eccentric ceiling angles, curving hallways, and an inviting wraparound front porch where you can start your day with morning coffee or retreat to in the afternoon and evening for drinks and interesting conversation.

Each morning, Honeysuckle Hill's guests are served a delectable breakfast in an elegantly comfortable breakfast room. The light and lovely guest rooms are exquisitely decorated with antiques, white wicker and luxurious linens.

"An old-fashioned sense of hospitality at this 1810 farmhouse ... loaded with tons of amenities ... comfortably elegant."—Editors Choice, Yankee Traveler Magazine

Baked Eggs with Wild Mushrooms, Sun-dried Tomatoes & Brie

Yield: 8—10 servings

2–3	Tbsp unsalted butter
½–¾	lb. mixed fresh, wild mushrooms (baby bellas, shiitake, crimini), thinly sliced
¼	cup oil-packed sun-dried tomatoes, finely diced
4–5	oz. Brie cheese, sliced into small cubes
14–16	large eggs
2	Tbsp fresh or prepared pesto

Preheat oven to 350 degrees F.

Melt butter in a medium pan and sauté mushrooms until most of their moisture has evaporated. Distribute the mushrooms evenly in an oval casserole dish (at least 2-inch depth) that has been very lightly oiled. Take the sun-dried tomatoes and toss with the Brie. Distribute evenly in the casserole dish containing the mushrooms. Break the eggs, one by one over the top of the mushroom, tomato, cheese mixture, until the entire casserole is covered with eggs. (I deliberately break the yolks as I am doing this.) With a spoon, take small amounts of pesto and randomly "dot" the top of the eggs.

Loosely tent casserole dish with aluminum foil, and bake for about 35–40 minutes, or until egg yolks are cooked completely.

(FYI: I also place a loaf pan filled with hot water in my oven when I bake these eggs to help keep the whites of the eggs from drying out. Make sure that you tent the foil, otherwise, the whites will stick to the foil.)

Inn at Cape Cod

INNKEEPERS	Mike and Helen Cassels
ADDRESS	4 Summer Street, PO Box 371, Yarmouth Port, MA 02675
TELEPHONE	508-375-0590	800-850-7301
CONTACT	stay@innatcapecod.com	www.innatcapecod.com
FEATURES	6 Rooms, 3 Suites; Private baths	Children age 16 and older welcome	Pets not allowed

The Inn at Cape Cod began its life in 1820 as the private home of the wealthy Sears family, but soon became the famous Sears Hotel, providing comfort and rest for weary stagecoach travelers between the Cape and Boston.

This historic B&B is unique with its 200-year tradition of fine hospitality, and is the perfect base from which to visit all the Cape's wonderful attractions. Set on two-and-a-half acres of lush landscaped grounds, and bordering 100 acres of nature preserve, this Cape Cod B&B is a gentle stroll from several world-class restaurants, museums, a sandy freshwater beach, and the shops and attractions of historic Yarmouth Port. This acclaimed Cape Cod inn is centrally located close to Barnstable, Hyannis, several ocean beaches, island ferries, whale-watching excursions and nature trails.

Contemplate your next adventure while enjoying a delightful gourmet breakfast, graciously served in the sun-drenched morning room.

"Cape Cod is fantastic, and so is this place—it really is special. After many weeks of traveling throughout the USA we had experienced some pretty amazing places, but the Inn at Cape Cod has raised the bar. All inns should be this way. Located in the charming mid-Cape town of Yarmouth Port, the inn is within walking distance of several great restaurants. The innkeepers really do care, and within twenty seconds of meeting them you feel like old friends."—Guest

Date & Walnut English Rock Cakes

Yield: 9 servings

1½ cups all-purpose flour
1½ tsp baking powder
1/8 tsp salt
1 stick butter cut into small pieces
½ cup sugar
½ cup chopped dates
½ cup chopped walnuts
1 extra large egg
2 Tbsp half & half
Mix of graham cracker crumbs and sugar (2:1)

Preheat oven to 365 degrees F. (or 340 degrees F. if convection oven is used)

In a blade mixer, blend flour, baking powder, salt, and butter until mix resembles breadcrumbs. In a large bowl combine sugar, dates, and walnuts. In a small bowl mix egg with half & half. Add flour mixture to sugar mixture, and combine thoroughly. Make a "well" in the center of combined mix. Pour the egg mix into well. With a fork, roughly combine egg mix into dry mix until fully combined to resemble sticky dough. Scoop onto parchment-paper-lined cookie tray using ice cream scoop. Sprinkle graham cracker mix on top of each cake.

Bake for 18–21 minutes, or until a toothpick comes out clean from center. Serve with or without butter—delicious either way!

INN AT STOCKBRIDGE

INNKEEPERS	Alice and Len Schiller
ADDRESS	30 East Street, Rt. 7 North, Stockbridge, MA 01262
TELEPHONE	888-466-7865
CONTACT	innkeeper@stockbridgeinn.com | www.stockbridgeinn.com
FEATURES	8 Rooms, 8 Suites; Private baths | Children age 12 and older welcome | Pets not allowed; Resident Standard Poodle

The Inn at Stockbridge offers a welcoming New England B&B experience in western MA, highlighted by extraordinary attention to detail. The inn is a family-owned and operated property with over 16 years of experience in providing excellence in hospitality.

Stockbridge is in the heart of the Berkshires, a town described by Norman Rockwell as "the best of America, the best of New England." Steeped in history, celebrity, romance, and intrigue, the town has a timeless appeal, with each season stamped with its own beauty and charm.

Situated on 12 acres, the 1906 estate features beautiful gardens, an outdoor heated pool, wraparound porch, original sculptures donated by Carl Kanter (a guest of the inn), and even a turn-of-the-century buggy to complete the ambiance.

Relax and indulge yourself with a wonderful breakfast prepared daily inside in the formal dining room or outside overlooking the beautiful grounds and porch. Linger over your coffee, or have a quick bite in preparation for your day.

2012 Trip Advisor Certificate of Excellence

Trip Advisor Rating #1 out of 12 Stockbridge B&Bs

Easy Potato Leek Soup

Yield: 8–12 servings

½ stick butter or ¼ cup vegetable oil
3 cups diced leeks or yellow onions
4 medium Yukon Gold potatoes, peeled and diced
6 cups water, milk, chicken broth or a combination
2 tsp salt
white pepper, to taste
¼–½ cup heavy cream (optional)
2–4 Tbsp parsley, minced, for garnish

Heat butter or oil in a large saucepan over medium heat. Add leeks or onions and toss to coat. Cook, covered, for about 10 minutes, until soft but not brown. Add potatoes, your choice of milk, water or broth, and salt. Season with white pepper. Bring to a boil, lower heat and simmer, partially covered, for 30 minutes.

Strain soup; return strained liquid to saucepan and purée the strained leek mixture. Add puréed leek mixture to saucepan. Bring to a simmer. Adjust seasonings, if needed, with salt and white pepper. If soup is too thick, add more liquid. Just before serving, stir in cream, if desired. Garnish with parsley to serve.

INN ON COVE HILL

INNKEEPER	Betsy F. Eck
ADDRESS	37 Mount Pleasant Street, Rockport, MA 01966
TELEPHONE	978-546-2701
CONTACT	Betsy25@verizon.net | www.innoncovehill.com
FEATURES	7 Rooms; Private baths | Children age 12 and older welcome | Pets not allowed

Rockport is noted for its stately homes, dramatic coastline, and white picket fences festooned with pastel beach roses. Behind one such fence, the Inn on Cove Hill awaits guests in search of old New England-style elegance and beautifully restored Federal- and Georgian-style architecture.

A magnificent entryway, featuring a gracefully handcrafted spiral staircase, greets visitors upon arrival. Beautiful, wide pumpkin pine floorboards, crown, and dentil molding and a wood-paneled hallway lead to rooms of exceptional character. This gracious house gently transports you back in time and provides a unique New England experience.

The Inn on Cove Hill has been selected as one of the 300 best examples of restored inns and bed & breakfasts in 24 states across the country by The Old House Lover's Guide to Inns, Bed & Breakfasts and Guest Houses.

Banana Oatmeal Almond Muffins

Yield: 12 jumbo or 24 regular muffins

*"I started with a recipe from the former owner
of the inn and made it my own."*

4–5	well-ripened bananas, mashed
¾	cup sugar
4	large eggs
¼	cup, plus 2 Tbsp vanilla yogurt
2	tsp vanilla extract
1¾	sticks melted butter
4	cups all-purpose flour
4	tsp baking powder
2	tsp baking soda
¾	cup Irish oats
¾	cup sliced almonds

Preheat oven to 375°F. Grease or paper line a jumbo or a regular muffin tin.

In a large bowl, combine banana, sugar, eggs, yogurt, and vanilla. Stir in melted butter. In a medium bowl, combine flour, baking powder, baking soda, oats, and almonds; add to banana mixture and stir until combined.

Pour batter into muffin cups. Bake for 25–30 minutes, or until a toothpick inserted in center comes out clean.

MORRISON HOUSE B&B

INNKEEPERS	Ron and Linde Dynneson
ADDRESS	221 Morrison Avenue, Somerville, MA 02144
TELEPHONE	617-627-9670 | 877-627-9670
CONTACT	hosts@morrisonhousebnb.com | www.morrisonhousebnb.com
FEATURES	4 Rooms, 1 Suite; Private baths | Children welcome | Pets not allowed

The Morrison House B&B, a charming Italianate turn-of-the-century house, is in the heart of one of America's most vibrant neighborhoods. The nearby subway stop provides quick and easy access to the entire Boston area. Walk to great restaurants, shops and entertainment. The inn is also conveniently located near Tufts, Harvard, and downtown Boston. The Minuteman Bikeway, which runs through Arlington and Lexington into Bedford, is a block away.

Your stay includes a continental-plus breakfast with fresh seasonal fruit, home-baked pastries, a variety of cereals, hard-boiled eggs, Greek yogurt, bread and all-fruit jams and peanut butter, fresh orange juice, gourmet coffee (& decaf), and regular and herbal teas. They also cater to special dietary needs with advance notice. Breakfast is served at a large table in the dining room where you can meet and socialize with the other guests.

"A really fantastic time in Boston which just wouldn't have been the same if we had not discovered Morrison House. What a treat! The best B&B we have ever stayed in."—Guest

Banana Bread with Streusel Topping

Yield: 1 loaf

"This is a standard at our B&B. It is an easy way to use leftover bananas. One day I topped the loaf with some leftover streusel mix. It was such a big hit, I've been making it that way ever since."

Bread:
- 1¾ cups all-purpose flour
- ¾ tsp baking soda
- 1¼ tsp cream of tartar
- ½ tsp salt
- ⅓ cup butter, softened
- ⅔ cup sugar
- 2 large eggs, well beaten
- 3 very ripe, large bananas, mashed
- ½ cup walnuts, coarsely chopped

Topping:
- ½ cup brown sugar, firmly packed
- 2 Tbsp flour
- ½ cup chopped walnuts
- 2 Tbsp butter, melted
- ½ tsp cinnamon

Preheat oven to 350°F. Grease a large loaf pan.

Place flour in a large bowl. Add baking soda, cream of tartar, and salt. Mix together well with a whisk. In a medium bowl, cream butter and sugar. Add eggs, one at a time. Blend well. If using a mixer, cut bananas in 1-inch chunks and add to mixer. If mixing by hand, mash bananas before adding to wet ingredients. Mix well. Add in dry ingredients, and mix just a couple of seconds. Stir in nuts. Pour into prepared loaf pan.

Topping: In a medium bowl, mix together brown sugar, flour, nuts, melted butter, and cinnamon. Mix to crumbly. Sprinkle over batter in loaf pan.

Bake for 50–60 minutes, until a toothpick inserted in the center comes out clean.

ONE CENTRE STREET INN B&B

INNKEEPER Carla Masse

ADDRESS One Centre Street, Yarmouth Port, MA 02675

TELEPHONE 508-362-9951 | 866-362-9951

CONTACT sales@onecentrestreetinn.com | www.onecentrestreetinn.com

FEATURES 4 Rooms, 1 Suite; Private and shared baths | Children age 12 and older welcome | Pets not allowed

One Centre Street Inn, an elegant 1824 parsonage, is a Cape Cod B&B with all the amenities of the present, while retaining the charm of the past.

This Cape Cod inn is situated among stately sea captains' homes and other historic parsonages. The inn is centrally located on Olde Kings Highway (Route 6A), which winds through the Center of Yarmouth Port like a gently meandering river. Olde Kings Highway is the most beautiful and scenic travel route on all of Cape Cod. One Centre Street Inn is a short walk or bike ride to antique shops, fine restaurants, art galleries, great golf courses, and Gray's Beach.

Guest rooms are uniquely decorated in historic colors and are named for prominent people who lived in Yarmouth Port around the 1800s. Each guest will receive personal, first-rate service and a delicious gourmet breakfast at this Cape Cod B&B.

"Our second visit was even better than our first!! We cannot begin to put into words how wonderful our visits have been. The food was incredible and the company and conversation even better. We look forward to visiting year after year."—Guest

Belgian Waffles with Bananas

Yield: 6–8 waffles

Waffles:

   2 cups all-purpose flour
   2 Tbsp sugar
   2 tsp baking powder
   1 tsp baking soda
  ¾ tsp salt
   2 cups well-shaken buttermilk
  ¾ stick (6 Tbsp) unsalted butter, melted and cooled to room temperature
   2 large eggs
      Vegetable oil for waffle iron

Topping:

   2 Tbsp unsalted butter
   2 firm, but ripe large bananas, cut diagonally into ⅓-inch-thick slices
 1¼ cups pure maple syrup
      Accompaniment: sour cream or whipped cream

In a large bowl, whisk together flour, sugar, baking powder, baking soda, and salt. In a separate bowl, whisk together buttermilk, melted butter, and eggs, then whisk into flour mixture until just combined.

Brush hot waffle iron lightly with vegetable oil and pour a slightly rounded ½ cup of batter into each waffle mold. Cook waffles according to manufacturer's instructions until golden and cooked through, about 3 minutes. Transfer to a rack in the oven to keep warm, keeping waffles in one layer to stay crisp. Make more waffles in same manner.

Topping: While last batch is cooking, heat butter in a 12-inch heavy skillet over moderately high heat until foam subsides, then add banana slices in one layer and cook until golden, about 1 minute per side. Remove from heat and add syrup to skillet. Spoon bananas over waffles, and then drizzle with warm syrup before serving.

Parsonage Inn B&B

INNKEEPERS	Jo-Anne and Richard Hoad
ADDRESS	202 Main Street, East Orleans, MA 02643
TELEPHONE	508-255-8217 | 888-422-8217
CONTACT	innkeeper@parsonageinn.com | www.parsonageinn.com | www.facebook.com/theparsonageinn
FEATURES	8 Rooms; Private baths | Children age 12 and older welcome | Pets not allowed.

Relax and unwind at the Parsonage Inn, a romantic inn nestled in the village of East Orleans, close to local restaurants, and just a mile and a half from Nauset Beach. Built around 1770 as an authentic full-Cape house, the building served as a vicarage in the 1800s. Today it is a cozy and elegant inn.

Breakfasts are inspired by seasonal, local, and organic produce whenever possible. The menu may consist of fruit salad with yogurt and granola on the side; Orange Zest French Toast served with warm maple syrup; quiche or scrambled eggs, cranberry cornmeal muffins with ginger-apricot butter, scones or orange sticky buns. Breakfast is served at individual tables in the dining room, on the brick patio, or in the privacy of your room.

"We enjoyed your hospitality, the fine breakfast, the nicely appointed and comfortable room, and the fun chatter at 6 p.m."—Guest

Feta, Pea, & Chive Tortilla with Roasted Grape Tomatoes

Yield: 4 servings

8 oz. organic red-skinned potatoes
4 organic cage-free eggs
6 oz. feta cheese, cubed
6 oz. frozen peas
  small handful chopped chives
  handful Parmesan cheese, grated
4 oz. organic grape/cherry tomatoes
  salt and pepper
  fresh basil
  Large glug of olive oil*

Preheat oven to 375°F.

Grate the potatoes coarsely and add to a heated and oiled 9-inch pan. Toss frequently until the potatoes begin to soften. In a bowl, beat the eggs; add feta, peas, and chives. Pour the mixture into the pan over the potatoes, and cook over a low to medium heat for about 10 minutes, or until the mixture starts to set. Sprinkle Parmesan cheese on top, transfer to the oven, and cook until golden, about 3–4 minutes.

Season the grape tomatoes with salt and pepper, drizzle with olive oil, and bake for 10 minutes. Cut the potato mixture (tortilla) into wedges, add tomatoes, sprinkle with fresh basil and serve.

Tips: For meat lovers, replace the frozen peas with 6 oz. chopped chorizo sausage.

A glug is approximately 2 tablespoons.

SEAGULL INN B&B

INNKEEPERS	Ruth and Skip Sigler
ADDRESS	106 Harbor Avenue, Marblehead, MA 01945
TELEPHONE	781-631-1893
CONTACT	host@seagullinn.com | www.seagullinn.com
FEATURES	3 Suites; Private baths | Children welcome | Dogs welcome; call ahead

The Seagull Inn B&B on Marblehead Neck offers casual elegance, glorious summer gardens, and spectacular views from the decks throughout the year. Luxurious suites, most with ocean and harbor views, complement the seaside setting. Each suite has been totally restored with cherrywood floors, Shaker furniture, and original paintings.

The charming New England community of Marblehead is well known as the "Yachting Capital of America" and the "Birthplace of the American Navy." Just 17 miles north of Boston, Marblehead is home to the most majestic and beautiful harbor on the eastern seaboard, and is an art and cultural center. Enjoy the water by collecting shells and sea glass, paddling a kayak, or just taking a quiet stroll along the beach; or you might rather immerse yourself in history by taking a walking tour of the town. Steeped in history, Marblehead has over 200 homes and buildings that predate the Revolutionary War.

In the morning, enjoy a view of the harbor with a breakfast of homemade granola, muffins and breads, fresh coffee, bagels, and smoked salmon.

> *"The rooms are lovely, sun-drenched spaces with tasteful décor. The stellar attraction is an apartment suite for five with access to a rooftop deck offering vistas of the ocean and Marblehead."*
>
> —Boston Magazine

Cranberry Scones

Yield: 16–20 scones

3 cups all-purpose flour

4 tsp baking powder

½ tsp baking soda

½ tsp salt

½ cup sugar

2 sticks unsalted butter, chilled and diced

3 large eggs

²/₃ cup buttermilk or plain yogurt

1 cup frozen or fresh cranberries, snip each one in half with scissors

1 tsp freshly grated orange zest

Preheat oven to 350°F.

Process flour, baking powder, baking soda, salt, sugar and butter in a food processor until mixture is the consistency of cornmeal. In a large bowl, beat eggs and buttermilk or yogurt with a mixer. Beat in flour mixture until a soft dough forms. Fold in cranberries and orange zest. Scoop dough with an ice cream scoop onto an ungreased baking sheet; bake for about 20 minutes, until lightly browned.

Tip: This dough freezes well and yields fresh-baked treats with minimal time in the morning. Simply scoop dough onto baking sheet, lightly cover with plastic wrap and freeze. When frozen, transfer to a plastic freezer bag. When ready to bake, place frozen, unbaked scones on an ungreased baking sheet and bake immediately in a preheated 350°F oven for 25 minutes.

SHERBURNE INN

INNKEEPERS	Susan and John Daniels
ADDRESS	10 Gay Street, Nantucket, MA 02554
TELEPHONE	508-228-4425
CONTACT	welcome@sherburneinn.com | www.sherburneinn.com
FEATURES	8 Rooms; Private baths | Children age 12 and older welcome | Pets not allowed

The Sherburne Inn is tucked away in a quiet corner of beautiful Nantucket. Built in 1835 as the headquarters for the Atlantic Silk Company, the inn is ideally located just minutes from Main Street and a short five-minute walk from Steamboat Wharf. The inn's rich history and original artworks enhance the warmth and beauty felt by guests.

Each morning, a delicious home-baked continental-plus breakfast is served, complete with homemade muffins and Nantucket-made breads.

The Sherburne Inn is a small and intimate property, owned and operated by people who know and love Nantucket. Guests here should feel welcome, but also be able to take advantage of knowledge and insights of the innkeepers, as well as the experience of previous guests, so they can have the most enjoyable experience possible of Nantucket.

"We are excited to tell you that the Sherburne Inn is featured in an episode of the new Travel + Leisure 90-Second Insider *video series."*—Innkeeper

Nantucket Cranberry Apple Crisp

Yield: 12 servings

- 6 cups chopped, peeled tart apples
- 4 cups cranberries, frozen or fresh
- 2 cups white sugar

Topping:
- 3 cups old-fashioned rolled oats
- 2 sticks butter, melted
- 1 cup light brown sugar
- $2/3$ cup all-purpose flour
  - Ice cream, for serving (optional)

For the apple crisp: Preheat oven to 350°F. Lightly butter a 9x13-inch baking dish.

Combine apples, cranberries, and sugar in a saucepan over medium heat; cook until cranberries pop or until apples have softened slightly, and there is still liquid in the pan. Spread apple mixture in baking dish.

In a bowl, combine oats, butter, brown sugar, and flour; sprinkle over apple mixture.

Bake for 30 minutes, or until topping is lightly browned and apple mixture is bubbling. Serve warm with ice cream, if desired.

THE WAUWINET

INNKEEPER	Bettina Landt
ADDRESS	120 Wauwinet Road, Nantucket, MA 02584
TELEPHONE	508-228-0145
CONTACT	wau@niresorts.com | www.wauwinet.com
FEATURES	32 Rooms, 4 Cottages; Private baths | Children and pets: inquire

Located just nine miles from bustling Nantucket Town and adjacent to the Great Point Wildlife Sanctuary, The Wauwinet is a serene retreat that combines the luxurious comfort of a wealthy friend's New England seaside estate with the sophistication of an elegant European inn.

The Wauwinet offers sophisticated accommodations surrounded by the relaxing, natural beauty of Nantucket Island. The historic inn features 32 luxury guest rooms, as well as four charming cottages. Each of the rooms is uniquely decorated with one-of-a-kind furnishings with hand-stenciled finishes, Pratesi linens, and a selection of fresh-cut wildflowers.

Rated as one of North America's finest restaurants and a continual recipient of the *Wine Spectator*'s "Grand Award" and *Wine Enthusiast*'s "Award of Excellence," Topper's restaurant offers guests an extraordinary dining experience with gracious personalized service.

"The Wauwinet is naturally beautiful. Wonderfully romantic. Unmistakably Nantucket."—Guest

Lobster Cobb Salad

Yield: 6 servings

Citrus vinaigrette:

- ¾ cup grape seed oil
- 2 Tbsp lemon juice
- 2 Tbsp orange juice
- 1 Tbsp chives, chopped
- 1 Tbsp shallots, minced
  - salt and pepper, to taste
  - minced zest of 1 lemon

Salad:

- ½ lb. pancetta, sliced ¼-inch-thick and diced into ¼-inch pieces
- 1 avocado, chopped into large dice
- ½ lb. haricots vert (green beans), trimmed and blanched
- 9 baby artichokes, cooked and halved
- 1 lb. assorted baby salad greens
- 3 (1½-lb.) lobsters, cooked, meat removed
- 6 radishes, thinly sliced
  - edible flowers, for garnish

For the vinaigrette: Whisk together all ingredients until thoroughly combined.

For the salad: Cook pancetta in a skillet over medium heat until crisp; set aside and keep warm. In a stainless steel bowl, toss avocado, green beans, and artichokes with ½ cup of citrus vinaigrette. In a separate bowl, toss baby greens with enough vinaigrette to coat greens. Place an equal amount of baby greens in the center of 6 plates.

In a bowl, toss lobster with remaining vinaigrette. Arrange lobster meat from ½ tail and 1 claw on each plate. Add green beans on plates, with beans coming through claw. Arrange avocado and 3 baby artichoke halves around lobster. Sprinkle with some pancetta and radishes. Drizzle a little vinaigrette over each salad, if desired. Garnish with edible flowers.

YANKEE CLIPPER INN

INNKEEPERS	Randy and Cathy Marks (and manager Michael Barnhard)
ADDRESS	127 Granite Street, Rockport, MA 01966
TELEPHONE	978-546-0001 | 800-545-3699
CONTACT	info@yankeeclipperinn.com | www.yankeeclipperinn.com
FEATURES	8 Rooms; Private baths | Children welcome | Pets not allowed

The seaside village of Rockport, with its views of Gloucester, attracts visitors from around the world. The Yankee Clipper Inn, overlooking the ocean, provides the perfect backdrop for a New England getaway. Jackie and John F. Kennedy, John Lennon and Yoko Ono, and numerous other celebrities have all been guests of the inn. Rolling lawns and country gardens frame colorful vistas to the open sea. Breathe deeply the salt air from the gazebo. Relax under the umbrellas on the terrace or swim laps in the sun-filled, heated, salt-water pool.

The Yankee Clipper Inn has won countless awards over the years. *Arrington's Bed and Breakfast Journal* has voted the Yankee Clipper Inn "The best inn on the eastern seaboard," "One of the best inns in the country," and "Most panoramic ocean views." *Boston Magazine* named the Yankee Clipper Inn "Best Nearby Escape." The inn has been featured in *Country Living Magazine* and on *The Country Inns* television program.

The Yankee Clipper Inn continues to be an award-winning establishment. In 2012, the inn won the Editor's Choice Award for Best Bed and Breakfast in North Shore Magazine *August 2012 Best of Issue.*

Oh Henry Bars

Yield: 36 bars

"This is a family recipe. They are messy and delicious.
Refrigerate them if you like."

1 stick, plus 2²/₃ Tbsp butter, softened
1 cup packed brown sugar
½ cup white Karo syrup
1 Tbsp vanilla extract
4 cups old-fashioned rolled oats
¾ cup peanut butter
1 (6-oz.) pkg. chocolate chips

Preheat oven to 350°F. Grease a 9x13-inch baking pan.

In a small bowl, cream together butter and sugar. Add Karo syrup, vanilla, and oats. Spread into baking pan. Bake for 18–20 minutes.

Melt peanut butter and chocolate chips over low heat or on top of double boiler. Spread peanut butter mixture on top of baked layer in pan. Cut into bars while still slightly warm.

"Mr. Darcy said very little, and Mr. Hurst nothing at all. The former was divided between admiration of the brilliancy which exercise had given to her complexion, and doubt as to the occasion's justifying her coming so far alone. The latter was thinking only of his breakfast."

— Jane Austen
Pride and Prejudice

Vermont B&Bs

AND THEIR SIGNATURE RECIPES

BRASS LANTERN INN B&B

INNKEEPERS	**Mary Anne and George Lewis**
ADDRESS	**717 Maple Street, Stowe, VT 05672**
TELEPHONE	**802-253-2229	800-729-2980**
CONTACT	**info@brasslanterninn.com	www.brasslanterninn.com**
FEATURES	**9 Rooms; Private baths	Call ahead for children's visits	Pets not allowed**

The Brass Lantern Inn began as a modest farmhouse with a separate carriage house and expansive farmland. The original brick house and wood-framed carriage house is circa 1810. In the structure of today you will see reminders of the past: exposed mortise and tenon, wood columns and beams, wide plank pine floors, and unique brickwork. The expansive back yard provides a level of privacy and unique views of Mt. Mansfield.

Over the years the house has been lovingly maintained and restored. In 1988 it was converted to quality accommodations as the Brass Lantern Inn. The inn is brimming with original antique details yet is coupled with the comfort and amenities expected of today.

The inn is a member of the Vermont Fresh Network—a collection of food service providers that work closely with local farmers and vendors to bring local foods to the breakfast table.

"The fresh homemade breakfast each morning was incredible. Parfait, fresh fruits, juices, coffee, tea, French toast, quiche, etc ... not to mention an amazing view of Mt. Mansfield while you eat!"—Guest

Apple Crêpes

Yield: 6 servings

Crêpes:

- 2 large eggs
- 1½ cups milk
- ½ tsp salt
- 1 cup all-purpose flour
- 2 Tbsp butter, melted

Filling:

- 3 Tbsp butter
- ⅔ cup packed brown sugar
- ¼ cup raisins
- grated zest of 1 orange
- 4½ Granny Smith apples, peeled and cut into ¼-inch-thick slices
- 2 Tbsp pure Vermont Maple Syrup
- 1 tsp cornstarch

For the crêpes: Blend all crêpe ingredients in a blender until smooth. Let batter stand for 30 minutes (this will yield more tender crêpes). Lightly coat a crêpe pan or skillet with vegetable oil and heat over medium-high heat. Pour about 3 tablespoons of batter into pan. Rotate pan to coat evenly with batter. Cook crêpe until golden brown, turn and cook other side briefly. Stack crêpes on a plate with waxed paper between each crêpe.

For the filling: Melt butter in a skillet over medium heat. Add brown sugar, raisins, and orange zest; simmer until sugar is dissolved. Add apples, and simmer gently for about 20 minutes. Remove apples. Pour the remaining pan syrup mixture into a small saucepan. Return apples to skillet and keep warm. Whisk cornstarch into pan syrup until smooth. Simmer over low heat until reduced to desired consistency. Fill crêpes with apple filling. Drizzle some pan syrup over crêpes.

CASA BELLA INN & RESTAURANT

INNKEEPERS	Susan and Franco Cacozza
ADDRESS	3911 Main Street, Route 100 North, Pittsfield, VT 05762
TELEPHONE	802-746-8943 | 877-746-8943
CONTACT	info@casabellainn.com | www.casabellainn.com
FEATURES	6 Rooms, 2 Suites; Private baths | Children age 10 and older welcome | Pets not allowed

The Casa Bella Inn & Restaurant offers "a little bit of Tuscany" in a Vermont country inn. Chef Franco welcomes you to his Chef-owned restaurant where northern Italian cuisine is featured.

Recent restorations have created modern accommodations while retaining the inn's original grandeur. The inn's setting, architecture, casual, relaxed atmosphere and wonderful food combine to create an unforgettable experience. Sit on one of the two-story porches overlooking the village green, or gaze at the mountains and forests and consider them your playground.

In the summer you'll escape with hiking, mountain biking, fishing and walking tours. Visit the Green Mountain National Forest or go tubing in the White River. In the winter months you can enjoy skiing, snowshoeing, and snowmobiling. The inn is located at corridor #100 on the VAST trails. There is ample parking for snowmobile trailers as well. Snowmobilers can come for dinner and a good night's rest, then leave their trailers and head off for a few days of fun.

> *"We came here because it sounded like the ideal Vermont B&B.*
> *Not only did it more than live up to our expectations, we accidentally*
> *discovered what may be the best Italian restaurant in Vermont."*
>
> —Guest

Calamari Alla Franco

Yield: 4 servings

"Shrimp may be substituted for calamari."

1 Tbsp olive oil
1 Tbsp fresh minced garlic
12 squid tubes, cleaned, washed and sliced into rings
1 Tbsp capers
½ cup pitted Italian black olives
  pinch of dried oregano for sauce
  pinch of red pepper flakes (optional)
  salt and pepper, to taste
2 cups tomato sauce
  dried or minced fresh oregano, for serving

Heat oil in a skillet over medium heat. Add garlic and cook just until golden. Add calamari (squid tubes), and cook for about 2 minutes, until opaque. Raise heat to medium-high, add capers and black olives; cook for 1 minute. Stir in oregano, red pepper flakes, salt and pepper. Add tomato sauce, and cook for an additional 30 seconds, or until tomato sauce is hot and calamari is white and no longer transparent (be careful not to overcook). Serve immediately sprinkled with a little fresh or dried oregano.

COMBES FAMILY INN B&B

INNKEEPERS	Ruth & Bill Combes
ADDRESS	935 East Lake Road, Ludlow, VT 05149
TELEPHONE	802-228-8799 | 800-228-8799
CONTACT	info@combesfamilyinn.com | www.combesfamilyinn.com
FEATURES	11 Rooms; Private baths | Children and pets are welcome

The Combes Family Inn B&B is a true family inn situated on a quiet country back road in the heart of Vermont's mountain and lake region. You are invited to explore the inn's 50 acres of rolling meadows and woods and to take advantage of the skiing, foliage, hiking and much more. Enjoy hearty, home-cooked meals, spectacular views, and a roaring fire on a cold night or a stroll along country back roads on a summer evening.

The aroma of fresh baked bread greets you upon entering the inn. If you've been relaxing on the porch, living room or bedrooms, tantalizing scents will have already piqued your appetite.

Your day begins with a hearty country breakfast that will fuel you through even the most grueling day of skiing, biking, walking, or touring. Breakfast could consist of pancakes, eggs, French toast or waffles, ham, sausage, or bacon, among other classics. When the dinner bell rings, a three-course, home-cooked meal is served that is "like going to your grandmother's house for Sunday dinner."

"Can't say enough about the Combes Family Inn. We have been going there for over 15 years. The kids loved it when they were small, and now as young adults they like coming back with us again for those great reunions."—Guest

Sour Cream Rhubarb Streusel Pie

Yield: 8 servings

"Our inn has a very large rhubarb patch. I make and freeze endless strawberry rhubarb pies, but the following sour cream rhubarb pie is a very popular dessert at the inn."

- 1 cup sour cream
- 1 large egg
- ¾ cup sugar
- 2 Tbsp all-purpose flour
- ¼ tsp salt
- 1 tsp vanilla extract
- 3 cups rhubarb, chopped
  - Ice cream, for serving

Topping:

- ½ cup packed brown sugar
- ¹/₃ cup oats
- ½ stick butter, softened
- 1 tsp cinnamon

Preheat oven to 350°F. In a large bowl, beat sour cream and egg. Add sugar, flour, salt and vanilla. Stir in rhubarb. Pour rhubarb mixture into an 8x8-inch baking pan. In a small bowl, combine topping ingredients until crumbly; sprinkle over rhubarb mixture. Bake for 30–35 minutes. Serve with ice cream.

DEER BROOK INN

INNKEEPERS	David Kanal & George DeFina
ADDRESS	4548 West Woodstock Road, Woodstock, VT 05091
TELEPHONE	802-672-3713
CONTACT	stay@deerbrookinn.com | www.deerbrookinn.com
FEATURES	4 Rooms, 1 Suite; Private baths | Children 8 years and older are welcome | Pets not allowed

Welcome to beautiful Woodstock and the Green Mountains. Enjoy a historic haven of hospitality and comfort surrounded by spacious lawns and gardens. Whether your vision of the idyllic New England bed & breakfast experience is replete with culture and recreation, or it involves simply sinking into a comfortable chair with a summer breeze or winter fire, the Deer Brook Inn sets the scene while allowing you to set the pace.

The inn offers a high degree of personalized service with only five guest accommodations. The focus and reason for success is in the fact that every guest is made to feel at home and truly important to the innkeepers. Enjoy a room filled with antique furnishings, original artwork and wide, honey pine floors.

Start your day with a full, candlelit breakfast. Breakfast is a much-talked-about event at Deer Brook. Served in the formal dining room or on the stone patio overlooking the lawn and wooded areas, it features fresh, local ingredients from neighboring farms whenever possible.

"For a B&B experience, the Deer Brook Inn, five miles west of Woodstock village, has a suite that includes a sofa bed for the children and a three-course breakfast featuring organic eggs from a neighbor's farm."—The New York Times

Autumn Brisket

Yield: 8–10 servings

*"Great comfort food for those cool days. Easy to make.
It gets even better when reheated on the second day."*

2	Tbsp vegetable oil
3–4	large onions, chopped
2	cloves garlic, chopped
6	lbs. brisket
1	cup packed dark brown sugar
¾	cup apple cider
1¼	cups ketchup
¼	cup water

Preheat oven to 350°F. In a large pot or Dutch oven over medium heat, heat oil. Add onions and garlic, and cook until soft. Remove onions and garlic from pot; set aside.

In the same pot over high heat, sear meat on both sides. Reduce heat and cover with onion mixture. Mix remaining ingredients in a bowl and pour over the meat. Cook, covered, over moderate heat for 2½ hours. Uncover and let cook for 1 hour longer, or until meat is fork-tender.

Tip: This brisket can be made 1–2 days in advance; covered, refrigerated, and then reheated—it's often best served this way.

ECHO LAKE INN

INNKEEPER	Laurence Jeffery
ADDRESS	Route 100 North, Ludlow, VT 05149
TELEPHONE	802-228-8602 | 800-356-6844
CONTACT	echolkinn@aol.com | www.echolakeinn.com
FEATURES	23 Rooms; 7 Suites; Private baths | Children welcome | Call ahead for pet stays; Resident dog

Located in Vermont's beautiful central lakes region, the Echo Lake Inn was built in 1840 as a Victorian summer hotel. Today it remains one of the few authentic country inns operating year-round in Vermont. The Vermont Country Inn's rich heritage includes frequent visits by President Calvin Coolidge, Henry Ford, Thomas Edison and many other historic figures.

The restaurant, recently featured in both *Gourmet* and *Bon Appetit* magazines, is well known for the excellent food and service provided by Chef Kevin and his staff. Chef Barnes has been the constant skill and creative force behind the success of the Echo Lake Inn restaurant for the past 10 years. His menus reflect the importance of attention to detail, creativity and the use of only the freshest ingredients. The delivery of fresh fish, meats, produce and herbs from our garden are the foundation for excellence.

"Dinner here is something of an event, cheerfully served under exposed beams on plum-colored linens, and accompanied by an affordable wine list. On weekends, so many people from Ludlow and other local communities dine here that two sittings are scheduled—a first-time visitor quickly understands why."—Vermont Magazine

Scallop-Stuffed Salmon en Papillote

Yield: 4 servings

"An elegant, but not difficult or time-consuming entrée. The secret is to fold the parchment paper tightly to seal in the flavors. Even though the salmon is baked, it is actually steamed in the paper."

- 4 (8-oz.) boneless salmon filets
- ½ lb. sea scallops
- 4 (12x16-inch) sheets parchment paper
- salt and pepper, to taste
- 1 lemon, thinly sliced
- 1 carrot, peeled and julienned
- 1 onion, peeled and julienned
- 1 rib celery, julienned
- 4 sprigs fresh dill
- ½ cup white wine
- 1 stick butter, cut into thin slices

Preheat oven to 425°F.

Slice salmon filets lengthwise down the center, about ¾ of the way through. Insert 3–4 scallops in each salmon filet. Center each salmon filet on ½ sheet of a parchment sheet.

Season salmon with salt and pepper. Cover each filet with a couple of lemon slices and some of the julienned carrot, onion and celery. Top vegetables with a sprig of dill, a sprinkle of wine and a few slices of butter.

Fold parchment tightly over salmon. Crimp edges by making overlapping folds every inch or so. Bake for 15 minutes. Serve sealed—allowing your guests to open these delicious packages!

GRÜNBERG HAUS

INNKEEPERS	Linda & Jeff Connor
ADDRESS	94 Pine Street, Route 100 South, Waterbury, VT 05676
TELEPHONE	802-244-7726 | 800-800-7760
CONTACT	info@grunberghaus.com | www.grunberghaus.com
FEATURES	9 Rooms, 2 Suites, 3 Cottages; Private & shared baths | Children age 5 and older welcome | Dogs & cats welcome in cabins

Warmly welcoming guests since 1972, the Grünberg Haus is a beautiful Austrian chalet, hand-built like a country inn hidden in the Alps and set among towering pines and sugar maple trees. Escape into the countryside and enjoy quiet relaxation in a mountainside setting midway between the resorts of Stowe and Sugarbush.

Breakfast features homemade breads and hearty entrées. Gaze out a 20–foot glass wall and watch wildlife while you savor pumpkin apple streusel muffins, maple-poached pears and ricotta-stuffed French toast.

Ben & Jerry's Ice Cream factory is nearby, as are Cold Hollow Cider Mill, Vermont Teddy Bear, Cabot Cheese, and Lake Champlain Chocolates.

"This was a very beautiful and relaxing place to have a little vacation. The cabins were very clean and the wood stove was amazing. Linda sure can cook!"—E.D., NY

Potato Cheddar Quiche

Yield: 6 servings

"This recipe is great for meeting the needs of both gluten-free diets and lactose intolerant diets. Plus, everyone likes it. (Including the cook, since it is so easy to prepare and freezes well.)"

Crust:
- 3 cups frozen cube-style hash browns, thawed
- ¼ cup onion, chopped
- 4 Tbsp butter, melted

Filling:
- 1 cup spinach, fresh
- 1 cup cheddar cheese, shredded

Custard:
- 3 large eggs, whisked
- ½ cup milk

Seasoned salt
tomato slices, to garnish
basil to garnish

Preheat oven to 400 °F. Combine potatoes and onion. Press into a 9-inch pie plate. Pour melted butter over all. Bake for 20–25 minutes until potatoes just begin to brown.

Remove from oven and reduce heat to 350°F. Spread spinach over the top. Spread cheese over the spinach. In a bowl, combine the egg and milk and pour over all. Top with seasoned salt. Let it settle. Return to oven for 25–30 minutes until golden brown.

Slice into 6 pieces and serve on plates garnished with tomato slices and basil.

HARTNESS HOUSE INN

INNKEEPERS	**The Blair Family**
ADDRESS	30 Orchard Street, Springfield, VT 05156
TELEPHONE	802-885-2115	800-732-4789
CONTACT	innkeeper@hartnesshouse.com	www.hartnesshouse.com
FEATURES	40 Rooms; Private baths	Children welcome	Pets not allowed

The Hartness House Inn is a historic country inn set on the beautiful 32-acre estate of a former governor, James Hartness of Vermont. The worldwide reputation of the Hartness House is due, in part, to the reputation of this visionary and inventor. Guests will see artifacts throughout the inn related to his many achievements.

Listed on the National Register of Historic Places, the inn offers landscaped grounds and gardens, an outdoor pool and park-like surroundings. A wide variety of accommodations are available, along with fine dining and casual restaurants, a tavern, and an extensive wine cellar. The Pushkin Restaurant at the inn offers authentic Russian cuisine with a variety of dishes direct from Moscow.

Near the inn, one can play tennis or golf, fly fish, antique shop, canoe, sail, hike, bike and enjoy glorious country drives with incomparable views.

"The Hartness House is one of Vermont's popular destinations for Thanksgiving, Christmas, and New Year's Eve. We open the holiday season with a traditional Thanksgiving feast surrounded by our gala holiday-decorated inn. During the Christmas season, the inn is decorated with brightly lit Christmas trees, hundreds of yards of garlands and festive lighting, and traditional holiday decorations throughout. For New Years, we offer a celebration feast with festive New Year's Eve decorations, live piano music and DJ music for your dancing pleasure."—Innkeeper

Pumpkin Layer Cheesecake

Yield: 8–12 servings

2 (8-oz.) pkgs. cream cheese, softened
½ cup sugar
½ tsp vanilla extract
2 large eggs
1 graham cracker crust
½ cup canned pumpkin
½ tsp cinnamon
¼ tsp ground cloves
¼ tsp ground nutmeg

Preheat oven to 350°F. Beat cream cheese, sugar, and vanilla with a mixer on medium speed until well blended. Add eggs and beat well. Transfer 1 cup of cream cheese mixture to a small bowl; set aside and reserve. Spread remaining cream cheese mixture in crust.

Add pumpkin, cinnamon, cloves and nutmeg to the reserved 1 cup of cream cheese mixture. Mix well, and carefully spread on top of cream cheese mixture in crust. Bake for 35–40 minutes. Cool and then cover and refrigerate cheesecake for at least 3 hours before serving.

HILL FARM INN

INNKEEPERS | Lisa and Al Gray
ADDRESS | 458 Hill Farm Road, Arlilngton, VT 05250
TELEPHONE | 802-375-2269 | 800-882-2545
CONTACT | stay@hillfarminn.com | www.hillfarminn.com
FEATURES | 5 Rooms, 6 Suites, 4 Cabins; Private baths | Children welcome | Pets not allowed; Resident goats, sheep, chickens, dog

Hill Farm Inn, one of Vermont's first bed & breakfast inns, specializes in warm country hospitality. This is the kind of place where there's always plenty to do, but never anything you have to do. And it's been this way for nearly 100 years. Set on 50 acres, with a mile of frontage on the famed Battenkill River, you'll enjoy spectacular mountain views in every direction.

The inn's convenient, but tucked away location between Manchester and Bennington provides easy access to a wide variety of cultural activities, shopping, dining, fishing, canoeing, hiking, skiing and fall foliage tours.

Each morning, guests will enjoy the full country breakfast that has become a Hill Farm Inn tradition. Breakfast is made to order, and may include muffins, scones, pancakes, eggs, bacon, granola, and more. Although dinner is not served at the inn, the Manchester and Arlington areas offer a wide variety of dining choices from casual to gourmet.

"Every afternoon we fill a table with a choice of teas, hot chocolate, coffee and home-baked cookies fresh from the oven. Then, in the evening, the table is replenished so that our guests might enjoy a little something after dinner."—Innkeeper

Salmon Pâté

Yield: 6–8 servings

"This is a great appetizer that even people who don't like fish—enjoy."

1 (16-oz.) can red sockeye salmon, drained and flaked
1 (8-oz.) pkg. cream cheese, softened
1 Tbsp lemon juice
1 Tbsp grated onion
2 tsp prepared horseradish
¼ tsp salt
¾ tsp Liquid Smoke
½ cup pecans, chopped
2 Tbsp fresh parsley, chopped
  cocktail rye bread or crackers, for serving

In a bowl, combine all ingredients, except pecans and parsley, by hand. If mixture is very soft, refrigerate for a few minutes. Combine pecans and parsley. Form salmon mixture into a ball and roll in pecan mixture. Chill for at least 3 hours. Serve with cocktail rye bread or crackers.

INN AT ORMSBY HILL

INNKEEPERS	Yoshio & Diane Endo
ADDRESS	1842 Main Street, Manchester, VT 05255
TELEPHONE	802-362-1163 | 800-670-2841
CONTACT	stay@ormsbyhill.com | www.ormsbyhill.com
FEATURES	10 Rooms; Private baths | Children age 14 and older welcome | Pets not allowed

This southern Vermont B&B is the premier romantic New England getaway to Manchester. The Inn at Ormsby Hill is a truly romantic and luxurious Vermont B&B country inn—a perfect New England vacation destination for intimate getaways, honeymoons, celebrations and relaxing escapes. The Inn at Ormsby Hill is proud to be the only inn in Manchester that provides AAA 4-Diamond service. We are one of only two 4-Diamond Vermont B&Bs. One luxurious evening with us and you'll know why.

Renowned for comfort, heartfelt hospitality and profound attention to detail, the Inn at Ormsby Hill is an ideal retreat where guests are totally pampered with exquisite accommodations, excellent food and unparalleled amenities. Whether you come for relaxation, romance or recreation, the Inn at Ormsby Hill will make your Vermont getaway an unforgettable event.

Imagine stylish décor of the highest quality—a canopy bed, a private Jacuzzi for two, a glowing fireplace. It is a potion for romance. Room design and ambiance was created with tranquility and comfort as the guiding principles.

"You say you are searching for a sumptuous room with a fireplace and a Jacuzzi big enough for two, plus a gourmet breakfast lavish enough to last all day? Look no further ..."
—Recommended Bed & Breakfasts of New England

Cranberry Bread Pudding

Yield: 10–12 servings

4 cups water	4 tsp cinnamon, divided
4½ cups sugar, divided	2 sticks butter, melted
3 Tbsp grated lemon zest	5 cups heavy cream
1 vanilla bean, split lengthwise	5 cups milk
2 lbs. cranberries	18 large eggs
2 (1-lbs.) loaves challah bread, cut into 1-inch chunks	powdered sugar to garnish

Preheat oven to 350°F. In a large saucepan, bring water, 2 cups of sugar, lemon zest and vanilla bean to a boil, stir to dissolve sugar. Add cranberries; simmer for 1 minute. Remove from heat. Scrape vanilla bean seeds into cranberry mixture; discard vanilla bean pod. Cool to room temperature. Put bread in a large bowl. Add 4 tablespoons of sugar, 2 teaspoons cinnamon and melted butter; toss to combine. Transfer to a baking sheet and bake for 24 minutes.

In a small bowl, combine 4 tablespoons sugar and 2 teaspoons cinnamon; sprinkle mixture into a well-greased 10-cup Bundt pan, coating both bottom and sides. Transfer bread to the Bundt pan. Drain cranberry mixture and spread over bread. In a large bowl, whisk together heavy cream, milk, eggs and remaining 2 cups of sugar; pour over bread. Cover and refrigerate overnight.

The next day, preheat oven to 350°F. Cover Bundt pan with foil. Set Bundt pan in a larger pan. Add enough hot water to come halfway up the sides of the Bundt pan. Bake for 1 hour, or until center is barely set. Remove Bundt pan from pan and let stand for 5 minutes. Sprinkle with powdered sugar before serving. Slice and serve with breakfast meat of choice.

LIBERTY HILL FARM INN

INNKEEPERS	**Beth Kennett and family**
ADDRESS	**511 Liberty Hill, Rochester, VT 05767**
TELEPHONE	**802-767-3926**
CONTACT	**beth@libertyhillfarm.com	www.libertyhillfarm.com**
FEATURES	**5 Rooms; 4 Shared baths	Children welcome	Pets not allowed**

For a quarter of a century, Liberty Hill Farm Inn has opened its doors and hearts to guests from around the world. Many of the guests return year after year and have become dear friends. Maybe it's because of Beth's incredible, home-cooked meals or the novelty of a genuine, working dairy farm. Perhaps it is the allure of the peace and quiet of this stunningly beautiful corner of Vermont or the chance to milk a real cow!

Some come to celebrate anniversaries, others family reunions. Whatever the reason for your visit, the Kennett family feels blessed to be able to share their home and their way of life with you. Are you looking for outdoor adventure or looking for a quiet retreat? Liberty Hill Farm offers the best of both. You are always welcome here!

Liberty Hill Farm has been selected to be one of the voices representing the family farm owners of Cabot Creamery Cooperative. Cabot Cheddar has won every major award for cheese and Liberty Hill Farm's Cabot butter is a blue ribbon winner as well.

Liberty Hill Farm was awarded Yankee Magazine's *"Best of New England" Editors' Choice Award in their "2010 Travel Guide to New England."*

Beth's Baked Oatmeal

Yield: 4–5 servings

"The big farm breakfast with pancakes and eggs and homemade sausage with my hot-from-the-oven coffeecakes and muffins are appreciated by all my guests, but the breakfast item that really gets rave reviews morning after morning is the Baked Oatmeal. So simple, so filling, so good for you."

- 1⅓ cups oats (must use old-fashioned, steel cut, never use quick oats)
- ¼ cup brown sugar or maple sugar
- 1 apple, peeled and diced
- ⅓ cup dried cranberries
- ½ tsp cinnamon
- ¼ tsp salt
- 2 Tbsp butter, melted
- 2 cups milk (for best flavor and nutrition use whole milk)

Preheat oven to 375 degrees F.

Stir all ingredients together in an ovenproof pan. Bake for 45 minutes. Serve in bowls with milk.

RABBIT HILL INN

INNKEEPERS	Brian & Leslie Mulcahy
ADDRESS	448 Lower Waterford Road, Lower Waterford, VT 05848
TELEPHONE	802-748-5168 | 800-762-8669
CONTACT	info@rabbithillinn.com | www.rabbithillinn.com
FEATURES	11 Rooms, 8 Suites; Private baths | Children age 14 and older welcome | Pets not allowed

Established in 1795, the Rabbit Hill Inn is an elegant, luxury country inn—a perfect Vermont destination for relaxing escapes, romantic getaways and honeymoons. Select from 19 romantic, lavishly appointed guest rooms and suites—most with flowing fireplaces, many with double whirlpool tubs, canopy beds, and antiques. All rooms are steeped with charm and elegance, designed with your needs and comforts in mind.

Your day starts with a full candlelit breakfast and a choice of two hot entrées. Afternoon tea is a "perfect cup" of tea and delicate pastries. Evening dining is again by candlelight. The offerings are innovative, seasonal, and sourced locally whenever possible.

"There are some inns that just seem to stir the romantic soul and this showpiece is most certainly one of them!"—The Travel Channel

Corn & Rye Whiskey Soup

Yield: 4 quarts (or 16 cups)

"Chef John Corliss crafted this totally awesome and unique fall soup. The dining crowd went crazy over it. Chef John encourages you to try this at home."

2 medium onions, sliced	**Corn Stock:**
6 cloves garlic, crushed	12 corn cobs
12 cobs of fresh sweet corn	3–6 sprigs fresh thyme
1 cup white wine	1 Tbsp whole black
1 cup Rye Whiskey	peppercorns
1 quart heavy cream	1 medium onion,
salt & pepper, to season	quartered

Remove the corn kernels from cobs. Set kernels aside. Reserve cobs.

In a large pot, heat a thin layer of oil. Add garlic and sliced onion. Over medium heat, sweat onion and garlic until softened. Add corn kernels. Sauté lightly. Remove pan from heat. Add wine and whiskey. Return to medium heat and reduce by 2/3. Add cream and reduce by ½. Let cool slightly. Place your corn & cream mixture into blender. Blend until smooth. As you blend, add your corn stock to achieve desired consistency. Work this process in batches if needed. Once desired consistency is reached, and all batches are together, add salt and pepper to taste.

Corn stock:
Place cobs in a pot just large enough to hold them and cover with cold water. Add thyme, peppercorns, and quartered onion. Bring to a gentle boil, then reduce to simmer for 40–60 minutes, or until you have a nice corn-flavored stock. Strain and set aside.

SINCLAIR INN B&B

INNKEEPERS	Nimmie & Don Huber
ADDRESS	389 Vermont Route 15, Jericho, VT 05465
TELEPHONE	802-899-2234 | 800-433-4658
CONTACT	sinclairinn@myfairpoint.net | www.sinclairinnbb.com
FEATURES	6 Rooms; Private baths | Children age 7 and older welcome | Pets not allowed

West of the Green Mountains and east of Lake Champlain, the Sinclair Inn invites guests to step back in time to a bygone era. Located just 15 miles from Burlington, this Queen Anne Victorian Inn was built in 1895 by Edward Sinclair. Edward, a wood craftsman and building contractor, built the home for his bride-to-be, Ruth. At the time, Edward was in his early 30s and Ruth was just sixteen. This historic, fully restored Victorian inn features original crown moldings, fret work, hardwood floors and stained glass windows.

On cold days, the living room's fireplace beckons guests to relax and curl up with a good book. In summer, stroll past the stone pond and cascading waterfall to the back of the gardens which overlook the Green Mountains.

"Loved the inn! Creature comforts abound. The innkeepers are so gracious and hospitable. The Sinclair Inn is ideally located for cross-country skiing and other winter sports, as well as antiquing, restaurants, scenic drives, and local Vermont shopping. Thanks so much for a truly wonderful visit!"—Guest

Drunken Bananas

Yield: 1 Serving

1 banana, unpeeled
  Kahlúa or Tia Maria, or other coffee-flavored liqueur
  cinnamon sugar
  Ben & Jerry's Ice Cream

Preheat oven to 350°F. Bake banana in its skin for 15–20 minutes, until black and soft. Cut banana open; serve in skin with a dash of Kahlúa or Tia Maria, and a sprinkle of cinnamon. Top with your choice of ice cream. (We suggest Ben and Jerry's.)

Tips:

* A quick way to ripen bananas is to put them in a paper bag with one ripe apple.

* To slow the ripening process, refrigerate the bananas. The skins will turn brown, but the flesh of the banana will not be affected.

* Overripe bananas can be frozen for future use in baking—peel and mash and place in a freezer bag or airtight container.

STONE HILL INN

INNKEEPERS	Linda & George Fulton
ADDRESS	89 Houston Farm Road, Stowe, VT 05672
TELEPHONE	802-253-6282
CONTACT	stay@stonehillinn.com | www.stonehillinn.com
FEATURES	9 Rooms, Private baths | Children age 18 and older welcome | Pets not allowed

A scenic mountain village awaits guests at the doorstep of the Stone Hill Inn, a place for couples who treasure their time together. Stowe, with its New England charm hinting of European influence and natural beauty, has been welcoming visitors for two centuries.

Breakfast, of course, is the most important meal of the day. So, Linda insists on everything homemade. Like the powdered sugar on your orange pecan waffle, sun dabbles the room through a cathedral of forty windows. Each evening an hors d'oeuvre is set out in the guest pantry. It's meant to be a nice pre-dinner treat.

"The Stone Hill Inn combines a coveted hilltop setting in the woods, tranquility, top-drawer construction, designer décor, gourmet breakfasts and gorgeous, spacious private baths. It's an intimate place with only nine guest rooms—picture perfect."—Montreal Gazette

Mediterranean Shrimp

Yield: 12 servings

*"You will need wooden skewers for grilling
or broiling these delicious shrimp."*

1½ cups olive oil
½ cup chopped fresh parsley
1½ Tbsp dried basil
1 Tbsp dried oregano
12 cloves garlic, minced
1½ Tbsp salt
2 Tbsp pepper
2 lbs. raw shrimp, peeled, (thawed, if frozen)
lemon wedges, for serving

In a small bowl, combine olive oil, parsley, basil, oregano, garlic, salt, and pepper for a marinade. Put shrimp in a glass baking dish or other non-reactive container. Pour ⅔ of marinade over shrimp; stir well to coat. Cover and refrigerate shrimp for at least 1 hour. Soak wooden skewers in water for at least 1 hour before using.

Preheat grill or broiler. Remove shrimp from marinade; discard used marinade. Put shrimp on skewers and grill or broil, basting with remaining marinade, for 3 minutes on each side. Serve with lemon wedges.

STRONG HOUSE INN

INNKEEPERS	Mary & Hugh Bargiel
ADDRESS	94 West Main Street. Vergennes, VT 05491
TELEPHONE	802-877-3337
CONTACT	innkeeper@stronghouseinn.com | www.stronghouseinn.com
FEATURES	15 Rooms; Private baths | Children age 8 and older welcome | Dogs welcome; call ahead

Built by Samuel Paddock Strong in 1837 and listed on the National Register of Historic Places, the Strong House Inn is ranked as one of the finest examples of early Greek Revival architecture in the area. Enjoy the ambiance of the enchanting English Garden Cottage. Or, celebrate a crimson sunset with the backdrop of the Adirondack Mountains.

The Adirondack Room is the ultimate romantic hideaway, reflecting the style of great turn-of-the-last-century Adirondack camps. The room features a magnificent canopied four-poster Adirondack bed and a floor-to-ceiling stone fireplace.

The Strong House Inn is located in Vergennes, Vermont, the smallest city in the U.S. in area (2½ square miles). It is just a half-hour south of Burlington. Hiking, biking, boating, fishing, birding, golfing and discovering the beauties of Vermont are just a few of the activities that abound. Vergennes and the surrounding area have the best restaurants and antique shops in all of Vermont. Come to the Strong House Inn and feel the spirit of Vermont.

"Our popular "Quilting in Vermont" retreats have been featured in The New York Times. *These retreat packages are packed with pampering, wonderful food, and ambiance; sharing ideas, making new friends and just having lots of fun."*—Innkeeper

Roasted Red Pepper Soup

Yield: 4–6 servings

4　large red bell peppers
4　cups chicken broth
2　cups tomatoes seeded, chopped
1　cup potato, diced
2　cloves garlic, minced
½　cup sour cream, room temperature
　　salt and pepper, to taste

Roast bell peppers on a grill, over the flame on a gas stove, or broil until outside of pepper is well charred. Place peppers in a paper bag for a few minutes. This steams them and makes them easier to peel. Peel, seed and coarsely chop peppers.

In a medium saucepan over medium-high heat, combine peppers, chicken broth, tomatoes, potato and garlic. Bring to a boil, lower heat and simmer until potatoes are tender. Remove soup from heat and purée in a blender or food processor. (Be careful—the soup will be very hot). Return soup to saucepan. Stir in sour cream. Season with salt and pepper. Serve hot or cold.

VERMONT INN

INNKEEPERS	McLemore-Smith Family
ADDRESS	Route 4, 78 Cream Hill Road, Mendon, VT 05701
TELEPHONE	802-775-0708 | 800-541-7795
CONTACT	thevermontinn@gmail.com | www.vermontinn.com
FEATURES	11 Rooms, 7 Suites; Private baths | Children welcome | Pets not allowed

The Vermont Inn is a small, circa-1840 country inn on five acres in the Green Mountains. The inn combines the charm of a family-run bed & breakfast with excellent New England and Continental cuisine. Guests enjoy year-round outdoor adventures, with exceptional skiing in winter and a myriad of summer and fall activities in the surrounding mountains.

The Vermont Inn offers clean and comfortable Killington-area lodging and ensures that guests feel at home. Each room is individually decorated with unique and tasteful decor that exudes warm country charm.

The highlight of the Vermont Inn is the fabulous, award-winning, gourmet cuisine. Guests of the inn are served a four-course dinner by a roaring fire in the huge fieldstone fireplace, accompanied by beautiful mountain views.

The inn was named one of the Top Fifty Inns of America by The Inn Times *and is featured in* Recommended Country Inns of New England *and* America's Wonderful Little Hotels and Inns.

Vermont Baked Veal

Yield: 4 servings

1 lb. veal top round
2 Tbsp olive oil
2 cloves garlic, minced
½ cup shallots, chopped
1 cup spinach, chopped
½ cup diced cooked bacon
2 cups cheddar cheese, grated
   salt and pepper, to taste
   ground nutmeg, to taste
½ cup all-purpose flour
4 large eggs, slightly beaten
½ cup breadcrumbs

Preheat oven to 350°F. Cut veal into ¼-inch-thick slices and pound lightly until very thin; set aside. Heat oil over medium heat. Add garlic, shallots and spinach; cook until shallots are soft, then remove from heat. Add bacon, cheese, salt, pepper, and nutmeg to spinach mixture; stir until well combined.

Place ¼ cup of spinach mixture in center of each slice of veal; roll up tightly. Secure with toothpicks, if desired. Dredge veal rolls in flour, dip in egg and then roll in breadcrumbs. Place veal rolls on a greased baking sheet. Bake for 15–20 minutes, or until golden brown.

WEST MOUNTAIN INN

INNKEEPERS	Mary Ann & Wes Carlson
ADDRESS	144 West Mountain Road, Arlington, VT 05250
TELEPHONE	802-375-6516
CONTACT	info@westmountaininn.com	www.westmountaininn.com
FEATURES	Features: 14 Rooms, 3 townhouse units; Private baths	Children welcome	Pets not allowed

Nestled on a mountainside, the century-old West Mountain Inn invites guests to discover its many treasures. Distinctively decorated guest rooms and comfortable common areas, along with 150 woodland acres with wildflowers, a bird sanctuary, and llamas, provide space to relax and rejuvenate the body and spirit. Miles of wilderness skiing or hiking trails and the Battenkill River provide seasonal outdoor activities. A hearty breakfast, complete with apple pie, and a fine country dinner in front of an open hearth, complete your stay.

The inn is pleased to have Chef Jeff Scott in charge of the inn's cuisine. A graduate of Johnson and Wales University, Jeff Scott has been the dedicated and creative head chef at the West Mountain Inn for over 7 years. His passion for local, fresh, organic ingredients has him seeking out only the finest local food producers Vermont has to offer. On any given week, you might find him picking out fresh creamy goat cheeses, or seasonal organic produce from local farms.

"My husband and I started staying at the West Mountain Inn many years ago to celebrate our wedding anniversary. We returned many times taking our children there for skiing trips in the winter. We stayed in the Norman Rockwell Room, and as they grew, we moved down the hill to the Mill House. We always feel at home and at peace at the inn. The food is fabulous!—Guest

Maple Pumpkin Bisque

Yield: 4–6 servings

"Since we live in Vermont, maple syrup is often our sweetener of choice, and in this soup the pumpkin and maple flavors blend well. The creamy orange color and the cinnamon and nutmeg really say Fall!"

- ¼ cup vegetable oil
- 1 large red onion, chopped
- 3 cloves garlic, minced
- 1 medium pumpkin, peeled, diced
- ½ bottle of Marsala wine
- ½ gallon vegetable stock or broth
- ½ gallon chicken stock or broth
- cinnamon, to taste
- nutmeg, to taste
- salt and pepper, to taste
- 1 pint heavy cream
- 2 cups Vermont maple syrup (the real stuff, not imitation!)

Heat oil in a soup pot over medium heat. Add onion and garlic; cook, stirring often, for 5 minutes. Add pumpkin and sweat for 5 minutes, stirring often. Add wine and simmer until reduced by half. Once reduced, add vegetable and chicken stock; bring to a boil and continue cooking until reduced by half. At this point, the pumpkin should be soft. If not, continue cooking until it is soft.

In a food processor, purée mixture and add cinnamon, nutmeg, salt and pepper to taste.

Add heavy cream and maple syrup. Pour back into soup pot and heat on stove if necessary. Serve.

White Rocks Inn B&B

INNKEEPERS	Will & Leigh Quigley
ADDRESS	1774 U.S. 7 South, Wallingford, VT 05773
TELEPHONE	802-446-2077 | 866-446-2077
CONTACT	info@whiterocksinn.com | www.whiterocksinn.com
FEATURES	5 Rooms, 2 Cottages; Private baths | Children 12 and older welcome in the main house | Children of all ages and pets are welcome in the cottages

Experience the warmth and charm of old Vermont at the White Rocks Inn Bed & Breakfast, a historic dairy farm. This classic Vermont farmhouse wraps you in warmth from the moment you enter the front door. The view of the mountains and valley from your window is virtually the same as it was in the 1800s.

The inn is central to shopping in the quaint villages along Route 7, scenic trips through the countryside, outdoor activities, downhill skiing at Pico, Okemo, or Killington and cross-country skiing on the inn's property.

Breakfast will be one of the highlights of your visit. It is a memorable experience, with three courses served on antique china in the candlelit dining room of the main house.

"Fresh homemade cookies await you in the afternoons and evenings. Guest favorites include chocolate chip, peanut butter, cinnamon snickerdoodles, and fresh ginger cookies. Apples, chips, pretzels, candy, and other snacks may also be available. A pot of hot water is always handy to make a variety of green, black, and herbal teas, as well as hot cocoa. On summer afternoons you may enjoy lemonade or raspberry iced tea on the side porch."—Innkeeper

Baked Peaches with Raspberries & Cream

Yield: 4 servings

"We serve this a lot in summer when peaches are fresh and plentiful. We nearly always serve it for breakfast the morning after we have a wedding at the inn. It's the perfect tribute to love and happiness."

- 2 large peaches, ripe but firm, peeled, pitted and halved
- 4 tsp raspberry preserves, plus extra for garnish
- ½ cup heavy cream
- 2 tsp powdered sugar
- ¼ tsp vanilla extract
- whipped cream, for serving
- fresh raspberries, for garnish

Note: the peaches need to be refrigerated overnight so start this recipe the night before. Fill each peach cavity with 1 teaspoon raspberry preserves. Put peaches on a greased baking sheet. Bake for 30–40 minutes, until peaches are very tender. Cool, then cover and refrigerate overnight.

The next day, preheat oven to 350°F. Whip together cream, powdered sugar, and vanilla, just until thick. Spread a pool of cream in each of 4 serving dishes. Place 1 peach half in the center of the cream in each dish.

With an eyedropper, drop 5 small dots of raspberry jam (thinned with a little water) in the cream around the edges of the dish. Draw the point of a sharp toothpick through each dot of jam, forming tiny hearts. (Wipe toothpick with a paper towel after forming each heart.) Top each peach with a dab of whipped cream and a fresh raspberry.

WILDFLOWER INN

INNKEEPERS	Jim & Mary O'Reilly
ADDRESS	2059 Darling Hill Road, Lyndonville, VT 05851
TELEPHONE	802-626-8310	800-627-8310
CONTACT	info@wildflowerinn.com	www.wildflowerinn.com
FEATURES	10 Rooms, 14 Suites; Private baths	Children welcome	Pets not allowed

Tucked into the rolling hills of the Northeast Kingdom of Vermont, the Wildflower Inn is a 570-acre Vermont country resort. The inn offers hiking and mountain biking, cross-country skiing, downhill skiing at Burke Mountain Resort, snowshoeing, snowmobiling, horse-drawn wagon and sleigh rides, extensive flower gardens and a petting barn.

Breakfast is not to be missed at the inn; and they are famous for their homemade chocolate chip cookies.

The Juniper Restaurant is an onsite restaurant at the inn, offering all natural beef dishes, farm fresh ingredients, and an extensive wine list.

"This grand inn high on a 1,000-foot ridge welcomes your family with warm hospitality and tons of kids' activities. The dining room is notable for its eclectic cuisine. The scenery and recreation are top-notch."—Yankee Magazine

Blackberry-Stuffed French Toast

Yield: 6 servings

"This recipe can be adapted to use any seasonal berries."

2 (8-oz.) pkgs. cream cheese, softened
1 cup blackberries
½ cup honey, warmed slightly (aids mixing)
   pinch of ground nutmeg
1 loaf homemade bread, sliced
6 large eggs
½ cup heavy cream
1 Tbsp vanilla extract
1 Tbsp cinnamon
   cinnamon sugar, for garnish
   Vermont maple syrup, for serving

In a medium bowl, stir together cream cheese, blackberries, honey and nutmeg until loosely blended. Spread cream cheese mixture on one side of half the bread slices. Cover with second slice (to make a sandwich). In a medium bowl, thoroughly beat eggs, cream, vanilla and cinnamon. Dip sandwiches into egg mixture. Cook on a flat buttered griddle or skillet until golden brown on both sides. Dust with cinnamon sugar and serve with warm Vermont maple syrup.

"I like breakfast-time better than any other moment in the day," said Mr. Irwine. "No dust has settled on one's mind then, and it presents a clear mirror to the rays of things."

— George Eliot
Adam Bede

New Hampshire B & Bs

AND THEIR SIGNATURE RECIPES

1785 INN & RESTAURANT

INNKEEPERS	Becky and Charlie Mallar
ADDRESS	3582 White Mountain Highway, North Conway, NH 03860
TELEPHONE	603-356-9025	800-421-1785
CONTACT	info@the1785inn.com	www.the1785inn.com
FEATURES	17 Rooms, 1 Suite; Private and shared baths	Children welcome	Pets not allowed

A visit to the 1785 Inn in the Mount Washington Valley of New Hampshire's White Mountains is an experience you'll long remember. From the charm and beauty of its original colonial construction to the cheerful, welcoming atmosphere of its Victorian lounge, you'll enjoy the tradition of friendly Yankee hospitality in a classic New England country inn.

The dining room at the 1785 Inn is renowned for its outstanding cuisine and service. Candlelight casts a romantic glow throughout the evening, inviting you to take your time and enjoy the pleasures of your meal. The restaurant's wine list has been awarded *Wine Spectator*'s "Award of Excellence" each year since 1986.

The 1785 Inn is convenient to North Conway and all the White Mountain attractions. The inn's cross-country ski trails offer interesting nature walks and fishing during the spring, summer, and fall seasons.

"So picturesque it belongs on a Christmas card ... a perfect place to stay."—Country Magazine

Smoked Salmon Ravioli

Yield: 6–8 servings

Pasta:
- 2 cups all-purpose flour
- 2 large eggs, beaten
- 2 egg yolks, beaten
- egg wash (1 egg beaten with 1 Tbsp of water)

Mousse:
- 1 lb. smoked salmon
- 2 eggs
- 1 cup whipping cream, chilled
- ½ tsp coarsely ground pepper
- 2 Tbsp chives, chopped

Serving:
- 2 cups grated Gruyère cheese
- 1 cup heavy cream

For the pasta: Put flour in a mound on a smooth work surface. Make a well in the center of flour. Pour eggs and yolks into the well; slowly pull flour into eggs until well incorporated. Knead dough by hand, adding more flour if needed for a smooth consistency. Divide dough in half and roll out each half or feed through pasta roller until thin (number 6 setting on a machine).

For the mousse: In a food processor, purée smoked salmon and eggs until smooth. Slowly add cream, pepper and chives; process until smooth.

Lay pasta on a floured surface. Place 24 mounds of mousse 2 inches apart on one sheet of pasta. Brush egg wash on pasta between mounds of salmon mousse and cover with second sheet of pasta. Cut raviolis apart and refrigerate or freeze until ready to use.

To serve: Preheat broiler. Bring a large pot of lightly salted water to a boil. Add raviolis and cook for about 6 minutes.

Sprinkle 2 tablespoons of Gruyère and 2 tablespoons of cream over each of 6–8 ovenproof plates. Broil until cheese melts. Put 3–4 ravioli on each plate and sprinkle with 2 tablespoons of Gruyère. Broil until cheese browns lightly.

ADAIR COUNTRY INN & RESTAURANT

INNKEEPERS	Judy and Bill Whitman, Ilja & Brad Chapman
ADDRESS	80 Guider Lane, Bethlehem, NH 03574
TELEPHONE	603-444-2600 | 888-444-2600
CONTACT	innkeeper@adairinn.com | www.adairinn.com
FEATURES	8 Rooms, 1 Suite; Private baths | Children age 12 and older welcome | Pets not allowed

Set on a grassy knoll on 200 acres of land near the White Mountains, this intimate inn has been hosting guests for nearly 75 years. Adair Country Inn, with its long drive bordered by stately pines, gleaming birch and stone walls, picturesque landscaping and graceful Colonial Revival design, is one of New England's most renowned inns.

Adair Country Inn & Restaurant is an intimate and romantic retreat for couples who wish to relax, observe wildlife, and take advantage of nearby hiking, skiing, and the natural attraction of New Hampshire's White Mountains.

With Head Chef, Orlo Coots, your dining experience will be predictably wonderful!

> *"This luxury inn calls to the weary traveler from a snowy hilltop. Each room is exquisitely decorated with antiques and reproductions and has its own private bath. Personal touches abound."*
> —Connecticut Magazine

Popovers a la Adair

Yield: 6 servings

6 large eggs
6 Tbsp butter, melted
   pinch of salt
2 cups milk (any kind but skim)
2 cups all-purpose flour

Beat the eggs in a medium bowl with a wire whisk. Add the butter and salt, and whisk in the milk. Stir in the flour, leaving small lumps. Do NOT over beat. Cover the batter with plastic wrap and refrigerate overnight.

Place the oven rack on the lowest level and preheat the oven to 400°F. Spray six ¾-cup ovenproof glass cups with cooking spray.

Remove the batter from the refrigerator and stir the batter until it is relatively smooth but still has some lumps. Ladle the batter into the cups, filling them ¾-full. Place the cups on a baking sheet, allowing some space between them, and place the baking sheet on the lowest oven rack. Bake the popovers for about 50 minutes, until puffed and brown. To prevent the popovers from collapsing, avoid opening the oven door during the first 40 minutes of baking. Serve immediately.

Tip: The chef suggests leaving the batter very lumpy—(more is better than less).

BENJAMIN PRESCOTT INN

INNKEEPERS	Sue and Charlie Lyle
ADDRESS	433 Turnpike Road (Rte. 124E), Jaffrey, NH 03452
TELEPHONE	603-532-6637
CONTACT	innkeeper@benjaminprescottinn.com | www.benjaminprescottinn.com
FEATURES	5 Rooms, 5 Suites; Private baths | Children age 12 and older welcome | Pets not allowed

Remember your grandmother's house? Do you recall the kitchen? Grandmother was always there—she would be baking a pie or pulling freshly made cookies from the oven. When you walked outside, the cows would "moo" at you and there was always a grassy hill to climb. Well, that's what life is like at the Benjamin Prescott Inn. Time travel back to the mid-nineteenth century. Immerse yourself in all that was good about that era.

Centrally located in the Monadnock region, and virtually in the shadow of the famed Mt. Monadnock, this inn provides you with an easy access to countless activities and entertainments. Golfing, horseback riding, and tennis, or swimming, boating, and fishing are all close by. Mt. Monadnock is said to be the most climbed mountain in America with over 40 miles of trails leading up to its 3,165-foot summit. In the winter there are nine cross-county ski trail areas and downhill skiing at Crotched Mountain.

"The perfect spot for a weekend getaway; Just what you think it should be and more with warm hospitality. We'll Be Back!"—Guest

Blueberry Cream Muffins

Yield: 18–20 muffins

2 large eggs
1 cup sugar
½ cup vegetable oil
½ tsp vanilla extract
2 cups all-purpose flour
½ tsp salt
½ tsp baking soda
1 tsp baking powder
1 cup sour cream
1 cup fresh or frozen (thawed) blueberries

Topping:
2 Tbsp sugar
1 tsp cinnamon

Preheat oven to 400°F. Spray muffin cups with nonstick cooking spray.

In a large bowl, beat eggs. Beat in sugar. Beat in oil and vanilla. In a medium bowl, combine flour, salt, baking soda and baking powder. Alternately mix flour mixture and sour cream into egg mixture. Gently fold in blueberries. Pour batter into muffin cups. Sprinkle topping over batter in muffin cups. Bake for 20 minutes.

For the topping: Combine sugar and cinnamon.

COLBY HILL INN

INNKEEPERS	Cyndi and Mason Cobb
ADDRESS	33 The Oaks, Henniker, NH 03242
TELEPHONE	603-428-3281 | 800-531-0330
CONTACT	innkeeper@colbyhillinn.com | www.colbyhillinn.com
FEATURES	12 Rooms, 2 Suites; Private baths | Children age 7 and older welcome | Pets not allowed

For those planning a wedding reception, business conference, or retreat, the Colby Hill Inn offers a wonderful slice of New England hospitality. The inn overlooks lovely historical perennial gardens, antique barns, and a charming garden gazebo. Colby Hill Inn provides classic B&B accommodations and much more, including an award-winning restaurant, which is unique for a small village inn. The restaurant has received the coveted Wine Spectator Award of Excellence every year since 2003, as well as being selected as a *Yankee Magazine* Editor's Pick and a "Best of New Hampshire" recipient by *New Hampshire Magazine.*

Located right in the middle of southern New Hampshire, Henniker is just 90 minutes north of Boston and 20 minutes west of Concord, the state capital. It is an hour from the seashore, and minutes to New Hampshire's mountains and lakes.

Chef Jeannine Carney's "cooking local" philosophy ensures that guests will enjoy fresh, creative, and seasonally prepared cuisine. Dishes might include steamed Narragansett mussels or farm-raised Bonnie Brae venison with maple sugar rub and spiced rhubarb chutney.

"Thank you for everything. There was absolutely nothing else we could have asked for. All the extra little touches were not only unexpected but made our stay here very special. This inn is definitely our favorite." —Guest

Sweet Potato Muffins or Bread

Yield: 36 muffins or 3 loaves

"One of our guests' favorites!"

2 cups sweet potatoes, peeled, cooked, mashed
1 cup vegetable oil
4 large eggs
1 cup water, rum or brandy (or a mix of any or all)
1 tsp vanilla extract
3 cups sugar
3½ cups all-purpose flour
2 tsp baking soda
½ tsp salt
1 tsp cinnamon
1 cup raisins, optional

Topping:
¾ cup chopped nuts (walnuts or pecans are good)
¾ cup packed brown sugar
½ stick butter, melted
1½ tsp cinnamon

Preheat oven to 350°F. Grease muffin cups or 3 (9x5-inch) loaf pans.

In a large bowl, combine sweet potatoes, oil, eggs, water, and vanilla. In a medium bowl, combine sugar, flour, baking soda, salt, and cinnamon; add to sweet potato mixture and stir until combined. Stir in raisins, if desired. Pour batter into muffin cups or loaf pans.

For the topping: Combine all topping ingredients until crumbly.

Sprinkle topping over batter. Bake muffins for about 30 minutes or loaves for about 1 hour.

Inn at Crystal Lake

INNKEEPERS	Bobby Barker and Tim Ostendorf
ADDRESS	2356 Eaton Road, Eaton Center, NH 03832
TELEPHONE	603-447-2120 | 800-343-7336
CONTACT	stay@innatcrystallake.com | www.innatcrystallake.com
FEATURES	11 Rooms, 1 Cottage; Private baths | Children age 12 and older welcome | Dogs welcome (1 room)

Keeping watch over the charming lakeside village of Eaton, the award-winning Inn at Crystal Lake is a touchstone for service and hospitality in the Mt. Washington Valley. Located at the historic 1884 Palmer House, just minutes from North Conway, this charming New England inn provides a traditional B&B atmosphere with the refinement of a small European hotel.

Every season offers unique ways to experience the White Mountains and Lakes Region, and the Inn at Crystal Lake and Palmer House Pub keeps you close to everything, but still tucked away in a quiet little village. No area in New England can match the number of vacation opportunities here in the Mt. Washington Valley and the Lakes Region. So make the Inn at Crystal Lake your number one choice for lodging in New Hamphire's White Mountains.

Our pub has a full liquor license and we specialize in classic cocktails like Martinis and Manhattans, but innkeeper Tim is usually behind the bar and willing to whip up almost any kind of drink! In addition, we also prepare nightly dinner specials to reflect the freshest local ingredients.

> *"You have created the model for the perfect New England inn. Attentive care, excellent food and charming ambiance."*
> —Guests, Lehigh Valley, PA

Bobby's Blueberry Bread

Yield: 8 servings

"This recipe was chosen by Yankee Magazine *for their 2002 B&B Guide."*

1 stick butter, softened
1½ cups sugar, plus extra for topping
1 cup sour cream
3 eggs
3 cups all-purpose flour, sifted
4 tsp baking powder
1 tsp salt
2 cups fresh blueberries

Preheat oven to 350°F. Grease and flour a tube or standard Bundt pan.

In a large bowl, combine butter, sugar, and sour cream. Add eggs and mix well. Add flour, baking powder, and salt, and mix just until batter comes together. Fold in blueberries. Pour batter into tube or Bundt pan. Sprinkle a layer of sugar over batter. Bake for 1 hour (check after 45 minutes), until a toothpick inserted in center comes out clean.

Tip: In the fall, substitute fresh cranberries and walnuts for the blueberries.

INN ON GOLDEN POND

INNKEEPERS	**Bill and Bonnie Webb**
ADDRESS	**Route 3, Holderness, NH 03245**
TELEPHONE	**603-968-7269**
CONTACT	**info@innongoldenpond.com	www.innongoldenpond.com**
FEATURES	**6 Rooms, 2 Suites; Private baths	Children age 12 and older welcome	Pets not allowed**

For more than 25 years this impressive Holderness B&B, just minutes from Squam Lake, has been the choice of discerning travelers looking for a warm and inviting New Hampshire lodging experience. Located at the northern edge of New Hampshire's Lakes Region and in the foothills of the White Mountains, the Inn on Golden Pond was originally built as a beautiful, private Colonial home. As an 8-room country inn it has been expanded and refurbished to provide the modern amenities that today's traveler expects and deserves.

During winter season, spend the day snowshoeing through the woods, downhill skiing at one of four ski areas nearby, or cross country skiing across Squam Lake. Or try something really different and take a sled dog excursion!

Spend the evening dining at one of the area's gourmet restaurants, enjoying a live performance at a local theater or simply relaxing next to a crackling fire in the sitting room.

"We think of breakfast as a time to get to know our guests and so the morning hour is filled with conversation, stories and laughter. It's also a time to help get our guests off to a good start for the day. We're always available to answer questions about local attractions or to give directions to get our guests to their next destination."—Innkeeper

Flat-Top Orange Date Muffins

Yield: 12 muffins

	rind of 1 orange
1	orange, quartered and pith removed
½	cup orange juice
1	stick unsalted butter, softened
1	large egg, lightly beaten
½	cup chopped dates
1½	cups all-purpose flour
1	tsp baking soda
¾	cup sugar
1	tsp baking powder
	Dash of salt

Preheat oven to 400°F. Grease muffin cups.

Chop orange rind in food processor. Add orange quarters, orange juice, butter, egg, and dates; chop and set aside. Sift together flour, baking soda, sugar, baking powder, and salt into a large bowl. Add orange mixture to flour mixture; stir just until moistened. Divide batter among muffin cups. Bake for 20–25 minutes.

LAKE HOUSE AT FERRY POINT

INNKEEPERS	John and Cindy Becker
ADDRESS	100 Lower Bay Road, Sanbornton, NH 03269
TELEPHONE	603-524-0087
CONTACT	innkeeper@lakehouseatferrypoint.com | www.new-hampshire-inn.com
FEATURES	10 Rooms; Private baths | Children age 10 and older welcome | Pets not allowed; Resident dogs

The Lake House at Ferry Point is the only lakefront B&B in New Hampshire's Lakes Region. On this quiet, scenic property, guests will be treated to idyllic views of Lake Winnisquam and its glistening water, the luscious gardens, and guardian mountains in the distance, as they enjoy relaxing on the big front porch.

Enjoy panoramic views from the summit of Mount Washington on the Mt. Washington Cog Railroad. A trip to the Flume Gorge and Visitor's Center includes sightseeing highlights such as Avalanche Falls and Liberty Gorge. Franconia Notch State Park and the White Mountain National Forest offer an assortment of activities such as camping, swimming, hiking and fishing in the summer, and cross-country skiing and snowmobiling in the winter.

Lake House at Ferry Point supports the farmers' market and uses local fresh ingredients and produce for their breakfast creations. They serve rich, extra dark amber syrup from the Just Maple Sugar House right down the road, and homemade brownies or cookies are always available. One of the guests' favorites is Cranberry White Chocolate Chip Cookies.

"Thank you so much for a relaxing couple of days. The hospitality was wonderful and the food was delicious. We wish you continued success here at the Lake House and hope to return soon!"—Guest

Memère's French Crêpes

Yield: 10 crêpes

"This is a very special recipe that has been in my family for generations. My grandmother taught my mother and my mother still teaches me. It has taken me about 20 years to learn the proper technique for cooking my grandmother's crêpes. When done to perfection, these crêpes should be thin, crisp and melt in your mouth."

2	cups all-purpose flour
1	tsp baking soda
½	tsp salt
3	eggs
1¾	cups milk
	solid shortening, enough to cook 10 crêpes
	fresh strawberry slices or raspberries, for garnish
	warm maple syrup, for serving

In a medium bowl, combine flour, baking soda, and salt. In a small bowl, beat eggs and milk with a whisk; stir into flour mixture until smooth and no lumps remain.

Melt 1 tablespoon of shortening in a cast-iron crêpe pan or skillet over medium-high heat. When shortening begins to smoke, carefully place 2 serving spoons of batter in pan in a circular direction. Using the back of the spoon, quickly spread batter to cover bottom of pan and fill any holes. Turn crêpe when underside browns and sides begin to curl. Brown the other side slightly. Repeat with remaining batter. Serve immediately garnished with strawberries or raspberries, and topped with warm maple syrup.

LAZY DOG INN

INNKEEPERS Steven and Lauren Sousa

ADDRESS 201 White Mountain Highway, Tamworth, NH 03817

TELEPHONE 603-323-8350 | 888-323-8350

CONTACT info@lazydoginn.com | www.lazydoginn.com

FEATURES 7 Rooms, 1 Suite; Private and shared baths | Children age 14 and older welcome | Dogs age 12 weeks and older welcome

Lazy Dog Inn is truly a "Dog Friendly B&B," providing guests and their dogs traditional New England comforts in a historically rich farmhouse built in 1845. The innkeepers pride themselves in anticipating their guests' needs. They welcome all dogs without your typical weight or breed restrictions. Doggie guests are welcome with open arms and an open heart. Come experience what all of their doggie guests are howling about. Doggie guests have access to a climate controlled "Doggie Lodge" where doggie daycare is provided (included in our rates). A secure fenced "Doggie Play Area" is available for fun and exercise. Guest rooms allow your best friend to join you for a good night's sleep.

"Details, details … right down to the doggie pen in my hand. What a fun place! Everything here was beyond expectation. Thanks for taking care of us."—Guest

Garlic Chive Potato Pancakes

Yield: 8–10 servings

3 lbs. potatoes (Yukon Gold are especially good),
   peeled and quartered
4 oz. cream cheese – low-fat or regular, softened
1 Tbsp chopped fresh chives
1 clove garlic, minced
   salt and pepper, to taste
   milk or half & half

Cook potatoes in salted boiling water until tender; drain and mash. Add cream cheese, chives, garlic, salt, and pepper; beat until smooth. Add enough milk or half & half to make a creamy consistency. Cover and refrigerate overnight.

Form potatoes into patties, using ¼–⅓ cup of potatoes per patty. Cook patties on a preheated, greased or buttered griddle or skillet until heated through and golden brown on both sides.

Mt. Washington B&B

INNKEEPER	Mary Ann Mayer
ADDRESS	421 State Route 2, Shelburne, NH 03581
TELEPHONE	603-466-2669	877-466-2399
CONTACT	mtwashbb@yahoo.com	www.mtwashingtonbb.com
FEATURES	7 Rooms; Private baths	Children welcome	Pets not allowed

Surrounded by the White Mountains, the Mt. Washington B&B is located on five acres in the Androscoggin River Valley. The inn sits on a hill overlooking Reflection Pond, which is fed by the Androscoggin River. To the south is the Presidential Range and Mount Washington. Hike, bike, canoe, ski, shop, or just relax on the porch. As you relax on our porch, you can gaze at Mount Washington, and on a clear day you can see the Observatory's towers and the smoke from the Cog Railway as it makes its way to the highest peak in the Northeast.

Rooms are named after birds in the area. Each is individually decorated with handmade quilts, antique furniture, fluffy robes, scented glycerin soaps and bath and shower scents.

Start your day with a full breakfast prepared by Mary Ann. You awaken to the aroma of freshly brewed coffee. Breakfast is served "Innkeeper's Choice" style using organic and locally grown products when available.

"It was a pleasure to stay in your B & B, Mary Ann. It is an enchanting inn, away from the town. The French toast with walnuts & cream cheese was delicious. I must try it at home. Thank you for your casual and warm hospitality."—Guest

Frangelico-Nutella French Toast

Yield: 8 servings

"A wonderful Valentine's Day breakfast for your special someone."

8 large eggs
½ cup half & half
1 shot (¼ cup) Frangelico or other hazelnut liqueur
2 loaves Italian bread, sliced ½–1 inch thick
   Nutella, to taste*
   powdered sugar, for garnish
   sliced fresh strawberries, for garnish
   maple syrup, for serving

Heat a lightly greased griddle or skillet.

In a mixing bowl, whisk eggs, half & half, and Frangelico until well blended. Dip bread in egg mixture, turning to coat. Place on griddle or skillet until browned on both sides. Spread Nutella on one side of each piece of French toast (thickly or thinly, to your taste). Sprinkle very lightly with powdered sugar. Garnish with sliced strawberries. Serve with warm maple syrup, if desired.

*Nutella is a delicious chocolate hazelnut spread that can be found in the peanut butter section of most grocery stores.

ROSEWOOD COUNTRY INN

INNKEEPERS	Dick and Lesley Marquis
ADDRESS	67 Pleasant View Road, Bradford, NH 03221
TELEPHONE	603-938-5253 | 800-938-5273
CONTACT	rosewoodinn@tds.net | www.rosewoodcountryinn.com
FEATURES	2 Rooms, 9 Suites; Private baths | Children age 12 and older welcome | Pets not allowed

This country inn was built around 1850 in the early Victorian style. The Rosewood is set on twelve hilltop acres in Bradford, part of New Hampshire's Dartmouth/Lake Sunapee Region (about 90 minutes from Boston). The inn offers fireplaces, whirlpool tubs, sunlit porches, and inviting common rooms.

The Rosewood's dining room has spectacular views of the gardens, pond and waterfall. What a wonderful way to start off the morning! Not only does Chef Lesley use vegetables and herbs grown on-site, there is also a strong focus on local ingredients. The Rosewood uses local cheeses and fresh-from-the-farm eggs, and maple syrup made right from the inn's sugar bush. Be sure to check out their online recipes and Chef Lesley's two cookbooks when visiting the Inn.

The Rosewood Country Inn was selected as "One of New Hampshire's Eight Most Romantic Inns" by Chronicle Books and Inn of the Year for 2002 by guidebook author Pamela Lanier. The Rosewood was also voted the Most Romantic B&B/Country Inn in America and one of the Most Romantic Hideaways by readers of Arrington's *Bed and Breakfast Journal*.

"The inn was wonderful. The rooms are so pretty; the breakfasts are delicious; and the people are so nice!"—Guest

Lemon-Poached Pears
with Raspberry Coulis

Yield: 8 servings

2 cups water
1/3 cup sugar
8 large firm pears, peeled, cored, and cut in half
    peel from 1 lemon

Place water and sugar in covered frying pan. Heat until sugar dissolves. Place pears and lemon peel in pan, and poach until tender, but not soft. Remove pears from syrup and chill. Serve with Raspberry Coulis or syrup.

Raspberry Coulis

½ cup sugar
3 tablespoons water
1 lb fresh raspberries or 1 (12 oz.) bag frozen raspberries, thawed
1 teaspoon Kirsch (optional) or 1 teaspoon framboise eau de vie (optional)

Heat the sugar and water in a small saucepan over medium heat, stirring from time to time, until the sugar dissolves completely, about 5 minutes. Put the raspberries and the sugar syrup in a blender and purée. Strain through a fine mesh sieve to remove the seeds. Stir in the Kirsch or framboise, if using. The sauce keeps well, tightly covered, in the refrigerator for 4–5 days and freezes perfectly for several months.

SUGAR HILL INN

INNKEEPERS	Steve Allen and Karen Cail
ADDRESS	116 New Hampshire 117, Sugar Hill, NH 03586
TELEPHONE	603-823-5621 | 800-548-4748
CONTACT	info@sugarhillinn.com | www.sugarhillinn.com
FEATURES	9 Rooms, 5 suites; Private baths | Children age 10 and older welcome | Pets not allowed

Everyone needs a perfect country inn getaway; let New Hampshire's Sugar Hill Inn be yours. The inn's Sugar Hill location is just north of Franconia Notch, right in the heart of the White Mountain National Forest. Take your pick of activities in every season—hiking, biking, natural wonders, apple picking, local crafts, antiques, Nordic and alpine skiing, snowshoeing, and so much more.

Relax on the front porch as day turns to evening. Then enjoy a drink fireside in our new Tavern Room before being seated for an elegant dinner. Finally retire to one of our 14 unique guest rooms, cottages or suites for a restful, refreshing sleep. The Sugar Hill Inn … everything a country inn should be. You may never want to leave.

"This rambling, romantic farmhouse, surrounded by woodlands and mountains, is known for its lingering, four-course prix fixe dinners. Chef Val Fortin's creative and sophisticated fare, with a focus on local sourcing, has won the hearts (or should we say stomachs?) of New Englanders and garnered a fair share of national accolades. When winter arrives, he turns to down-to-earth, hearty, comfort fare, like the braised pork osso bucco, horseradish crusted tenderloin (they do their own butchering and make all their own sauces and stocks), and roasted Vermont quail and venison."—The Boston Globe

Gingerbread Pancakes

Yield: 6–10 servings

- 1 cup whole-wheat flour
- 1 cup all-purpose flour
- ¼ tsp nutmeg
- ¼ tsp ground ginger
- ½ tsp salt
- 1 Tbsp baking powder
- ½ tsp cinnamon
- 2 Tbsp packed brown sugar
- ½ cup molasses
- 2 eggs, separated
- 3 Tbsp butter, melted
- 1 cup milk
  New Hampshire maple syrup, for serving
  freshly whipped cream, for serving

In a large bowl, combine whole-wheat and all-purpose flour, nutmeg, ginger, salt, baking powder, cinnamon, and brown sugar. In a small bowl, combine molasses, egg yolks, butter, and milk. In a medium bowl, beat egg whites until stiff. Gently fold molasses mixture into egg whites. Gently stir egg white mixture into flour mixture. Cook pancakes on a preheated, greased griddle or skillet until golden brown on both sides. Serve with maple syrup and whipped cream.

SUNSET HILL HOUSE

INNKEEPERS	Nancy and Lon Henderson
ADDRESS	231 Sunset Hill Road, Sugar Hill, NH 03586
TELEPHONE	603-823-5522	800-786-4455
CONTACT	stay@sunsethillhouse.com	www.sunsethillhouse.com
FEATURES	21 Rooms; Private Baths	Children: inquire	Pets: inquire

Sunset Hill House traces its history to the grand resort hotels of the New Hampshire White Mountains. In the nineteenth and early twentieth centuries, residents of Boston, New York and other East Coast cities traveled by train and horse-drawn coach to stay for the season at the old resort hotels. These resorts were referred to as "houses" despite their huge scale. There, the wealthy and influential exchanged the humidity, heat and pollution of coal-age America for the cool mountain air of New Hampshire.

Sunset Hill House in Sugar Hill, New Hampshire, was particularly well situated as a house. Its location, high atop Sunset Hill Ridge, has been long recognized as having the best accessible mountain views in New England. Construction of the inn began in 1880 after the railroad came to neighboring Lisbon Village (Sugar Hill Station), and by about 1910, the Sunset Hill House Grand Hotel—with its restaurants, pool and golf course—could accommodate over 350 guests, 300 staff and all the animals needed to transport and feed a small town.

"My husband and I decided to spend our five-year anniversary at Sunset Hill House. You just can't get any more romantic than a remote mountain view getaway, in a quaint little town, in the most beautiful, historic inn ever!"—Guest

Pumpkin Soup

Yield: 8 servings

*"For your dining enjoyment, and a little taste of
Sunset Hill House, we present our Pumpkin Soup recipe,
compliments of Joseph Peterson, former Executive Chef."*

- 1 stick butter, cut into small pieces
- 1 cup onion, diced
- 1 cup celery, diced
- ½ cup all-purpose flour
- 1 cup sherry
- 2 quarts chicken stock
- 1 medium pumpkin, poached and peeled
  (or one large can of pumpkin purée)
- ¼ cup New Hampshire Maple Syrup
  salt and pepper, to taste
- 3 cups cream

Melt butter in a soup pot. Add onion and sauté until translucent. Add celery and sauté. Add flour and form roux. Add sherry and de-glaze pot. Add chicken stock; bring to a boil while mixing. Reduce heat to a simmer. Add pumpkin, maple syrup, salt, and pepper and blend. Add cream, stir and serve.

"The cup of tea on arrival at a country house is a thing which, as a rule, I particularly enjoy. I like the crackling logs, the shaded lights, the scent of buttered toast, the general atmosphere of leisured coziness."

— P.G. Wodehouse
The Code of the Woosters

Maine B&B s

AND THEIR SIGNATURE RECIPES

1802 HOUSE B&B

INNKEEPERS	Teri and Roger Walker
ADDRESS	15 Locke Street, Kennebunkport, ME 04046
TELEPHONE	207-967-5632 | 800-932-5632
CONTACT	info@1802inn.com | www.1802inn.com
FEATURES	5 Rooms, 1 Suite; Private baths | Children age 12 and older welcome | Pets not allowed

One of Kennebunkport's finest inns, 1802 House, offers understated, casual luxury accommodation in its nineteenth century restored colonial inn. Nestled in a quiet neighborhood, it is only a short stroll from Kennebunkport's Dock Square. Secluded among towering pines and lush private gardens, this Kennebunkport B&B offers the perfect place to relax and enjoy everything that coastal Maine has to offer.

A three-course breakfast is served daily in the main dining room. The food is sourced as fresh as possible so that guests get some of the best that Maine has to offer from local growers. Start the morning with assorted fruit juices and freshly brewed tea and coffee. The menus change daily and include classics such as Maine Blueberry Pancakes and Eggs Benedict. Daily entrées are alternated between savory and sweet.

"Nestled along the 15th hole, 1802 House offers a prime location and luxury accommodation for golfers who come to Kennebunkport to play the historic Cape Arundel Golf Club. Founded in 1896, Cape Arundel is listed on the U.S. Register of Historic Places. Known as the "home of Presidential golf," this prestigious course counts George H.W. Bush and George W. Bush as members, in addition to hosting former Presidents Bill Clinton and Richard Nixon."—Innkeeper

Apple Raisin Bread Pudding

Yield: 6 servings

*"Minus the ice cream, this delicate pudding
makes a wonderfully indulgent breakfast."*

2 cups whole milk
1 cup sugar
4 large eggs
3 Tbsp unsalted butter, melted
¼ tsp cinnamon
1/8 tsp salt
7 slices white bread (crusts removed), cut into ¾-inch cubes
1 large Granny Smith apple, peeled and cut into ½-inch cubes
2/3 cup raisins
    Vanilla ice cream, for serving

Preheat oven to 350°F. Butter a 7x11-inch or 8x8-inch glass baking dish. In a large bowl, whisk together milk, sugar, eggs, melted butter, cinnamon and salt. Fold in bread, apples and raisins.

Pour bread mixture into prepared baking dish. Bake for 30 minutes, then sprinkle with additional cinnamon. Continue baking until top of pudding is golden and the center is set, about 35 minutes longer. Spoon pudding into bowls. Top with vanilla ice cream and serve.

BEAR MOUNTAIN INN

INNKEEPERS	**Jim and Christie Kerrigan (and Family)**
ADDRESS	**364 Waterford Road, Waterford, ME 04088**
TELEPHONE	**207-583-4404	866-450-4253**
CONTACT	**innkeeper@bearmtninn.com	www.bearmtninn.com**
FEATURES	**8 Rooms, 2 Suites, 1 Cottage; Private baths	Children welcome	Pets allowed**

The Bear Mountain Inn is a spectacular four-season lakefront B&B resort nestled in the foothills of the White Mountains. The dramatic 25-acre property in Waterford, Maine, offers the charm of a country inn, with the breathtaking natural beauty of the lakes and mountain region. The historic homestead, surrounded by sprawling lawns and forest, overlooks a private sandy beach, and a large deck with fieldstone fireplace providing splendid vistas of Bear Lake.

In the summer, enjoy kayaking and canoeing on Bear River, or take a relaxing stroll along a wooded trail on the river's edge. Burn off breakfast with a rigorous hike up Bear Mountain, or take a nap in our hammock to more gently enjoy the tranquility of nature around you. Many of our guests favor the winter months with snowmobiling, alpine and cross-country skiing and snowshoeing.

"Bear Mountain Inn is everything you would expect from a B&B. It's clean, cozy, and well-maintained. The innkeepers are friendly and helpful, and customer service is their main objective. We had a wonderful time canoeing and kayaking on the lake."—Guest

Sour Cream Peach & Blueberry Pancakes

Yield: 6 servings

"This dish is a cross between a French crêpe and a Maine pancake. It is light and delicious."

1	cup sour cream
5	large eggs
1	Tbsp water
1	tsp vanilla extract
½	tsp butter extract
1	tsp baking soda
1	tsp baking powder
½	tsp salt
¼	cup white sugar
3½	Tbsp packed brown sugar
1	cup unbleached all-purpose flour
½	tsp cinnamon
	peaches, thinly sliced peeled, to garnish
	fresh Maine blueberries, to garnish

Preheat oven to 350°F. In a medium bowl, with a mixer at medium speed, beat sour cream, eggs, water, vanilla and butter extract for 2 minutes. Slowly mix in remaining ingredients, with the exception of the garnishes.

Pour batter onto a preheated, greased griddle or skillet. Once pancakes begin to bubble, top with a few peach slices and some blueberries. Turn pancakes and cook for 1 more minute, or until done.

BLUE HARBOR HOUSE

INNKEEPERS	Terry and Annette Hazzard
ADDRESS	67 Elm Street, Camden, ME 04843
TELEPHONE	207-236-3196 | 800-248-3196
CONTACT	info@blueharborhouse.com | www.blueharborhouse.com
FEATURES	6 Rooms, 5 Suites; Private baths | Children and pets: inquire

This mid-coast Maine B&B was built in 1810. Today, its historic charms blend perfectly with its modern comforts. The elegant yet casual atmosphere is a relaxing retreat for romantic getaways, families, and business travelers. Expect pampering while staying here. A generous complimentary breakfast is served each morning in the dining room. Start with freshly brewed coffee or tea and an assortment of juices. The first course includes favorites such as Poached Pears in Raspberry Coulis with Vanilla Cream, Caribbean Bananas, and Spiced Fruit with Yogurt and Toasted Almonds. The main entrées are house specialties such as Eggs Florentine, Bacon & Leek Quiche, and Blueberry Pancakes. A delicious way to start your day!

Then, it is time to explore Camden. Here you will find mountain trails to hike, country roads to bike, and waters to paddle or sail. Enjoy a round of golf overlooking the bay. Swim in warm lake waters or the brisk Atlantic. If you're ready to shop 'till you drop, the harbor front streets are lined with intriguing shops selling many made-in-Maine crafts as well as treasures from around the world. Purchase artwork directly from artisans in their studios. Browse the antiques shops and flea markets. There are great country auctions, too!

"Fresh-catch dining is a highlight for Camden. Stop in to one of our many restaurants and pubs for some delicious fresh Maine seafood or fabulous traditional cuisine. A Foodies delight!"—Innkeeper

Crab Cakes

Yield: 4–5 servings

1	Tbsp olive oil
¼	cup minced onion
2	cloves garlic, minced
¼	cup cooked corn (optional)
2	Tbsp celery, chopped
4	oz. shiitake mushrooms, chopped
¼	cup white wine
1	tsp seasoning salt, to taste*
¼	cup finely chopped parsley
6–10	oz. fresh crabmeat, picked over for shells
1	egg, beaten
¼	cup mayonnaise
1	Tbsp chopped fresh basil
	unseasoned dry or fresh breadcrumbs
1	Tbsp butter

Heat oil in a skillet over medium heat. Add onion, garlic, corn and celery; cook until onion is soft. Add mushrooms and wine; cook until liquids are absorbed. Add seasoning salt to taste and parsley. Remove from heat and let cool.

Shred crabmeat into a medium bowl. Mix in beaten egg, mayonnaise, basil and sautéed mushroom mixture. Mix in enough breadcrumbs so mixture holds together (mixture should be firm but not dry). Form into about ½-inch-thick patties. Melt butter in a skillet over medium-low heat. Add crab cakes and cook until golden brown on both sides. Serve hot.

Tip: To make your own seasoning salt, try a mixture of ground nutmeg, cinnamon, allspice, ground ginger, garlic salt, thyme, crushed red pepper flakes, and a little cayenne pepper.

BLUE HILL INN

INNKEEPER	Sarah Pebworth
ADDRESS	40 Union Street, Blue Hill, ME 04614
TELEPHONE	207-374-2844 | 800-826-7415
CONTACT	Sarah@bluehillinn.com | www.bluehillinn.com
FEATURES	11 Rooms, 2 Suites; Private baths | Children welcome | Pets allowed in suites

At the Blue Hill Inn, individualized guest attention is the first priority. Innkeeper Sarah Pebworth and the staff of the inn will make suggestions, assist with itineraries, help with directions, and make reservations. They are familiar with the area and can direct guests to great boating, live music, beautiful picnic spots, husband-friendly shopping, and delicious lobster rolls.

Complimentary breakfasts at the Blue Hill Inn are designed with guests in mind. Choices range from vacation-decadent to watching one's waistline. Special menus to accommodate individual food allergies or restrictions are easily arranged. Dining at the inn is a culinary experience you won't want to miss. The chef at The Blue Hill Inn is passionate about working with local farmers, fishermen, and purveyors.

"We feel so lucky to have discovered Blue Hill and the Blue Hill Inn, both of which are idyllic. Thank you for a wonderful stay, it was perfect in every way—nicely appointed rooms and baths with many little extras … An inn with 'good taste' in all senses. Our stay could not have been nicer. Best blueberry pancakes and scones ever!"—Guest

Flourless Chocolate Cake with Toasted Nut Crust

Yield: 12 servings

"Guests often mention that Chef Devin Finigan's inspired creations are the highlight of their trip."

- 2 Tbsp melted butter
- 1 cup toasted nuts (almonds, pecans, pistachios, walnuts, or hazelnuts)
- 9 oz. milk chocolate (we recommend Ghirardelli)
- 9 oz. bittersweet chocolate
- 1 cup unsalted butter
- 6 eggs
- ¾ cup sugar
- ½ cup heavy cream
- whipped cream flavored with cinnamon to garnish

Preheat oven to 300°F. While the oven preheats, place a baking pan filled with water in the oven. This will be the bath in which the cake cooks. Fill with enough water so that it will rise around the cake pan, but not spill into it. Melt 2 tablespoons butter. While butter melts, pulse nuts in food processor until they reach the consistency of fine crumbs. Add melted butter and mix thoroughly. Press mixture into the bottom of a springform pan. Wrap the bottom of the pan in tin foil so no water can get in.

Over a double boiler, melt both types of chocolate and butter. Remove from heat and let sit 5 minutes. In another bowl, whisk together eggs and sugar. Whisk in the melted chocolate, followed by the heavy cream.

Pour the cake mix into the springform pan, and gently place cake into the water bath.

Bake 40–60 minutes until cake has set, with a slight wiggle in the very middle. Remove from oven, and take out of water bath. Remove tin foil, and let cake cool to room temperature.

Refrigerate for at least 5 hours before serving.

CAPTAIN BRIGGS HOUSE B&B

INNKEEPERS	**Bev and Chuck Tefer**
ADDRESS	**8 Maple Avenue, Freeport, ME 04032**
TELEPHONE	**207-865-1868	888-217-2477**
CONTACT	**info@captainbriggs.net	www.captainbriggs.com**
FEATURES	**6 Rooms, 1 Suite; Private baths	Children welcome	Call ahead for pet stays**

A beautifully restored 1853 shipbuilder's home, the Captain Briggs House B&B is located on a quiet side street, just three blocks from L.L. Bean and within easy walking distance of Freeport's many fine shops and restaurants. Spend a day visiting lighthouses and museums or hiking trails in coastal parks. Scenic cruises offer fine opportunities to see Maine's coastline and wildlife.

At the Captain Briggs House B&B, guests are treated like family. Start your day out right with a hearty full breakfast—at no extra charge.

Breakfast fare consists of fresh fruit, homemade pastries, cereals, and a hot entrée. Some of the guests' favorites are Belgian waffles, Eggs Benedict, quiches, omelets and casseroles. The innkeeper can accommodate special dietary requests with advance notice.

"Thank you for your hospitality during our stay in your lovely home. We enjoyed our week visiting Wolf's Neck State Park, Winslow Memorial Gardens, the Maine Museum, the Observatory and Longfellow's House & Museum. Your B&B is lovely. The accommodations are excellent and the breakfasts are the ideal start to the day."—Guest

Laurie's Breakfast Casserole

Yield: 12 servings

- 1 stick butter
- 1 (24-oz.) pkg. frozen hash browns
- 2 cups cubed ham or 1 lb. sausage or bacon
  Additional options: peppers, onions, pimiento, chives, tomatoes, and mushrooms
- 12 eggs
- 1 cup milk
- 4 cups sharp cheddar cheese, grated
- 2 tsp pepper

Preheat oven to 350°F.

Melt margarine or butter in 9x13-inch pan. Add thawed hash browns and ham (or sausage or bacon) and any optional ingredients desired. Beat eggs with milk—using an electric mixer makes them fluffier. Pour over potatoes. Sprinkle cheese on top and season with pepper. Bake for 45–60 minutes. Eggs will set better if casserole is made the night before.

Tip: Try sprinkling tomatoes, extra cheese, bacon, or parsley on top for the last few minutes of baking for presentation.

CAPTAIN LINDSEY HOUSE INN

INNKEEPERS	Captains Ken and Ellen Barnes and Patricia Payeur
ADDRESS	5 Lindsey Street, Rockland, ME 04841
TELEPHONE	207-596-7950	800-523-2145
CONTACT	info@lindseyhouse.com	www.lindseyhouse.com
FEATURES	9 Rooms; Private baths	Children welcome	Pets not allowed

Built in 1835 by a Maine sea captain as his home, this Harbor District Federal-style inn combines the attributes of a boutique hotel and an inn right in the heart of Rockland's waterfront district. Meticulous care is evident in each of the nine spacious rooms with private bathrooms. Many of the rooms have their own fireplace.

Guests enjoy afternoon baked refreshments with port wine or tea, available fireside or outside in the private walled-in garden. Breakfast is the specialty. A large English breakfast is served buffet-style every morning. Coffee and teas are ready by 7:00 a.m. Guests are treated to a hearty array of homemade granola, fresh baked breads, yogurt, juices, breakfast meats, egg dishes, Belgian waffles, fruit compotes, and more.

After breakfast you can be off exploring the charming seaside port of Rockland. The front door faces a quiet side street, and it is only a few steps to Main Street. Downtown contains an eclectic collection of stores from art to antiques, baked goods to books, clothes to coffee, handmade jewelry to handmade soap, and sporting goods to souvenirs. You will find shops specializing in Maine-made goods, or items from exotic foreign countries. Our vibrant shopping district truly has something for everyone.

Ellen's cookbook, A Taste of the Taber, *illustrated by Ken, has become a classic both afloat and ashore and her appearance on the Food Network airs frequently.*

Blueberry Sour Cream Cake

Yield: 8 servings

"We grow the best wild blueberries in Maine. They are small and very tasty. During the season—late July and August—I try to use our home-grown blueberries as much as possible."

1½ cups all-purpose flour
½ cup sugar
1 stick butter, softened
1 egg
1½ tsp baking powder
1 tsp vanilla extract
1 quart fresh blueberries

Topping:
½ cup sugar
1 tsp vanilla extract
2 cups sour cream
2 egg yolks

Preheat oven to 350°F. In a large bowl, combine flour, sugar, butter, egg, baking powder, vanilla, and blueberries; pat into a 9-inch springform pan. For the topping: combine all topping ingredients and blend well. Pour topping over batter. Bake for 75 minutes, or until a toothpick inserted in the center comes out clean.

CHADWICK B&B

INNKEEPERS	E. Scot Fuller and Laura McDowell
ADDRESS	140 Chadwick Street, Portland, ME 04102
TELEPHONE	207-774-5141 | 800-774-2137
CONTACT	info@thechadwick.com | www.thechadwick.com
FEATURES	4 Rooms; Private baths | Children over the age of 14 welcome if accompanied by a family member | Pets not allowed

The perfect Portland getaway, the Chadwick B&B provides thoughtful touches that invite a sense of pampering and romance in unsurpassed comfort and elegance. With endless events and activities offered in the greater Portland area, guests can keep active or spend time relaxing in the comfort of this classically appointed home away from home.

Whether visiting Maine for a long weekend, vacation, rest and relaxation, honeymoon, anniversary, or business, the Chadwick B&B strives to provide a level of personal service that goes above and beyond, leaving guests with a rich and memorable experience. The Chadwick staff take great pride in providing tastefully appointed guest rooms—each with a private bathroom—beautifully landscaped grounds, and a five-star gourmet breakfast each and every morning.

"My husband and I stayed at the Chadwick for our 5th Anniversary. The service was amazing and so friendly. We have both worked in many areas of customer service, and are not easily impressed … they went the extra mile, more than once. Everything is so clean. I would whole-heartedly recommend this B&B!"—Guest

Crab Quiche

Yield: 6 servings

- 1 (9-inch) pre-baked pie crust
- 8 oz. crabmeat
- 1 cup Swiss cheese, grated
- 2 green onions, finely chopped
- ¼ cup sliced almonds
- ½ tsp grated lemon zest
- 4 large eggs
- 2 cups half & half
- ½ tsp salt
- ¼ tsp dry mustard
- dash of mace

Preheat oven to 425°F. Sprinkle crabmeat, cheese, green onions, almonds, and lemon zest into crust. In a bowl, combine eggs, half & half, salt, dry mustard, and mace; pour over ingredients in crust. Bake for 15 minutes. Lower oven temperature to 300°F and bake for 30 minutes longer. Let stand for 10 minutes before slicing and serving.

CRAIGNAIR INN & RESTAURANT

INNKEEPERS	Joanne and Michael O'Shea
ADDRESS	5 Third Street, Spruce Head, ME 04859
TELEPHONE	207-594-7644 | 800-320-9997
CONTACT	innkeeper@craignair.com | www.craignair.com
FEATURES	20 Rooms; Private and shared baths | Children welcome | Pets welcome; call ahead

Set on a granite ledge rising from the sea and surrounded by flower gardens, Craignair was built in 1928 to house workers from the nearby quarries. Little has changed here since the turn of the century, and you can still feel the mood of a once lively and active working town. The union hall still stands, as well as the old general store and post office. The chapel, where the stonecutters and their families once worshiped, is now an annex to the inn. Evidence of the quarry-workers' time is also portrayed in the beautiful granite causeway that stretches across the water to Clark Island, where a great quarry was once the center of this picturesque village. Clark Island granite was used in the construction of the Central Park bridges and gate houses, and in the Brooklyn Battery Tunnel, both in New York City, and the Library of Congress in Washington, just to name a few. The boarding house was converted to an inn in 1947.

"Craignair Inn has been hosting weddings and special events for over 60 years. The restaurant offers gourmet dinners on special evenings—like Valentine's Day. But we are especially enthusiastic about our casual Friday night Burger menu.—Innkeeper

Craignair Inn
Breakfast Frittata

Yield: 12 servings

16 eggs
2 cups heavy cream
2 cups vegetables, your choice, chopped into bite-sized pieces
   (Broccoli and fennel are our favorites, but any vegetable will work.)
   salt and pepper, to taste
2 cups cheese, shredded (your choice, cheddar, swiss, mozzarella)

Preheat oven to 375°F. Grease a 9x13-inch baking dish.

Mix eggs and cream with a hand or stand-up mixer until well combined. Pour egg mixture into baking dish. Distribute vegetables throughout the dish. Season with salt and pepper; spread cheese on the top. Cook, uncovered for about 40–45 minutes. Check to see if the egg dish appears to be set. Pull from the oven and serve immediately.

DOCKSIDE GUEST QUARTERS

INNKEEPERS	The Lusty Family
ADDRESS	22 Harris Island Road, York, ME 03909
TELEPHONE	207-363-2868 | 800-270-1977
CONTACT	info@docksidegq.com | www.docksidegq.com
FEATURES	15 Rooms, 6 Suites; Private baths | Children welcome | Pets not allowed

For over 50 years, the Lusty family has welcomed guests to the Dockside Guest Quarters and Restaurant. Situated on a private, seven-acre peninsula bordering York Harbor and the ocean, the inn offers 21 rooms and suites. This Maine house is a classic New England cottage with a large wraparound porch. The view from the porch is quintessential coastal Maine, overlooking the harbor and the Atlantic Ocean.

The Dockside Restaurant is set on the shores of Harris Island and is known for creatively prepared fresh Maine seafood in a yacht club atmosphere.

This beautiful York Harbor inn is ideal for short stays, and even better for extended Maine vacations, weddings, or family reunions. Appealing accommodations, bountiful breakfasts, and creative cuisine offer guests in search of the ideal southern Maine vacation all the ABCs for a relaxing and rejuvenating getaway.

"Breathtaking views, superb service, and the pleasure of working with Phil Lusty during those few months leading up to our Wedding Day. 'Cocktails on the Lawn' was a great way for guests to mingle during pictures and enjoy the view."—Newlywed Guest

Maine Maple Syrup Pie

Yield: 8 servings

"This is great on a cold day! A very rich and filling dessert—delicious by itself or a la mode."

  1 cup maple syrup
  1 lb. brown sugar
1½ cups heavy cream
  2 Tbsp butter, softened
  4 eggs
  1 (9-inch) piecrust
    Vanilla ice cream, for serving

Preheat oven to 350°F. In a mixing bowl, beat together maple syrup, sugar, cream, butter, and eggs. Pour into crust and bake for about 45 minutes, until a toothpick inserted in the center comes out clean. Serve with ice cream, if desired.

GALEN C. MOSES HOUSE B&B

INNKEEPERS	Jim Haught and Larry Kieft
ADDRESS	1009 Washington Street, Bath, ME 04530
TELEPHONE	207-442-8771 | 888-442-8771
CONTACT	stay@galenmoses.com | www.galenmoses.com
FEATURES	4 Rooms; Private baths | Children age 13 and older welcome | Pets can be accommodated only in carriage room, which is being renovated in 2013

There are surprises throughout the Galen C. Moses House, from the elegant gardens and rooms filled with tasteful antiques to the full theatre located on the third floor (once used to entertain officers from the nearby Naval Air Station during World War II).

The house contains a number of spirits, other than the sherry served at 5 p.m. Our ghosts, assuredly friendly, are likely to make their presence felt on a frequent basis. Early evening finds guests relaxing on the porches that surround the house, or taking a leisurely stroll along the waterfront.

"This was our first B&B experience and I'm certain there will never be one as memorable and lovely. So many of your beautiful touches reminded me of my mother's things. The breakfasts were divine. I felt so spoiled by your service to us and by your talent in the kitchen."—Guests

Baked Eggs in Maple Toast Cups

Yield: 4 servings

2 Tbsp maple syrup
2 Tbsp butter
8 slices white bread, crusts removed
8 large eggs
   salt and pepper, to taste

Preheat oven to 400°F. Grease a large muffin tin.

In a small saucepan over medium-low heat, combine maple syrup and butter. Heat until butter is melted; stir to combine. Roll out bread slices with a rolling pin until they are thin enough to press into a muffin cup. Brush each slice with the maple syrup mixture and press into greased muffin cups. Break 1 egg into each muffin cup. Sprinkle with salt and pepper. Bake for 15 minutes.

HARRASEEKET INN

INNKEEPER	Nancy Gray
ADDRESS	162 Main Street, Freeport, ME 04032
TELEPHONE	207-865-9377 | 800-342-6423
CONTACT	harraseeke@aol.com | www.harraseeketinn.com
FEATURES	93 Rooms; Private baths | Children welcome | Small dogs allowed

The Harraseeket Inn is a family-owned, luxury inn featuring two great restaurants, 23 fireplaces, an indoor heated pool, and pet-friendly lodging.

The two restaurants at the Harraseeket Inn use only the finest organic and natural Maine produce, wild seafood and game, and make all their breads and desserts daily. Sample the award-winning cuisine in the Maine Dining Room. The atmosphere is refined yet cozy, warmed by two fireplaces.

Of course, Maine lobsters are always available and Sunday brunch is not to be missed. It's an elegant array featuring a carving station, whole poached salmon, Belgian waffles with seasonal fruits and gourmet specialties such as caviar, pates, terrines, and artisan cheeses.

The Harraseeket Inn has won many awards. Among them are: Top 500 hotels in the world by *Travel + Leisure Magazine* 2010; Top 100 Hotels in the U.S., *Conde Nast Traveler,* 2011; Top 45 Hotels in the Northeast, *Conde Nast Traveler* Readers Poll 2012.

"Scallop fritters, espresso/ancho-rubbed ribeye, chilled Maine lobster—when it comes to setting the table for Sunday brunch, the Harraseeket Inn knows how to satisfy hungry Mainers—and, apparently, Down East *readers."*—Down East Magazine

Spicy Buffalo Chili

Yield: 10–12 servings

"Spicy Buffalo Chili makes a perfect winter meal served with tortillas or corn bread. Prep time, 15 minutes. Substitute beef for bison if desired, tho bison is healthier. Use your favorite beans or two different varieties!"

1	Tbsp vegetable oil
2½	lbs. ground buffalo meat
1	large onion, chopped
3	cloves garlic, minced
2	jalapeño, seeded and diced
1	red bell pepper, diced
1	can (28-oz.) tomato purée
½	cup chili powder
1	Tbsp ground cumin
½	tsp ground chipotle pepper
¼	tsp cinnamon
1½	tsp salt
½	tsp ground black pepper
½	tsp cayenne
2	cups beef broth, or water
2	(15-oz.) cans pinto beans, drained
	water as needed

In a large pot, over medium-high heat, cook the buffalo in the oil until browned and broken in small pieces. Add the onions and sauté for 5 minutes. Add the garlic and cook for one minute.

Add all remaining ingredients, except the beans, and bring to a boil. Reduce the heat to low and simmer 1 hour, stirring occasionally. Add the beans and cook for 15 minutes more. Water can be added during the cooking to adjust for thinner or thicker chili.

Hartwell House Inn

INNKEEPERS	Danette Kerrigan and the Hartwell House staff
ADDRESS	312 Shore Road, Ogunquit, ME 03907
TELEPHONE	207-646-7210	800-235-8883
CONTACT	innkeeper@hartwellhouseinn.com	www.hartwellhouseinn.com
FEATURES	12 Rooms, 4 Suites; Private baths	Children age 14 and older welcome if accompanied by adult	Pets not allowed

The Hartwell House Inn B&B has been welcoming guests since it was built in the mid-twentieth century. The inn offers elegant accommodations with authentic New England charm. Rooms are furnished with a distinctive collection of early American and English antiques. Most have French doors leading to terraces or balconies over-looking sculpted flower gardens.

The inn's expansive landscape, with its picturesque lily pond and manicured croquet lawn, offers the beauty and tranquility of the Maine countryside. Yet, the inn is ideally located within walking distance of all that Ogunquit has to offer.

Breakfast is a social event when the varied guests gather in the morning in the sunlit dining areas. A full, gourmet breakfast and after-noon tea are served each day.

> *"We wanted to let you know that we thoroughly enjoyed our recent visit to the Hartwell House. Danette gave us some wonderful recom-mendations for dining out and places to see in the area. The staff was extremely helpful and responsive to any of our requests. This was a repeat visit for us, after several years."*—Guest

Blueberry Sage Scones

Yield: 24 scones

*"Capturing the bountiful harvest of local Maine blueberries,
these scones are delightful for breakfast and afternoon tea alike.
The perfect combination of sweet and savory."*

5¼	cups all-purpose flour
¾	cup, plus 1 Tbsp sugar
2	Tbsp plus 1½ tsp baking powder
2¼	tsp salt
2	sticks plus 2 Tbsp butter, chilled and cubed
6–7	oz. dried blueberries
1	Tbsp fresh sage, finely chopped
2	cups plus 1½ Tbsp heavy cream

Preheat oven to 350°F. Sift together flour, sugar, baking powder and salt in a large bowl or an electric stand mixer. Add butter and mix with a mixer just until pea-sized clumps form. Add blueberries, sage and 2 cups of heavy cream; mix just until combined.

Scoop dough with an ice cream scoop onto a cookie sheet or roll out to 7/8-inch thick and cut with 3-inch biscuit cutter or a glass. Brush with remaining 1½ tablespoons of heavy cream. Bake for 10 minutes, or until golden brown. Allow to cool 10 minutes before serving.

Inn at English Meadows

INNKEEPERS	Eric and Liz Brodar
ADDRESS	141 Port Road, Kennebunk, ME 04043
TELEPHONE	800-272-0698	207-967-5766
CONTACT	innkeeper@englishmeadowsinn.com	www.englishmeadowsinn.com
FEATURES	5 Rooms, 4 Suites, 1 Private bungalow; Private baths	Children age 10 and older welcome	Pets welcome for an additional fee

The Inn at English Meadows, a Victorian Greek revival home, was originally built in 1860 by a local farmer. The land was used to run a dairy business after the Civil War, keeping the cattle in the attached barn and renting rooms in the main house. This recently renovated historic inn has welcomed travelers from all over the world for more than 75 years.

The inn is located within walking distance of the Kennebunkport Village, otherwise known as Dock Square. Kennebunkport has many shops, galleries, restaurants and historic homes. If you want to explore the area's natural beauty, visit the vast ocean beaches and rocky coastline, less than a mile away from the inn. During the evening, choose from a wide variety of dining experiences at Dock Square.

The Inn at English Meadows features a breakfast that is truly one of the highlights of your stay. Guests of the inn have expressed on several occasions that the freshly prepared, three-course gourmet breakfast is nothing short of divine.

"We are proud to share the news that Select Registry announced that the Inn at English Meadows has joined its portfolio of celebrated B&Bs. Only 330 properties throughout North America have qualified for the Select Registry designation."—Innkeeper

Ginger Cake

Yield: 8 servings

1½ cups unbleached all-purpose flour
2 tsp ground ginger
1 tsp ground cinnamon
½ tsp baking soda
¼ tsp ground cloves
¼ tsp salt
½ cup unsalted butter, at room temperature

1 Tbsp minced fresh ginger
¼ cup granulated sugar
¼ cup packed dark brown sugar
1 large egg, at room temperature
½ cup unsulfured mild molasses
½ cup buttermilk, at room temperature

Position a rack in the center of the oven and preheat the oven to 350°F. Butter the sides of an 8x8-inch square cake pan and line the bottom of the pan with parchment.

In a medium bowl, mix the flour, ground ginger, cinnamon, baking soda, cloves, and salt. Set aside.

Using a hand mixer or a stand mixer fitted with the paddle attachment, beat the butter on medium speed until light and fluffy, about 1 minute. Add the fresh ginger and mix until just combined. Add both sugars and beat on medium speed until well combined and fluffy, about 1 minute. Stop the mixer and scrape down the sides of the bowl. Add the egg and mix on medium speed until well combined. Turn the mixer to low and slowly add the molasses. Add about one-third of the dry ingredients and mix until just combined. Add one-third of the buttermilk and mix until just combined. Add the remaining dry and wet ingredients in four more additions, finishing with the buttermilk and mixing until just combined after each addition. Scrape the batter into the cake pan and spread it evenly.

Bake the cake until a skewer inserted into the center comes out clean, 30–35 minutes. Let the cake cool completely in the pan, at least an hour.

INN AT SOUTHWEST

INNKEEPER	Sandy Johnson
ADDRESS	371 Main Street, Southwest Harbor, ME 04679
TELEPHONE	207-244-3835
CONTACT	reservations@innatsouthwest.com	www.innatsouthwest.com
FEATURES	5 Rooms, 2 Suites; Private baths	Children age 8 and older welcome	Pets not allowed

The Inn at Southwest is a circa-1884 Victorian B&B that overlooks the serene waters of Southwest Harbor. Near the center of town and close to Bar Harbor and Acadia National Park, the inn offers comfortable yet elegant lodging and is within walking distance of shops, restaurants, and the marina.

The wicker-filled verandah is the perfect spot to enjoy the gardens or watch boats slip in and out of Southwest Harbor. Rooms have down-filled duvets, ceiling fans, and luxurious linens and towels. Some rooms feature limited water views and gas log stoves.

Freshly baked cookies and refreshments welcome you back from a day's activities.

"Of course, eating lobster pulled from the local waters is a must, whether in the casual atmosphere of a lobster pound where you can watch lobstermen return with their catch, or at one of the upscale Southwest Harbor or Bar Harbor restaurants."—Innkeeper

Blueberry Gingerbread

Yield: 9 servings

½ cup vegetable oil
1 cup, plus 2 Tbsp sugar
1 egg
½ cup molasses
2 cups all-purpose flour
1 tsp baking soda
1 tsp cinnamon
½ tsp ground ginger
½ tsp nutmeg
½ tsp salt
1 cup buttermilk
1 cup fresh or frozen blueberries

Preheat oven to 350°F. Grease a 9x9-inch baking pan.

In a large bowl, beat oil, sugar, and egg with a mixer on medium speed until light. Add molasses and beat at high speed for 2 minutes. In a medium bowl, combine flour, baking soda, cinnamon, ginger, nutmeg and salt; add to molasses mixture alternately with buttermilk and beat until smooth. Fold in blueberries. Pour batter into prepared baking pan. Bake for about 60 minutes, or until middle is set and a toothpick inserted in center comes out clean. Cool slightly before serving.

Maine Stay Inn & Cottages

INNKEEPERS	Judi and Walter Hauer
ADDRESS	34 Maine Street, Kennebunkport, ME 04046
TELEPHONE	207-967-2117	800-950-2117
CONTACT	innkeeper@mainestayinn.com	www.mainestayinn.com
FEATURES	4 Rooms, 3 Suites, 10 Cottages; Private baths	Children welcome	Pets not allowed

One of only a few small Kennebunkport hotels, Maine Stay Inn offers romantic lodging with the intimacy of a charming B&B inn. This distinguished B&B offers year-round historic New England lodging, exceptional hospitality and the unsurpassed beauty of the sandy coast of Kennebunkport, Maine. Whether you seek a romantic getaway or family vacation, the warmth and hospitality at Maine Stay Inn will make your visit to the southern Maine coast a most memorable experience.

Perfectly located in the quiet residential Historic District, it is just a short stroll along tree-lined streets to the multitude of fine shops, galleries, and restaurants in Kennebunkport's Dock Square. The expansive property, peaceful gardens, and proximity to town set the Maine Stay Inn and Cottages apart from other Kennebunkport hotels. Nature trails, sandy beaches, and quiet coves provide tranquility that will soothe your soul.

Make your next escape to a Maine B&B a warm memory with a visit to the Maine Stay Inn, a perfect lodging choice.

"We love that each one of our rooms and suites has a distinct personality—you certainly won't find that at a hotel!"—Innkeeper

Judi's Spinach Quiche

Yield: 8 servings

¾ cup chopped green pepper
¾ cup chopped onion
1½ cups chopped celery
2 cups chopped zucchini
1½ tsp minced garlic
3 Tbsp oil
7 eggs
1 (8-oz.) pkg. cream cheese, softened and diced
3 cups cheddar cheese, shredded
1 tsp salt
1/8 tsp pepper
 basil, to taste
1 (10-oz.) pkg. frozen spinach chopped, cooked, and drained
1-1½ cups grated Parmesan cheese

Preheat oven to 350°F.

Sauté peppers, onions, celery, zucchini, and garlic in hot oil. In a large bowl, beat eggs and combine with cream cheese, cheddar cheese, and seasonings. Add spinach and Parmesan cheese to egg mixture; add vegetables. Mix well. Bake in 10-inch springform pan (or make two thin pies by using two smaller pans) for one hour or until pie is set in center. Cool ten minutes before cutting.

PRIMROSE INN

INNKEEPER	Melissa Collier DeVos
ADDRESS	73 Mt. Desert Street, Bar Harbor, ME 04609
TELEPHONE	207-288-4031	877-846-3424
CONTACT	relax@primroseinn.com	www.primroseinn.com
FEATURES	8 Rooms, 7 Suites; Private baths	Children welcome in suites	Pets not allowed

This romantic B&B is ideally located just a few blocks from the center of downtown Bar Harbor and one mile from magnificent Acadia National Park. When staying here, guests will be just a leisurely stroll away from all of the wonderful restaurants, shops, galleries, museums and activities that make Bar Harbor a world-class destination. Additionally, the historic B&B is just a few minutes from the entrance to the park (by car or the free Island Explorer bus) and its miles of renowned carriage roads for enjoying hiking, biking, running, leisurely walks and even horseback riding.

Built in 1878, the historic Primrose Inn is decorated in an updated Victorian style with select antiques and enhanced with today's most requested guest amenities. Guests will enjoy the comfortable elegance of the spacious rooms, each with a private bathroom. Many of the rooms also feature cozy gas fireplaces, spa tubs, adjoining sitting rooms, and private porches and balconies.

Guests of the Primrose Inn will enjoy a hearty full breakfast each morning with a choice of hot entrées served fireside in our dining room or on the outdoor wraparound front porch.

"Our 'Afternoon Tea' featuring an assortment of freshly baked treats from the Primrose Inn's kitchen is very popular with our guests and many plan their day around returning to the inn to relax and enjoy it before dinner."—Innkeeper

Crab & Shrimp Egg Toasts

Yield: 4 servings

1	(6½-oz.) can crabmeat (or use fresh crabmeat)
10–12	medium shrimp, cooked, peeled and chopped
1	(3-oz.) pkg. cream cheese, cubed
2	oz. goat cheese, crumbled
9	hard-boiled eggs, peeled and chopped
2	Tbsp chives or green onions, finely chopped
¼	cup mayonnaise
1–2	Tbsp Dijon mustard
	dash of salt
	dash of Old Bay seasoning (optional)
4	English muffins, split and toasted
	Paprika for garnish (optional)

Preheat broiler. In a medium bowl, combine crab, shrimp, cream cheese, goat cheese, eggs, and chives; toss lightly to mix. In a small bowl, combine mayonnaise, mustard, salt, and Old Bay seasoning; gently fold into crab mixture. Spoon onto toasted English muffin halves and sprinkle with paprika. Broil about 6 inches from heat source until heated through.

PRYOR HOUSE B&B

INNKEEPERS	**Don and Gwenda Pryor**
ADDRESS	**360 Front Street, Bath, ME 04530**
TELEPHONE	**207-443-1146	866-977-7967**
CONTACT	**gwenda6@juno.com	www.pryorhouse.com**
FEATURES	**3 Rooms; Private baths	Children age 12 and older welcome	Pets not allowed**

The Pryor House is a lovely, circa 1820, Federal-style home over-looking the Kennebec River in Bath, the historic "City of Ships." Located just a few blocks from the heart of town, this classic New England home features an elegant double staircase, wide pine floors, and original fireplaces. Its comfortable atmosphere invites guests to escape from everyday life.

Guests can choose from three distinctive rooms, each with a private bath. The Captain's Room boasts a king-size, four-poster bed, decorative fireplace, and a window seat overlooking the river. There is also an inviting parlor area for guests to relax in, and a dining room where some of the most delicious breakfasts are served.

If you plan to visit the Bath area, see how ships were built with a trip to the Maine Maritime Museum, or visit the Chocolate Church Arts Center, Waterfront Park, or stroll along streets of the city to discover great restaurants and antique shops.

> *"This was a perfect stay. Thank you!"*—Guest
>
> *"Beautiful, comfortable rooms and fantastic food! We loved it!"*
> —Guest

French Banana Crêpes

Yield: 5–6 servings

Crêpes

- 1 cup all-purpose flour
- ¼ cup powdered sugar
- 1 cup milk
- 2 eggs
- 3 Tbsp butter or margarine, melted
- 1 tsp vanilla extract
- ¼ tsp salt

Filling

- ½ stick butter or margarine
- ¼ cup packed brown sugar
- ¼ tsp cinnamon, plus extra for garnish
- ¼ tsp ground nutmeg
- ¼ cup light cream
- 5–6 firm bananas, halved lengthwise
- whipped cream, for serving (optional)

For the crêpes: Sift together flour and powdered sugar into a bowl. Add milk, eggs, butter, vanilla, and salt; beat until smooth. Let batter stand for 30 minutes (this yields more tender crêpes). Heat a lightly greased 6-inch skillet over medium heat. Add about 3 tablespoons of batter, rotate pan so batter almost covers bottom of skillet. Cook until lightly browned; turn and lightly brown other side. Stack crêpes between sheets of wax paper on a wire rack. Repeat with remaining batter (makes 10-12 crêpes).

For the filling: In the same skillet, melt together butter, brown sugar, cinnamon, and nutmeg over low heat. Stir in cream and cook until slightly thickened. Add ½ of halved bananas to skillet; cook for 2-3 minutes, spooning sauce over them; remove bananas and keep warm. Repeat with remaining bananas.

To serve: Roll a crêpe around each banana half; place on a serving platter; spoon sauce over crêpes. Top with whipped cream.

Windward House B&B

INNKEEPERS	Kristi and Jesse Bifulco
ADDRESS	6 High Street, Camden, ME 04843
TELEPHONE	207-236-9656 | 877-492-9656
CONTACT	bnb@windwardhouse.com | www.windwardhouse.com
FEATURES	5 Rooms, 3 Suites; Private baths | Children welcome | Pets not allowed

This Maine lodging offers a great night's sleep on hand pressed, high-thread-count sheets in a traditional Greek revival house that will feel like putting on your favorite old sweater—and more. It is a fantastic location in Camden with many free amenities including wi-fi throughout the house and backyard, complimentary tea, coffee, and baked goodies in the afternoon, off-street parking, and air conditioning. Many rooms even have Vermont Castings gas-fired wood burning stoves.

A full-menu breakfast made to order is included with each room. Windward House is the only B&B in Camden that offers a complimentary menu breakfast. In addition to using local and organic ingredients in the menu items, Windward House uses Gilchrest & Soames BeeKind products.

"We serve our own coffee blend, Windward House Blend Fair Trade Shade Grown Organic. We offer vegan options such as Sticky Rice with Coconut Milk. Gluten free and vegetarian are available upon request. And we proudly serve Moo Milk, Maine's own organic milk, farm-fresh and Maine-produced and processed."—Innkeeper

Wicked Good Belgian Waffles with Maine Blueberry Compote

Yield: 8–10 waffles

"Belgian waffles were introduced to America at the 1964 World's Fair in New York, while Maine blueberries have been a staple of family meals for generations. The two come together in this recipe."

Belgian waffles

2¼	tsp active dry yeast
2¾	cups warm milk, divided, plus ¼ cup lukewarm milk
3	large eggs, separated
1½	sticks unsalted butter, melted and cooled
½	cup sugar
1½	tsp salt
2	tsp vanilla extract
4	cups all-purpose flour

Maine blueberry compote

2	cups fresh Maine blueberries
¼	cup pure Maine maple syrup

In a small mixing bowl, whisk together yeast and ¼ cup of warm milk; let stand for about 5 minutes. In a large bowl, whisk together egg yolks, ¼ cup of lukewarm milk, and butter. Whisk yeast mixture, sugar, salt, and vanilla into egg yolk mixture. Add flour in three parts, alternating with remaining 2½ cups of warm milk in two parts. In a medium bowl, beat egg whites until soft peaks form; fold into batter. Cover tightly with plastic wrap and let stand in a warm place (such as an unheated oven) for about 1 hour, until doubled in size. Stir down batter. Bake waffles on a preheated waffle iron until golden brown. Serve with warm blueberry compote.

For the blueberry compote: Bring blueberries and maple syrup to a boil in a saucepan. Lower heat and simmer until thickened.

YORK HARBOR INN

INNKEEPER	Garry Dominguez
ADDRESS	480 York Street, York Harbor, ME 03911
TELEPHONE	207-363-5119	800-343-3869
CONTACT	info@yorkharborinn.com	www.yorkharborinn.com
FEATURES	22 Rooms; Private baths	Children welcome	Pets allowed only in sister inn, Harbor Crest

The York Harbor Inn is an oceanfront B&B on the rocky coast of Maine. The inn belongs to a family of inns comprising six separate lodges. The main inn offers 22 elegantly appointed guest rooms, including several luxury units with ocean-view decks. A complimentary breakfast is included for all guests staying in the inn.

Beyond breakfast, dining at the York Harbor Inn is truly a special experience. The "1637 Restaurant" has fantastic ocean views, historic, intimate dining rooms, and a lively Tavern Bar and Tap Room (often with live entertainment) all centered around a large fieldstone fireplace. The Ship's Cellar Pub offers a "one of a kind" atmosphere with its décor and construction and live entertainment.

For things to do, Harbor Beach is directly across the street from the inn. Known as the "locals" beach, it often is full of children riding the waves and families picnicking in the sand. The summit of Mount Agamenticus is a 15–20 minute drive and on a clear day you can see the skyscrapers of Boston to the south. If you are a history buff, the town of York is one of the most historically well-preserved and documented towns in New England.

Over the last 31 years, York Harbor Inn has been featured in numerous types of media on countless occasions. Some of this wonderful media has included Gourmet Magazine, Food & Wine Magazine, *and* Great Country Inns of America *on* The Travel Channel.

Lobster-Stuffed Chicken with Boursin Cheese Sauce

Yield: 8 servings

Stuffing:

2	Tbsp butter, clarified
2	oz. onion, finely diced
2	oz. celery, finely diced
2	Tbsp dry sherry wine
1½	tsp garlic, minced
1½	tsp Worcestershire sauce
10	oz. Ritz crackers, crushed
1	Tbsp green onion, sliced
1	Tbsp parsley, chopped
1	tsp salt
1	tsp white pepper

Chicken:

1	lb. lobster meat, cooked, cut into medium dice, and divided
8	(6-oz.) boneless, skinless chicken breasts, lightly pounded
2	cups heavy cream
10	oz. garlic and herb Boursin cheese

For the stuffing: Heat butter in a skillet over medium heat. Add onion, celery, and cook until limp. Transfer to a bowl. Add remaining stuffing ingredients to the bowl and thoroughly combine.

For the chicken: Preheat oven to 350 degrees F. Place ⅛ of stuffing and ⅛ of lobster in center of each chicken breast. Fold in sides of chicken and secure with toothpicks. In 2-quart saucepan, bring cream to a boil. Whisk in the Boursin cheese. Lower heat and cook very gently, scraping bottom of pan with a rubber spatula often, so cheese does not burn. Cook until sauce is lightly thickened (sauce may be held for a short time in warm water bath). Bake chicken for about 18 minutes, until done. Top chicken with Boursin cheese to serve.

Breads, Muffins & Scones

Well, I can't eat muffins in an agitated manner. The butter would probably get on my cuffs."

— Oscar Wilde
The Importance of Being Earnest

Recipes in this Section:

Recipes in the Signature Recipes Section:

Westbrook Inn B&B
Cranberry Orange Scones

Yield: 10 scones

2	cups flour
10	tsp sugar, divided
1	Tbsp grated orange peel
2	tsp baking powder
½	tsp salt
¼	tsp baking soda
1/3	cup cold butter
1	cup cranberries
¼	cup orange juice
¼	cup half & half
1	egg
1	Tbsp milk

Glaze (optional):

½	cup confectioners' sugar
1	Tbsp orange juice

Orange Butter:

½	cup butter, softened
2–3	Tbsp orange marmalade

Preheat oven to 400°F.

In a large bowl, combine flour, 7 teaspoons sugar, orange peel, baking powder, salt, and baking soda. Cut in butter until the mixture resembles coarse crumbs; set aside. In a small bowl, combine cranberries, orange juice, half & half, and egg. Add to flour mixture and stir until a soft dough forms. On a floured surface gently knead the dough 6–8 times. Pat dough into an 8-inch circle. Cut into 10 wedges. Separate wedges and place on an ungreased cookie sheet. Brush with milk, then sprinkle with remaining sugar.

Bake for 12–15 minutes until lightly browned. Combine glaze ingredients, if desired, and drizzle over scones. Combine orange butter ingredients, and serve with warm scones.

Blue Hill Inn
Maple Glazed Date Scones

Yield: 12 scones

2½ cups (12 oz.) all-purpose flour (substitute up to ¾ cup
     whole-wheat flour, if desired)
1½ tsp baking powder
½   tsp salt
½   cup unsalted butter, diced/grated, and chilled
1½ cups half & half
¼   cup maple syrup, plus 2 Tbsp maple syrup (to brush on top)
½   cup dates (approximately 7), chopped

Preheat oven to 400°F. Grease a cooking sheet.

In a food processor,* combine flour, baking powder, and salt. Add butter and process until consistency of coarse breadcrumbs. Empty into a large bowl and add the half & half and ¼ cup maple syrup. Use your hands to bring ingredients together into a cohesive, slightly crumbly dough. Work dates into the dough. On a lightly floured surface, roll out into a circle, about ¾-inch thick. (If you prefer small, round scones, portion the dough with a scoop and press flat by hand, or roll out the dough and use a biscuit cutter.) Transfer to cookie sheet.

Bake 15 minutes, then brush top with maple syrup. Bake 5–10 more minutes, until the center is fully cooked. Serve warm.

*If a food processor is not available, grate cold butter and return butter to fridge. Combine flour, baking powder, and salt in a large bowl. Stir in cold grated butter and continue as directed above with addition of half & half and maple syrup.

Scranton Seahorse Inn

Rum Raisin Scones

Yield: 12 scones

½   cup raisins
½   cup dark rum (I use Meyers)
1¾ cups all-purpose flour
1   Tbsp + ½ tsp baking powder
¼   cup granulated sugar
½   tsp kosher salt

6   Tbsp unsalted butter, chilled, cut into small pieces
¾   cup heavy cream + 2 Tbsp to brush the scones before baking
1–2 Tbsp demerara sugar

Preheat oven to 375°F.

To prepare the raisins: Place the raisins in a small saucepan and cover with water. Bring to a boil and strain. Place the raisins in a small bowl. Cover with the rum and let it set for at least 1 hour. Strain the raisins again, reserving the rum.

In a mixing bowl, whisk together the flour, baking powder, sugar, and salt. Toss in the cut up butter and place the bowl in the freezer for 10 minutes. Using the paddle attachment, mix on low speed until the batter is broken up into pebble-sized pieces (3 minutes). Add the raisins to the flour mixture and beat just once or twice to evenly distribute them. With the mixer still on low speed, add ¼ cup of the rum and the heavy cream until the dough comes together. Using your hands, knead the mixture in the bowl until the dough comes together completely.

Turn the dough out on a lightly floured surface and roll it into a 7-inch round (about ¾-inch thick). Using a sharp knife cut in 12 equal wedges. The wedges will look small but they will spread and rise in the oven. Place the pieces on a baking sheet at least ½-inch apart. Cover with plastic wrap and freeze for 15 minutes. Brush the scones with heavy cream and sprinkle with demerara sugar. Bake for 20 minutes, turning the baking sheet halfway through. Transfer to a wire rack to cool. Serve warm.

Morrison House B&B
Cranberry Walnut Scones

Yield: 10–12 scones

2¾	cups flour
1	Tbsp baking powder
¾	cup sugar + extra for sprinkling
¾	tsp salt
½	cup (1 stick) firm butter
½	cup milk
2	eggs, beaten
1½	cups fresh or frozen cranberries, washed and coarsely chopped
½	cup walnuts, coarsely chopped

Preheat oven to 425°F. Spray cookie sheet with cooking spray or use a nonstick baking sheet.

In a large bowl, whisk together flour, baking powder, sugar, and salt. Cut the butter into the flour using a pastry cutter or 2 knives, until mix is crumbly. Mix milk and eggs together. Stir cranberries and nuts into flour mix. Add milk and eggs. Stir only until just mixed. Don't overwork the dough. Dough should stick together, but it should not be sticky. Drop ¼-cup of dough onto prepared cookie sheet. Shape into rounded mounds with a spoon. Sprinkle a little sugar on top of each scone. Bake for 10–12 minutes.

ONE CENTRE STREET INN B&B
Walnut & Raisin Scones

Yield: 8 scones

2	cups flour
3	Tbsp sugar
1	Tbsp baking powder
1¼	cups heavy cream
1	tsp vanilla extract
¾	cup raisins
¾	cup finely chopped walnuts

Topping:

1	Tbsp sugar
1	tsp cinnamon

Preheat oven to 425°F. Lightly grease a cookie sheet.

In a large bowl, mix flour, sugar, and baking powder. Add cream and vanilla; mix until lightly combined. Stir in the raisins and walnuts. On a floured surface, shape into a large rectangle. Cut into 8 triangles. Mix the topping ingredients together and sprinkle over the scones. Bake for exactly 14 minutes.

Scones are a classic Scottish single-serving cake. They differ from cakes and sweet buns because they do not use yeast as an ingredient. Traditionally, the scones would be cut from a large round cake (now called a bannock), and each serving size would be called a scone.

Liberty Hill Farm Inn
Cabot Cheddar Scones

Yield: 8–10 scones

2 cups King Arthur flour
½ cup Cabot butter, cold, cut in pieces
2 tsp baking powder
½ tsp baking soda
⅓ cup sugar
 salt, a pinch
1 cup Cabot sharp cheddar cheese, shredded, divided
1 large egg
¼ cup milk

Preheat oven to 425°F. Lightly butter baking sheet.

In a medium bowl combine flour, butter, baking powder, baking soda. With your fingers, combine ingredients until crumbly. Add sugar and salt; continue to combine with a fork. Add ½ cup cheese. Mix well. In a small bowl, whisk together egg and milk, reserving 1 Tbsp for egg wash. Slowly add egg mixture to flour, stirring with a fork until flour mixture holds together and forms dough.

Turn dough out onto floured surface and knead dough slightly. Too much will make it tough. Roll or pat out to ¾–1-inch thick. Cut with small round cutter or juice glass. Place on baking sheet. Brush tops of scones with reserved egg wash. Sprinkle with remaining shredded cheese. Bake for approximately 12 minutes until golden brown.

Westbrook Inn B&B

Grandma Zimmerman's Coffee Cake

Yield: 12–16 servings

2	sticks plus 2 tsp butter, softened
1¾	cup sugar
1	(8-oz.) pkg. cream cheese
1	cup sour cream
3	eggs
1½	tsp real vanilla extract
3	cups flour
1½	tsp baking powder
1½	tsp baking soda
1/3	tsp kosher salt
1/3	cup half & half
2	cups blueberries

Streusel Topping:

½	cup sugar
1/3	cup pecans, chopped
1	Tbsp cinnamon

Preheat oven to 350°F. Grease and flour a 9x13-inch baking pan.

In a large bowl, blend butter, sugar, and cream cheese together. Add sour cream, eggs, vanilla, flour, baking powder, baking soda, salt, and half & half. Blend well. Pour batter into prepared baking pan. Top with blueberries.

Mix ingredients for topping in a small chopper. Sprinkle on top of blueberries.

Bake for 50–55 minutes until toothpick comes out clean.

Cool thoroughly on wire rack.

Tip: If making the night before, cover the cooled dish with aluminum foil. In the morning divide into squares with a metal spatula and serve.

Inn at English Meadows

Sour Cream Coffee Cake with Toasted Pecan Filling

Yield: 16 servings

Streusel Topping
- 2 oz. (4 Tbsp) unsalted butter
- 3 oz. (²/₃ cup) all-purpose flour
- ¼ cup toasted pecans, coarsely chopped
- 2 Tbsp granulated sugar
- 2 Tbsp light brown sugar
- ½ tsp ground cinnamon
- ¼ tsp baking powder
- ¼ tsp table salt

Filling:
- 1 cup toasted pecans, coarsely chopped
- 3 Tbsp granulated sugar
- 3 Tbsp light brown sugar
- 1½ tsp ground cinnamon
- 1 tsp Dutch-processed or natural cocoa powder

Cake:
- 11¼ oz (3 cups) sifted cake flour
- 1½ tsp baking powder
- 1 tsp baking soda
- ¾ tsp table salt
- 10 oz. (1¼ cups) unsalted butter, slightly softened
- 11½ oz. (1²/₃ cups) superfine sugar
- 4 large eggs
- 2 tsp pure vanilla extract
- 16 oz. (2 cups) sour cream

Position rack in the center of the oven and preheat to 350°F (325°F if using a dark nonstick pan). Generously grease a 10-inch tube pan with a removable bottom.

Topping: In a 2-quart saucepan, heat the butter over medium heat until almost melted. Remove from the heat and cool to tepid. In a medium bowl, combine the flour, pecans, both sugars, cinnamon, baking powder, and salt and stir with a fork. Add the flour mixture to the butter and stir until evenly moistened and crumbly. Set aside.

Filling: In a food processor, pulse the pecans, both sugars, cinnamon, and cocoa 4–6 times, to combine; set aside.

(continued on next page)

Cake: In a medium bowl, whisk the flour, baking powder, baking soda, and salt. In the bowl of a stand mixer fitted with the paddle attachment, beat the butter on medium speed until smooth and creamy, 1–2 minutes. Add the sugar slowly, beating until combined. Scrape the bowl. Beat in the eggs one at a time, blending each one completely before adding the next. Scrape the bowl and blend in the vanilla. On low speed, alternate adding the dry ingredients and the sour cream, adding the flour in four parts and the sour cream in three parts, beginning and ending with the flour, and scraping the bowl as needed.

Layer and marble the batter and filling by spooning 2 generous cups of the batter into the prepared pan. Smooth with the back of a soup spoon, spreading the batter to the side of the pan first, and then to the center. Sprinkle about ½ cup of the filling evenly over the batter. Cover the filling with about 2 cups batter, dropping dollops around the pan and smoothing with the spoon. Sprinkle another ½ cup filling evenly over the batter and cover with 2 more cups of batter. Layer on the remaining filling, then the remaining batter. (You'll have four layers of batter, and three layers of filling). Insert a table knife 1 inch from the side of the pan straight into the batter going almost to the bottom. Run the knife around the pan twice with the blade, spacing the circles about 1 inch apart. Smooth the top with the back of the soup spoon.

Take a handful of the streusel crumbs squeezing firmly to form a large mass. Break up the mass into smaller clumps, distributing the streusel evenly over the batter. Repeat with the remaining streusel. Press the streusel lightly into the surface of the cake.

Bake 70–75 minutes, until the top of the cake is golden brown, the sides are beginning to pull away from the pan, and a wooden skewer inserted into the center of the cake comes out clean. Transfer to a wire rack and let cool for at least an hour before removing from the pan.

This cake keeps at room temperature well wrapped or under a cake dome for up to 5 days. You can freeze it for up to 3 months.

Marshall Slocum Inn
Beer Coffee Cake

Yield: 6 servings

"I found something involving beer for the most important meal of the day—so for all you beer lovers who want to bring some beer into your breakfast—here is an option."

2 cups all-purpose biscuit mix	**Topping:**
½ cup sugar	½ cup flour
½ tsp ginger	⅓ cup sugar
⅔ cup beer	1 tsp cinnamon
1 egg, slightly beaten	¼ cup chopped pecans
	⅓ cup butter

Preheat oven to 400°F. Lightly grease a 9-inch round cake pan.

In a large bowl, combine biscuit mix, sugar, and ginger. In a separate bowl, combine the beer and egg. Add the wet ingredients to the dry ingredients, stirring lightly, just until moistened. In a small bowl, combine flour, sugar, cinnamon, and pecans for the topping. Cut in butter until mixture is crumbly. Pour batter mixture into prepared cake pan. Sprinkle topping mixture over the batter. Bake for 20–25 minutes. Serve warm or cold.

Beer is often used in baking, although many people overlook its usefulness. In breads and cakes, it adds buoyancy and lightness. It can also be used to marinate meat, to baste foods for roasting, or to reconstitute instant or freeze-dried food.

Marshall Slocum Inn
Cliffwalk Cottage Cheese Coffee Cake

Yield: 8–10 servings

"Cliffwalk is a 3.5 mile walkway along the Newport shoreline. It was created in 1975 as a National Recreation Trail. To keep your energy up while spending time on Cliffwalk, start your day with a slice of this coffee cake."

3	cups all-purpose flour
2	cups sugar
1	tsp baking soda
1	tsp baking powder
3	eggs
½	cup butter, melted
1	cup buttermilk
1	Tbsp vanilla extract
1	cup cream cheese, softened

Filling:

1	cup sugar
½	cup cottage cheese
1	Tbsp cinnamon

Preheat oven to 350°F. Grease and flour a standard Bundt pan.

In a large bowl, combine flour, sugar, baking soda, and baking powder. In a separate bowl, combine eggs, butter, buttermilk, vanilla, and cream cheese. Add the dry ingredients and combine until incorporated. In a small bowl, combine all filling ingredients until well blended. Spoon half the batter into the prepared Bundt pan. Spoon the filling into the middle of the pan and cover with remaining batter. Bake for 45–50 minutes.

CAPTAIN BRIGGS HOUSE B&B

Cinnamon Bread

Yield: 2 loaves

½ cup vegetable oil
2 cups + ½ cup sugar
2 eggs
2 cups buttermilk
2 tsp baking soda
4 cups all-purpose flour
2 Tbsp ground cinnamon
½ tsp salt

Preheat oven to 350 °F. Spray two 9x5x3-inch loaf pans with nonstick spray.

In a large bowl, mix together oil, 2 cups sugar, eggs, buttermilk, baking soda, and flour. Pour a quarter of batter in each prepared pan. Combine ½ cup sugar, cinnamon, and salt in a small bowl. Sprinkle a quarter of sugar mixture into each pan on top of batter. Pour remaining batter equally between pans. Sprinkle with remaining sugar. Swirl a knife through batter.

Bake 1 hour, or until a knife inserted in center comes out clean. Cool for 10 minutes and remove bread from pans and place on waxed paper. Slice when completely cool.

Grünberg Haus B&B
Pumpkin Cranberry Bread

Yield: 12–16 slices

*"A big favorite here at breakfast. They often go so fast,
it is challenging to keep the bread baskets filled."*

    3 cups flour
    5 tsp pumpkin pie spice
    2 tsp baking soda
 1½ tsp salt
    3 cups sugar
    1 (15-oz.) can pumpkin
    4 eggs
    1 cup vegetable oil
   ½ cup orange juice
    1 (6-oz.) pkg. Craisins

Preheat oven to 350°F. Grease two 9x4-inch loaf pans.

In a large bowl, combine flour, pumpkin pie spice, baking soda, and salt. In a separate bowl, combine sugar, pumpkin, eggs, oil, and orange juice. Add wet ingredients to dry ingredients; mix well. Fold in the Craisins. Fill the loaf pans with the batter and bake for 1 hour.

SCRANTON SEAHORSE INN
Spiced Banana Bread with Chocolate

Yield: 8–10 servings

- 3 very ripe bananas
- 2 large eggs
- 1½ cups unbleached all-purpose flour
- 1 cup granulated sugar
- 1 tsp baking soda
- 2 tsp ground cinnamon
- 1 tsp pure vanilla extract
- ¾ cup semisweet chocolate chips

Topping:
- 2 Tbsp granulated sugar
- ⅛ tsp ground cinnamon
- ⅛ tsp cardamon
- ⅛ tsp all spice
- ⅛ tsp nutmeg

Preheat oven to 375°F. Butter or spray an 8-inch loaf pan.

In a large bowl, mash the bananas well with a fork or potato masher. Add the eggs, and stir well to combine. Add the flour, sugar, baking soda, cinnamon, and vanilla, and stir to mix. Fold in the chocolate chips. Pour the batter into the prepared pan, and set aside.

In a small bowl, stir together the topping ingredients. Sprinkle the mixture evenly over the batter in the pan. Optionally, you can add an additional ¼ cup chocolate chips to the top. Bake for 35–40 minutes, or until a toothpick inserted in the center comes out clean.

INN AT ORMSBY HILL

Japanese Bread

Yield: 8 mini loaves or 2 large loaves

"A delicious mini-loaf served at every breakfast."

Roux

- ⅓ cup flour
- 1 cup milk

Dough

- 1 cup warm milk
- 4 tsp active dry yeast
- 4 Tbsp extra fine sugar —You may substitute granulated sugar
- 5½ cups bread flour
- 2 tsp salt
- 4 Tbsp non-fat dry milk powder
- 3 large eggs—One is for an egg wash after the loaves are shaped
- 4 Tbsp unsalted butter at room temperature

Preheat oven to 350°F. Grease eight mini-loaf pans or two large loaf pans.

Roux: Whisk together the flour and milk in a small saucepan over medium-low heat until the mixture thickens to a runny, paste-like consistency. Do not let it boil or it will become too thick. Remove from heat. Place a piece of plastic wrap on the surface to prevent a skin from forming while cooling. Let cool to room temperature.

Dough: In a small bowl or large measuring cup, whisk together the warm milk, yeast, and sugar. In a stand-mixer bowl or bread machine, combine the flour, salt, and powdered milk. Add two eggs to the yeast mixture; whisk to combine. Add the cooked roux, and whisk until smooth. Pour the yeast and roux mixture over the flour mixture.

If using a bread machine, or a stand-mixer with a dough hook, or kneading by hand, add the butter after the ingredients have combined, but are not yet ball shaped. If using a bread machine to knead and bake, this will make a 2-pound loaf. You can just use the dough setting, and shape into mini loaves after the first rising. If using your hands, or a dough hook, knead until dough is a firm ball shape. Put dough in a large bowl, cover with plastic wrap or a towel, and let rise in a warm spot for 45 minutes, or until the dough has doubled in size.

For 8 mini loaves, cut the dough in half, and each half in quarters to get 8 even-sized pieces. Roll each piece gently with a rolling pin until it is approximately 10 inches long and 5 inches wide (a couple rolls with the pin). Starting from the top, roll the dough toward you like a jellyroll. Put the rolled up dough into a greased mini-loaf pan. Repeat with the other pieces of dough. Place the mini-loaf pans on a cookie sheet, cover with plastic wrap or a towel and let rise in a warm spot for an additional 45 minutes. For two large loaves, follow instructions above, fitting four mini rolls of dough sideways into each greased loaf pan.

Lightly beat the remaining egg with a fork, and brush it on the tops of the loaves. Bake for 20 minutes, or until the tops are brown and shiny, or 30 minutes for two large loaves.

Japanese bread is a soft, slightly sweet bread found in many Asian markets. The roux mixture is an old Japanese technique to improve the texture of the bread. The bread made with this technique doesn't get hard within a day like some breads. Instead, it stays soft and fluffy for several days.

Captain Freeman Inn
English Muffin Bread

Yield: 2 large loaves

"This bread is easy to make and does taste exactly like an old-fashioned English muffin. We use it as a base for our Eggs Benedict."

- 6 cups unbleached flour, divided
- ½ oz. active dry yeast (2 pkgs.)
- ¼ cup sugar
- 1 tsp salt
- ½ tsp baking soda
- 2½ cups warmed milk
- ½ cup warmed water
- 2 Tbsp fresh herbs or ½ cup fresh Parmesan cheese
  cornmeal, for dusting pans

Preheat oven to 400°F. Grease two large loaf pans.

In a large bowl, blend 3 cups flour with yeast, sugar, salt, and baking soda. Add milk and water. Blend until smooth. Gradually add remaining flour and herbs or cheese. A stiff dough will form. Knead the dough on a floured board for 8–10 minutes by hand or for 3–4 minutes in an electric mixer with a dough hook. Divide the dough between two bread pans that have been greased and dusted with cornmeal. Allow the bread to rise in the pans for 45 minutes, then bake for 20–25 minutes. Remove from the pans and cool on racks before cutting.

English muffins (better known in the U.K. as just muffins) are a popular breakfast food, first written about in the 18th century. They may date as far back as the 10th century, but they became popular during the 18th century. Many muffin factories sprouted up in the early 19th century, and the "muffin man" became a common sight.

CAPTAIN FREEMAN INN
Nanna's Blueberry Muffins

Yields: 12 muffins

½ cup unsalted butter
1 cup sugar
2 eggs
2 tsp baking powder
1 tsp vanilla
½ tsp lemon zest
1¾ cups flour
¼ cup yellow cornmeal
¼ tsp salt
1/8 tsp cinnamon
½ cup milk
2 cups blueberries

Preheat oven to 375°F. Lightly grease a 12-count muffin pan.

Mix butter and sugar. Add eggs one at a time, beating well after each addition. Add baking powder. Mix well. Add vanilla and lemon zest. In a separate bowl, combine flour, cornmeal, salt, and cinnamon. Add ½ of this mixture to batter; mix lightly. Add milk and remaining flour mixture. Stir well. Fold in blueberries. Fill each muffin tin 2/3 full. Sprinkle with sugar. Bake 25–30 minutes.

Morrison House B&B
Linzer Muffins—Gluten Free

Yield: 12 muffins

1 cup almonds, ground	¼ tsp cinnamon
¾ cup sugar	1 cup unsweetened almond milk
¾ cup millet flour	6 Tbsp butter, melted and cooled
¾ cup white rice flour	1 large egg
2 tsp gluten-free baking powder	½ tsp Boyajian Pure Lemon Oil
¾ tsp xanthan gum	(or fresh grated lemon zest)
½ tsp salt	⅓ cup raspberry jam

Preheat oven to 400°F. Lightly grease a 12-count muffin pan.

In a large bowl, whisk together the ground almonds, sugar, flours, baking powder, xanthan gum, salt, and cinnamon. In a smaller bowl, whisk together the milk, butter, egg, and lemon oil. Stir the wet ingredients into the dry ingredients. Do not stir it too much, just as much as needed to blend the two together.

Put a scant ¼ cup batter into each muffin cup. Top each with 1 rounded teaspoon of jam. Divide the remaining batter among the cups. Try to cover the jam completely.

Bake about 20 minutes or until the muffins are lightly browned and a toothpick inserted comes out clean. You should feel resistance when you insert the toothpick. Cool in pan 5–10 minutes before removing from pan.

> *Boyajian is a brand of infused olive oils founded by a man named John Boyajian in the Canton, MA, area. His products are sold in all 50 U.S. states and in several other countries. The company also makes Asian oils, vinegars and vinaigrettes, pure citrus oils, natural flavorings and extracts, and smoked salmon.*

Sugar Hill Inn
Maple Muffins

Yield: 16 muffins

1¾ cups all-purpose flour
2 tsp baking powder
1 tsp baking soda
½ tsp salt
½ cup walnuts, chopped
½ cup unsalted butter, cubed
¾ cup maple syrup (We suggest Grade A Dark Amber Sugar Hill Maple Syrup.)
1 cup sour cream
1 egg

Preheat oven to 400°F. Grease a large muffin tin.

In a large bowl, sift together flour, baking powder, baking soda, and salt.

Add the nuts to the dry ingredients.

Beat butter in electric mixer with paddle attachment until light and airy. Slowly add the syrup and beat well. Beat in the sour cream and egg. Add to dry ingredients and stir just until blended. Fill muffin cups and bake 16 minutes.

Maple syrup is divided into two major grades in the United States: Grade A and Grade B. Grade A is then divided further into three subgrades: light amber, medium amber, and dark amber. Extra light and Grade A syrups have a milder flavor than Grade B syrups, which are darker and richer in maple flavor. The dark grades are typically used for cooking and baking, although some specialty dark syrups are made for table use.

Marshall Slocum Inn
Apple Cinnamon Muffins

Yield: 6 muffins

1½	cups all-purpose flour
¾	cup granulated sugar
½	tsp salt
2	tsp baking powder
1	tsp ground cinnamon
⅓	cup vegetable oil
1	egg
⅓	cup milk
2	apples, peeled, cored, and chopped

Topping:

½	cup granulated sugar
⅓	cup all-purpose flour
½	cup butter, cubed
1½	tsp ground cinnamon

Preheat oven to 400°F. Grease 6 muffin cups or line with paper liners.

In a large bowl, mix flour, sugar, salt, baking powder, and cinnamon. Add the oil, egg, and milk. Mix until lightly blended. Fold in the apples. In a small bowl, combine sugar, flour, butter, and cinnamon for topping.

Spoon the batter into muffin cups, filling to the top. Sprinkle topping mixture over unbaked muffins. Bake for 20–25 minutes, or until a toothpick inserted in the center comes out clean.

WHITE ROCKS INN B&B
Goat Cheese Popovers

Yield: 24 Popovers

	vegetable oil
6	eggs
1½	cups all-purpose flour
1	tsp salt
½	tsp pepper
	pinch of nutmeg
2	cups milk
½	cup heavy cream
4	oz. herbed goat cheese, chilled and cut into 24 pieces

Preheat oven to 400°F. Brush muffin cups with oil and place in oven to get hot.

Blend eggs, flour, salt, pepper, and nutmeg in a blender for about 10 seconds, until well combined. Scrape down sides. With blender running, slowly pour in milk and cream; blend until smooth.

Remove muffin tins from oven. Fill each muffin cup ½-full with batter. Place a piece of goat cheese in the center of the batter in each muffin cup. Top with enough batter to fill cups ²/3-full. Bake for about 40–50 minutes until puffed and golden. Serve hot.

Popovers are the American version of Yorkshire pudding, made in England in the 17th century. The name comes from the fact that the batter "pops" over the edge of the muffin cups while baking. Popovers can also be served as sweets, topped with fruit and whipped cream.

WHITE ROCKS INN B&B
Yeast Biscuits

Yield: 12–16 biscuits

"This dough keeps up to a week in the refrigerator."

 5 cups flour
¼ cup sugar
 1 tsp baking soda
 3 tsp baking powder
 1 tsp salt
 1 cup shortening
 2 cups buttermilk
 1 pkg. yeast dissolved in ¼ cup warm water

Preheat oven to 400°F.

In a large bowl, mix all dry ingredients. Cut in shortening and make a well in the center of the flour mixture. Pour in buttermilk and yeast and stir until mixture forms a ball. Turn dough mixture out onto floured surface. Roll to desired depth (½-inch recommended) and cut with round cutter or juice glass. Place on baking sheet, spacing them at least an inch apart. Let biscuits rise for a few minutes and bake until golden, approximately 12–15 minutes.

Yeast is used as a leavening agent in baking. It converts fermentable sugars in the dough into carbon dioxide gas, causing the dough to rise. Bread gets its spongy texture from the air bubbles that form from the release of carbon dioxide gas and the yeast dying once it is baked.

French Toast, Pancakes, Waffles & Granola

"All happiness depends on a leisurely breakfast."

— John Gunther

Recipes in this Section:

Recipes in the Signature Recipes Section:

Scranton Seahorse Inn
Hawaiian Waffles

Yield: 6 waffles

"Macadamia nuts and shredded coconut aren't the only things that make this dish a summertime favorite. I serve a tropical salsa alongside it to finish it off. Use whatever fruit is ripe and fresh at the supermarket. Some of my favorites include mango, pineapple, and kiwi. Don't be afraid to try something different like star fruit or papaya to wow your family or guests."

- 2 large eggs
- ½ cup butter, melted
- 1¾ cups milk
- 2 cups all-purpose flour
- 4 tsp baking powder
- ½ tsp table salt
- ¾ cup shredded coconut
- ¾ cup raw macadamia nuts, coarsely chopped

Whisk the eggs until foamy and then whisk in the butter and milk. Add the flour, baking powder, and salt to the egg mixture and whisk until smooth. The batter should not be so thick that you cannot run your whisk through it. You can thin it out by adding a tablespoon or two of milk. Fold in the coconut and nuts. I like to let the mixture sit for 10 minutes before using.

Follow the instructions for your waffle iron to cook. But a general rule of thumb is when the steaming from the iron stops, your waffles are done!

Chop your fruit salsa into small bite-size pieces just like a salsa and serve a heaping mound with each waffle.

Tip: Instead of maple syrup, which can overpower the flavors of the coconut and macadamia nuts, try a light or amber agave nectar.

MARSHALL SLOCUM INN
Blueberry Sour Cream Waffles with Peaches

Yield: 10–12 servings

Waffles:

- 4 eggs, separated
- 2 cups milk
- 3 oz. butter, melted
- 4 cups sour cream
- 1 tsp baking soda
- 3 tsp baking powder
- 4 cups all-purpose flour
- 1 Tbsp salt
- 3 Tbsp sugar
- 2 cups fresh blueberries

Topping:

- 5 oz. butter
- 1 Tbsp nutmeg
- 2/3 cup brown sugar
- 1/4 cup cinnamon
- 2 lbs. sliced peaches
- powdered sugar

Preheat Belgian waffle iron.

In a large bowl, mix together egg yolks, milk, butter, sour cream, baking soda, baking powder, flour, and salt. In a separate bowl, beat egg whites until soft peaks form, add the sugar, and beat until stiff. Fold egg whites into batter mixture. Pour ¾ to 1 cup batter into waffle iron. Place 10–12 blueberries on top of the batter. Cook until waffles are crisp and golden brown.

For the topping: Melt butter in a large skillet. Add nutmeg, brown sugar, and cinnamon. Add peaches and cook over medium heat until peaches are very soft. Spoon peach mixture over waffles and sprinkle with powdered sugar.

One Centre Street Inn B&B
Lemon Ricotta Pancakes

Yield: 8–10 pancakes

1½	cups whole-milk ricotta cheese
¼	cup (½ stick) unsalted butter, melted and cooled
6	large eggs, separated
1	tsp pure vanilla extract
½	cup all-purpose flour
1	tsp baking powder
¼	cup sugar
½	tsp salt
	zest of 2 large lemons
1	Tbsp poppy seeds
	vegetable oil
	maple syrup, warmed
	berries, for garnish

In a large bowl, beat together ricotta, butter, egg yolks, and vanilla. In a medium bowl, whisk together flour, baking powder, sugar, salt, lemon zest, and poppy seeds. Using a rubber spatula, stir flour mixture into ricotta mixture. Place egg whites in the bowl of an electric mixer fitted with the whisk attachment. Beat until it forms firm, glossy peaks. Fold one large spoonful at a time of whipped egg whites into ricotta mixture.

Coat a griddle or large skillet with oil and heat over high heat until very hot, and then reduce heat to medium. Working in batches, place ¼ cup batter for each pancake on griddle, leaving space as they will spread. Cook until golden and top begins to bubble, about two minutes. Gently turn and continue cooking until bottoms are light brown. Transfer to a serving plate and keep warm until all the pancakes have cooked. Serve with maple syrup and berries.

An Innkeeper's Place

Cinnamon Pumpkin Pancakes

Yield: 18 pancakes (4-inch)

2	cups all-purpose flour
2	Tbsp brown sugar
1	Tbsp baking powder
1	tsp salt
1	tsp ground cinnamon
¼	tsp ground nutmeg
¼	tsp ground ginger
1¾	cups milk
½	cup pumpkin purée, fresh or canned
1	large egg
2	Tbsp vegetable oil
1½	cups maple syrup, warmed for topping

Whisk together all dry ingredients in a large bowl. In a separate bowl combine milk, pumpkin, egg, and oil. Mix well. Add the dry mixture to the wet, and stir just until combined.

Heat a griddle to medium-high heat. Butter griddle lightly. Spoon level ¼ cup batter onto griddle for each pancake. Cook until lightly brown and bubbles begin to form, 3–4 minutes. Turn and cook other side. Keep warm in 200°F oven until ready to serve.

Marshall Slocum Inn
Pumpkin Pancakes

Yield: 8–10 pancakes

2⅓ cups pancake mix
2½ Tbsp white sugar
⅓ tsp ground cinnamon
⅓ tsp ground nutmeg
¼ tsp ground ginger
2 eggs
1¼ cup milk
⅓ cup canned pumpkin
¼ cup vegetable oil

Topping:
1 cup whipping cream
2 Tbsp white sugar
¾ tsp vanilla extract
½ tsp ground nutmeg

In a large bowl, whisk together the pancake mix, white sugar, cinnamon, nutmeg, and ginger; set aside. In a separate bowl, beat together the eggs, milk, pumpkin, and vegetable oil. Combine the two mixtures, stirring just until all ingredients are moistened. Heat a lightly oiled griddle or frying pan over medium-high heat. Using approximately ¼ cup for each pancake, pour batter onto the griddle. Cook until the edges of the pancakes start to look dry, and a bubble popped near the edge holds its shape. Flip the pancakes over, and continue cooking until the other side is golden brown. Repeat with remaining batter. Stack the pancakes on a plate and keep warm until served.

For the topping: Place whipping cream in a small, deep, chilled bowl. Add sugar, vanilla, and nutmeg. Beat using a mixer with chilled beaters on medium-high speed until soft peaks form.

Serve pancakes with whipped topping for garnish.

INN ON GOLDEN POND
Puffed Apple Pancakes

Yield: 6–8 servings

6	eggs
1½	cups milk
1	cup flour
3	Tbsp sugar
1	tsp vanilla extract
½	tsp salt
½	tsp cinnamon
1	stick butter
3	large apples, peeled and sliced
¼	cup brown sugar

Preheat oven to 425°F.

In a medium bowl, mix eggs, milk, flour, sugar, vanilla, salt, and cinnamon. Melt the butter in a 13x9x2-inch glass baking dish. Add sliced apples. Pour batter over the apples and sprinkle with brown sugar. Bake for 30–35 minutes. Serve hot with warm New Hampshire maple syrup.

New Hampshire maple syrup maintains a higher standard of product density, similar to Vermont, but it does not use a separate grading scale. Compared to honey, maple syrup has about 15 times more calcium and 1/10 as much sodium. Many people use maple syrup as a substitute for sugar in some baking recipes.

GRÜNBERG HAUS
Applesauce Pancakes

Yield: 6–8 pancakes

*"This is the recipe our grandkids request every day when they are
visiting Vermont even if I have a different menu plan for guests.
The most important thing to remember about this one is: don't even
start to prepare it if you don't have the lemon juice on hand.
That is the secret recipe ingredient for light and fluffy pancakes."*

- 2 cups Bisquick®
- 1 tsp ground cinnamon
- 2 eggs
- 1 cup applesauce (I use Mott's® original)
- ½ cup milk
- 1 tsp lemon juice

Preheat electric griddle to 350°F.

Combine dry ingredients in a large bowl. Combine wet ingredients
in a separate bowl. Mix wet ingredients into the dry ingredients until
thoroughly blended. Pour ⅓ cup batter for each pancake onto electric
griddle. Serve with Vermont Grade A Dark maple syrup.

> *Vermont is the largest producer of pure maple syrup in the U.S. Ver-
> mont Grade A Dark syrup is a darker amber color, and it has a hearty
> maple flavor. It is a very popular choice around the breakfast table.
> Vermont uses a separate grading system than the U.S. grading system.
> Vermont syrups have 0.9 percent more sugar and less water than the
> U.S. versions.*

Grünberg Haus
Featherlight Buttermilk Pancakes

Yield: 18 pancakes

*"The secret to making these amazing pancakes is the lumpy batter.
So, whatever you do, do not over mix the batter! To cook the pancakes use
a heavy large griddle. A very low-sided griddle makes sliding your spatula
underneath the pancakes and turning them easy. The griddle's large surface
area allows you to cook a large batch of pancakes at a time."*

- 2½ cups all-purpose flour
- ¼ cup sugar
- 2 tsp baking powder
- 2 tsp baking soda
- 1 tsp salt
- 2 cups buttermilk (Please, use real buttermilk. You will be happier with the results.)
- 2 cups sour cream
- 2 large eggs
- 4 tsp vanilla extract

Combine dry ingredients in a large bowl. Combine wet ingredients in a separate bowl. Mix wet ingredients into the dry ingredients Do not over mix; there should be lumps. Use a ⅓ cup measuring cup as a scoop for each pancake. Turn when edges look dry and peeking under reveals a golden brown.

Tip: Once the liquid and dry ingredients are combined, the pancakes should be prepared within an hour.

Marshall Slocum Inn
Strawberry Stuffed French Toast

Yield: 4–6 servings

1 (8-oz.) pkg. cream cheese, softened
2 Tbsp strawberry purée or sliced strawberries
1 Tbsp grated orange zest
4 eggs
1 cup whipping cream
8 slices very thick bread, such as Italian, challah, Texas toast, etc.
1 Tbsp butter
  sliced fresh strawberries
  powdered sugar (optional)
  maple syrup or strawberry syrup

Preheat oven to 300°F. In a small bowl, stir together the cream cheese, strawberry purée, and orange zest until smooth; set aside. In a separate bowl, beat the eggs. Stir in the whipping cream. Pour into a shallow dish; set aside. Using a paring knife, slice a pocket into the side of each slice of bread, without cutting through the bread. Fill the pockets with a heaping tablespoon of the cream cheese mixture.

Melt the butter in a large skillet over medium heat. Dip the filled bread slices into the egg mixture. Place it on the skillet and let it brown for 1–2 minutes on each side until golden and crispy. Keep warm on a baking sheet in the oven until ready to serve. Serve hot with maple syrup, powdered sugar, and sliced strawberries.

Challah is a special braided bread eaten on Sabbath and holidays. Challah is typically made without dairy products. Two loaves are eaten at each holiday meal. Each loaf is woven with six strands braided together, making twelve strands altogether, representing the twelve tribes of Israel.

Thimble Islands B&B
Crème Brûlée French Toast

Yield: 1 serving

*"Multiply the portions by as many individual
servings as you wish to prepare."*

½ cup half & half	3–4 slices French baguette, ¾" thick
1 extra large egg	and cut in half (7 pieces)
¼ tsp vanilla	raw sugar or brown sugar
1/8 tsp salt	to sprinkle on top
1 tsp white sugar	maple syrup

Preheat oven to 425°F. and put oven rack in middle position. Generously grease one 8-ounce soufflé dish per serving.

Whisk together half & half, egg, vanilla, salt, and white sugar in a wide shallow bowl. Add bread slices to the custard mixture and turn over once or twice to coat. Let stand at room temperature 30 minutes.

Transfer bread slices to the individual soufflé dishes. Pour custard mixture into a vessel with a spout (such as a measuring cup) and pour custard into each soufflé dish to within ¼ inch of top. Sprinkle tops lightly with raw sugar (or brown sugar). Place soufflé dishes in a large Pyrex baking dish (like a lasagna pan) and pour boiling water up to ½ inch. Bake until custard is set and tops are golden brown, about 28 minutes.

Serve with pure maple syrup. Caution your guests that the dish will be very hot.

Tip: You may also make this recipe for multiple people in a large baking dish, cooked a bit longer, but it doesn't have the same presentation impact.

1802 House B&B

Baked Orange French Toast with Marmalade Glaze

Yield: 12 servings

1	loaf French or Italian bread	¼	tsp nutmeg
9	eggs		
1	cup orange juice		**For the Marmalade Glaze:**
2	cups light cream, half & half, or whole milk	1	cup good quality orange marmalade
2	Tbsp sugar	½	cup orange juice
1	tsp ground cinnamon	8	Tbsp unsalted butter
½	tsp ground ginger		

Grease a 9x13-inch glass baking dish. Tear bread into bite-sized chunks and place evenly in baking dish. In a large bowl, beat eggs. Add the orange juice, milk/cream, sugar, and spices and blend well. Pour over the bread making sure to cover all of the bread well.

Cover with plastic wrap and refrigerate at least 4 hours or overnight. Before baking, remove from refrigerator and allow to sit for an hour to come up to room temperature. Remove plastic wrap, cover with tin foil, and bake in preheated 350°F oven for 30 minutes. Remove tin foil and bake for another 30 minutes uncovered.

Remove French toast from oven, cover with tin foil and allow to sit for 15 minutes before cutting. Plate each slice, drizzle with marmalade glaze to serve.

For the topping: Place marmalade and orange juice into a pan and bring to a boil over medium heat, stirring continuously. Reduce heat to low, add butter, and bring back to a simmer, melting the butter. Be careful not to let it boil.

Tip: The French toast is richer when made with cream or half & half, but whole milk will also give good results.

GATEWAYS INN

Challah French Toast Soufflé with Fresh Berries and Crème Frâiche

Yield: 6–8 servings

10 cups (approx) of challah bread, crusts removed, cubed	8 extra large or jumbo eggs
5 Tbsp butter, softened	fresh blueberries and raspberries
1 (8-oz.) pkg. cream cheese, softened	slivered almonds
½ cup pure maple syrup	6–8 small pieces of butter
1½ cups half & half	crème fraîche
1 tsp vanilla extract	maple syrup, for serving

Generously butter a 9x13-inch glass baking dish. Put the cubed bread in a very large mixing bowl and set aside. In a separate bowl, beat the butter, cream cheese, and syrup together until it is smooth and uniform. Add the half & half and vanilla. Beat to aerate and combine. Add the eggs, one at a time, beating after each addition to incorporate. Pour this mixture over the cubed bread and toss to coat fully. Allow to sit for a few minutes, then toss again. Pour bread mixture into prepared pan, sprinkle with berries, cover, and refrigerate overnight.

In the morning, preheat oven to 350°F. Remove prepared pan from the refrigerator, remove cover, and sprinkle with almonds. Place the baking pan in a larger pan and add water to the larger pan about ⅓ of the way up the glass pan (water bath). Dot the top with butter and bake for about 50–60 minutes. Remove the pan from the water bath and continue to bake another 15–20 minutes until you see the bottom and sides of soufflé begin to brown. Soufflé is done when a small deep slit with a sharp knife made in the center comes out moist, not wet.

Allow to cool a few minutes, slice and serve with crème frâiche drizzled over the top, berries, and warmed maple syrup on the side.

Inn at Cape Cod
Pecan Streusel French Toast

Yield: 8–10 servings

French or Italian bread, cut into one-inch slices
8 eggs
3 cups half & half (or use light cream)
¾ cup light brown sugar
1½ tsp cinnamon
2½ tsp vanilla extract
¼ tsp salt

For the Streusel:
4 oz. butter, very soft
¾ cup light brown sugar
2 Tbsp all-purpose flour
½ tsp cinnamon
1 cup pecans, chopped

Spray two 8-inch glass dishes with nonstick cooking spray. Pack the bread into dishes, filling gaps with smaller pieces of bread. In a bowl, mix eggs, half & half, sugar, cinnamon, vanilla, and salt together thoroughly. Pour egg mix over bread, cover and refrigerate overnight.

For the streusel: Combine butter, brown sugar, flour, and cinnamon thoroughly; stir in pecans. Keep streusel mix covered in the refrigerator overnight.

The next morning, preheat oven to 350°F. Carefully drain off any excess egg mix from bread. Heat streusel mix in microwave to soften/melt it. Spread streusel mix evenly over bread. Bake for 45–60 minutes, until cooked and not runny in middle. Cut into pieces and serve with pure maple syrup, fresh raspberries, and crispy bacon.

Birchwood Inn

Peach Nectarine Upside-Down French Toast

Yield: 8 servings

½ cup unsalted butter
1 cup brown sugar, firmly packed
2 Tbsp light corn syrup
2 peaches, ripe but firm, cut into ½-inch slices
2 nectarines, ripe but firm, cut into ½-inch slices

1 loaf challah (egg bread)
4 eggs
1 cup whole milk
1 Tbsp vanilla extract
  cinnamon sugar
  melon slices or berries for garnish

Over medium-low heat, melt the butter in a saucepan. Stir in the brown sugar and corn syrup, until the sugar has dissolved. Cook for 3–5 minutes until the mixture is thick and bubbly. Remove the pan from the heat, and add the peaches and nectarines, stirring gently until all fruit is coated. Grease two 8x8 or 9x9-inch glass pans with cooking spray. Spread the fruit mixture evenly in the pans. Slice the top and side crusts off the challah, and cut the challah into 8 1-inch slices. Place the slices in one layer on top of the fruit. Cover and refrigerate overnight.

In the morning, remove the pans from the refrigerator an hour or so before baking. Preheat oven to 375°F.

Whisk the eggs, milk, and vanilla together and pour over the bread slices. Sprinkle with cinnamon sugar. Bake for 60 minutes, until the tops are golden brown and crisp. Remove from the oven and let sit for 5 minutes before cutting.

Cut the French toast into 8 servings, inverting each serving on individual plates, fruit side up. Spoon the pan liquid over the top and serve with colorful melon slices or berries. When peaches or nectarines aren't in season, substitute apples for Caramel Apple French Toast.

1802 House B&B
Breakfast Cranachan

Yield: 4 servings

*"Cranachan is a Scottish pudding (dessert) made with heavy cream
and whiskey. This is the 1802 House healthy breakfast version
and is very popular with our guests."*

- 1 cup fresh or frozen raspberries
- 1 pint plain greek yogurt
- 3 Tbsp honey (or to taste)
- 1 cup granola (We use a French vanilla-flavored granola.)

If using fresh raspberries, put ½ cup into freezer for 30 minutes. If using frozen raspberries, allow to defrost until just beginning to soften. In a bowl, make a purée by crushing berries with a fork. In a separate bowl, mix yogurt and honey; blend well. Fold the berries into the yogurt until just mixed and the berry juice begins to marble. Swirl the pink color through the yogurt. Do not over mix.

In a dessert glass, alternate layers of granola with the yogurt and berry mixture.

Top with fresh raspberries. Keep cold in refrigerator until ready to serve.

Tip: For a more individualized serving, bring dishes of each ingredient to the table to allow guests to assemble their dessert to taste. Serve in tall dessert glasses for presentation. Cranachan was originally a summer dish, but is now more likely to be served on special occasions or year-round. A fun variant for weddings is to serve the cranachan in individual glasses with one containing a ring in the mixture. Whoever receives the dish with the ring will be the next to marry.

INN AT ENGLISH MEADOWS

Ricotta Blintzes with Mixed Berry Sauce

Yield: 8–10 servings

For the crêpes:

- 2 cups whole milk
- 6 large eggs
- 1⅓ cups all-purpose flour
- 3 Tbsp unsalted butter, melted and cooled
- 2 Tbsp sugar
- ½ teaspoon salt
  vegetable oil

For the filling:

- 1 (8-oz.) container whipped cream cheese, room temperature
- 2 large eggs
- 2 tsp grated lemon peel
- ½ tsp vanilla extract
- ¼ cup sugar
- 1 (15 oz.) container ricotta cheese

For the mixed berry sauce:

- 1½ cups fresh or frozen raspberries, divided
- 1½ cups fresh or frozen strawberries, divided
- 1 cup fresh or frozen blueberries, divided
- ¾–1 cup sugar, to taste
- 1–2 Tbsp fresh squeezed lemon juice, to taste

For the crêpes: Blend milk and eggs in blender until smooth. Add flour, butter, sugar, and salt; blend until batter is smooth. Chill 1–2 hours. Re-blend before using. Heat an 8-inch bottom nonstick skillet over medium-high heat; brush with oil. Pour 3 tablespoons of batter in skillet; rotate skillet to spread batter over bottom. Cook until the crêpe is brown at edges and appears dry on top. Quickly turn crêpe over, cook until brown spots appear, about 10 seconds. Turn crêpe onto cooling rack; stack crêpes with paper towel in between each. Repeat. Should make about 24 crêpes.

For the filling: With mixer, beat together cream cheese, eggs, lemon peel, and vanilla with ¼ cup sugar. Beat in ricotta. Chill at least 2 hours or overnight.

For the berry sauce: Combine 1 cup of raspberries, 1 cup of strawberries, and ¾ cup of blueberries, ¾ cup of sugar, and 1 tablespoon of lemon juice in a saucepan and bring to a simmer over medium heat.

Simmer until the sugar dissolves, about 10 minutes. Taste; add more sugar and lemon juice, if necessary. Purée the sauce with an immersion blender. Return the sauce to a simmer and adjust flavor by adding additional lemon juice if necessary. Add the remaining berries and simmer until the sauce is very hot. The sauce can be stored in the refrigerator. It will thicken slightly. It keeps up to 10 days.

Preheat oven to 375°F. Butter a 15x10x2 glass baking dish. Place 1 crêpe, spotted side up, on a work surface. Drop ¼ cup of filling into a 3" long log in center of crêpe. Fold bottom of crêpe over filling, then fold sides in and roll up (like a burrito). Place seam side down in buttered pan. Repeat with remaining filling & crêpes. Cover dish with foil and bake blintzes until thermometer inserted into center of fillings reaches 160–170°F, approx 45 minutes. Place 2 blintzes on each plate. Serve with berry topping.

Crêpes are thin pancakes, usually made with wheat flour, originating from France. The common ingredients include flour, eggs, milk, butter, and a pinch of salt. Blintzes differ from crêpes in that they typically lack a leavening agent. Blintzes were popularized in the U.S. by Jewish immigrants who used them in their cuisine.

Scranton Seahorse Inn
Seahorse Inn Granola

Yield: 6–8 servings

*"Our suggestion is to try to use as many local ingredients as possible.
We use local maple syrup and honey. And we recommend pecans
and almonds for nuts."*

3 cups rolled oats
1 cup, any combination of
  your favorite nuts
½ cup shredded
  unsweetened coconut
½ cup quinoa
1½ Tbsp cinnamon
1 tsp freshly grated
  nutmeg

1 tsp kosher salt
¾ cup maple syrup
½ cup honey
1 Tbsp pure vanilla extract
2 Tbsp unsalted butter
½ cup golden raisins
1 cup of your favorite dried
  fruit(s)

Preheat oven to 350°F. In a large bowl, mix together oats, nuts, coconut, quinoa, and spices. Combine syrup, honey, vanilla, and butter in a microwave-safe bowl. Heat until butter is melted.

Stir together the warmed syrup mixture to combine well. Add to the oat and nut mixture. Stir until well coated.

Spread mixture on a rimmed baking sheet covered with a nonstick baking sheet. If you don't have a nonstick baking sheet, coat the baking sheet with cooking spray. Set oven timer to 7 minutes. Every 7 minutes for approximately 30 minutes remove the pan and stir. The mixture should be evenly cooked to a dark golden brown. Once cooled, add the dried fruit to the granola. The granola can be kept refrigerated in an airtight container for up to 3 weeks. Enjoy with milk, soymilk, or plain yogurt.

Gateways Inn
Gateways Granola

Yield: 16–20 servings

5 cups rolled oats
1 cup quinoa
1 cup sliced almonds
1 cup broken walnuts
1 cup broken pecans
1 cup shredded unsweetened coconut
1 cup unsalted sunflower seeds
2 Tbsp ground cinnamon
1 cup canola oil
1 cup local honey
¾ cup molasses
3 Tbsp pure vanilla extract
1 cup dates, chopped and pitted
1 cup dried apricots
1 cup raisins
1 cup dried cranberries
1 cup dried blueberries
1 cup dried cherries

Preheat oven to 325°F.

In a large bowl toss together and mix well the oats, quinoa, almonds, walnuts, pecans, coconut, sunflower seeds, and cinnamon. Heat canola oil, honey, molasses, and vanilla together in a medium saucepan, stirring constantly to warm through and combine.

Pour liquid mixture over dry ingredients and mix thoroughly until well coated. Spread evenly on a lined and lightly greased rimmed baking sheet. Bake for 30–40 minutes, stirring and turning over every 10 minutes to ensure even browning, being careful not to burn the granola. Remove from the oven when browning begins, but mixture is still moist. Add dried fruit. Store in airtight container when completely cooled.

Adair Country Inn & Restaurant

World Famous Adair Maple Granola

Yield: 12–16 servings

7	cups rolled oats, uncooked
1	cup toasted coconut
1	cup wheat germ
1	cup almonds, sliced or broken
1	cup pecans or walnuts, chopped or broken up
1	cup sunflower seeds, raw or toasted
½	cup Baker's Special dry milk (or use regular powdered milk)
½	tsp salt
½	cup vegetable oil
1	cup maple syrup
1	Tbsp vanilla extract
1	cup raisins
	additional dried fruit/nuts as desired

Preheat oven to 250°F.

In a large bowl, combine the oats, coconut, wheat germ, nuts, seeds, and milk powder. Mix well. In a separate bowl, whisk together the salt, oil, maple syrup, and vanilla. Pour over dry mixture in bowl, stirring and tossing until everything is well combined.

Spread granola on a couple of large, lightly greased baking sheets. Bake in oven for 2 hours, tossing and stirring mixture every 15 minutes or so. Remove pans from oven and cool completely. Transfer granola to a large bowl, and mix in raisins and additional dried fruit as desired.

Hill Farm Inn
Hill Farm Granola

Yield: approximately 3½ cups

*"This granola has no added fat or oil.
It's been a Hill Farm favorite for many years."*

 1 cup old-fashioned rolled oats
 ⅓ cup chopped nuts
 ⅓ cup wheat germ
 ⅓ cup sesame seeds
 ⅓ cup sunflower seeds
 ⅓ cup shredded coconut
 ⅓ cup banana chips
 ⅓ cup dried cranberries
 ¼ cup packed brown sugar

Put oats and nuts in a large, heavy skillet over low heat; cook for 5 minutes, stirring often. Add wheat germ, sesame seeds, sunflower seeds, coconut, banana chips, and dried cranberries; cook for 10 minutes. Add brown sugar and cook for 2 minutes longer. Transfer granola to a bowl and cool. When granola is completely cool, store in an airtight container.

Breakfast Entrées

"He that but looketh on a plate of ham and eggs to lust after it hath already committed breakfast with it in his heart."

— C.S. Lewis

Recipes in this Section:

Recipes in the Signature Recipes Section:

Butternut Farm
Casserole Florentine

Yield: 6 servings

1 (10-oz.) pkg. frozen chopped spinach, thawed and squeezed dry
1 can Campbell's® Condensed Cream of Mushroom Soup
1 clove garlic, minced
½ tsp dried tarragon
½ tsp dried marjoram
   salt and pepper to taste
4 cups cooked noodles or other cooked pasta
1 lb. sweet Italian sausage, cooked, drained, and chopped
1 large onion, coarsely chopped
1 egg
1 (15-oz.) container ricotta cheese
1 tomato, seeded, chopped
   parsley, chopped

Preheat oven to 375°F.

Combine spinach, soup, garlic, and seasonings in a small bowl; spread evenly over pasta in buttered 3-quart flat casserole dish. Distribute sausage over the spinach mixture and sprinkle with onion. In a separate bowl, blend egg into ricotta and spread on top of casserole.

Bake for 25–30 minutes or until golden, then allow to cool slightly. Top with garnish of tomato and parsley.

Campbell's Soup Company was founded in 1869, originally producing canned tomatoes, vegetables, jellies, soups, condiments, and minced meats. The brand expanded in the mid-20th century to include popular brands such as Pepperidge Farm, V8, Swanson broths, and Godiva chocolates. Many of the soups in the Campbell's condensed soup line are considered staples to casserole and comfort food recipes.

INN AT SOUTHWEST
Eggs Florentine

Yield: 6 servings

1 (8-oz.) pkg. frozen chopped spinach
8 eggs
¼ cup butter, melted
½ lb. Swiss cheese, grated
½ lb. feta cheese, crumbled
⅛ tsp nutmeg

Preheat oven to 350°F. Grease 6 individual ramekins.

Microwave spinach until heated through. Drain the spinach and pat dry with paper towels. Set aside. In a large bowl, beat the eggs well. Add the melted butter, cheeses, and nutmeg; mix well. Add the spinach and blend thoroughly. Pour into ramekins and place on a cookie sheet in the oven. Bake until nicely puffed and set, about 20 minutes.

Florentine simply means of or relating to Florence, the capital city of Tuscany, Italy. Traditional cuisine in Florence is related to peasant-style eating, rather than complex rarefied dishes. Many dishes are based primarily on meat. However, the common English meaning of Florentine means cooked or served with spinach.

Rosewood Country Inn

Eggs Florentine with English Muffins

Yield: 8 servings

- 3 Tbsp butter
- 3 Tbsp flour
- 3 cups milk
- ¼ tsp salt
- ¼ tsp pepper
- dash nutmeg
- 1 Tbsp onion, chopped fine
- 1 cup cheddar cheese, grated
- 8 English muffins, split and lightly toasted
- ½ (10-oz.) pkg. fresh baby spinach, steamed and patted dry
- 8 eggs, hard-boiled and sliced
- Parmesan cheese
- paprika
- parsley
- breadcrumbs

In a medium saucepan, melt butter. Add flour and stir for one minute. Add milk. Cook until thickened. Add salt, pepper, nutmeg, onion, and cheese; blend. Place split toasted muffins on a large baking sheet. Place a few spinach leaves on muffins and top with sliced cooked eggs. Pour cheese mixture over top. Sprinkle with Parmesan cheese, a dash of paprika, parsley, and a dusting of breadcrumbs. Broil until lightly browned.

1802 House B&B
Eggs Florentine Frittata

Yield: 12 servings

- 10 eggs
- 4 Tbsp butter, melted
- ¼ cup sour cream
- ¼ tsp fresh ground nutmeg
- 1 tsp ground white pepper
- ½ cup Gruyère cheese, grated
- ½ cup feta cheese, crumbled
- 1 cup cottage cheese
- 2 cups fresh baby spinach leaves, chopped

Preheat oven to 350°F. Grease a 9x13-inch baking pan. Whisk eggs in a bowl. Add melted butter, sour cream, nutmeg, and pepper and beat well. Fold in the cheeses and spinach until well mixed. Pour into prepared baking dish and bake for 45 minutes. Top should be lightly browned. Remove from oven, cover with tin foil. Let sit for 10 minutes before cutting and serving.

Tip: We serve with roasted tomatoes and sausage.

Frittata comes from the Italian, meaning "to fry." Outside of Italy, the frittata was synonymous with omelette until the mid-1950s. Unlike an omelette, a frittata is not folded to enclose its contents, and the added ingredients are often mixed in to the raw eggs before being beaten to add fluff. Frittatas are often divided into slices for serving multiple people.

DOCKSIDE GUEST QUARTERS
Breakfast Frittatas

Yield: 16 servings

"Frittatas have delicious southwestern flavors and are easy to prepare. They also can be made the day before, which really helps with planning and organization when having a group for breakfast."

¼	cup (½ stick) butter
½	cup onions, chopped
1	(17-oz.) can corn, drained
1	(8-oz.) can green chilies, chopped
1	(8-oz.) can rotelle tomoatoes
1¼	tsp chili pepper
1/8	tsp cayenne pepper
½	tsp salt
18	eggs
1	cup sour cream, plus more for topping
1/3	cup all-purpose flour
3	cups sharp cheddar cheese, grated
2½	cups Monterey Jack cheese, grated
	salsa to serve

Preheat oven to 350°F. Grease 2 (9-inch) pie plates.

In a skillet over medium heat, melt the butter and sauté the onions until soft. Add corn, chilies, tomatoes, chili pepper, cayenne pepper, and salt. Simmer until flavors are well blended, about 15 minutes.

In a large bowl, whisk together the eggs and sour cream. Add the flour and beat until smooth. Add the sautéed mixture and cheeses. Stir until well blended. Divide the mixture evenly between the 2 pie plates.

Bake 40 minutes or until set and browned. Cut the frittatas into wedges, and serve with salsa and sour cream.

1802 House B&B
Crabby Brie Soufflés

Yield: 6 Servings

For the soufflé:
- 4 Tbsp butter, divided
- 2 Tbsp chopped onions
- 1 cup Maine crabmeat
- ¼ lb. Brie cheese, sliced
- ¼ cup all-purpose flour
- 1¼ cups milk, warmed
- 4 egg yolks
- 6 egg whites

For the chive sauce:
- ½ cup whipping cream
- ½ cup sour cream
- juice of ½ lemon
- 5 Tbsp fresh chives, snipped

For the soufflé: Preheat oven to 350°F. Grease 6 individual soufflé dishes. Fold each of 6 sheets of foil into thirds (like folding a letter). Grease one side of each piece of foil and wrap around soufflé dish, greased-side-in, to form a collar extending one inch beyond height of rim.

Melt 2 tablespoons butter in a skillet over medium heat. Add onions and cook until translucent. Add crabmeat and cook until warmed through. Lay slices of Brie on top of crabmeat mixture; cover skillet and cook until cheese is melted.

Melt remaining 2 tablespoons of butter in a small saucepan over medium-low heat. Add flour and cook, stirring, for 4–5 minutes. Slowly add milk and cook, whisking constantly, for 8–10 minutes, until thickened. Whisk in egg yolks. Cook, whisking, for 2 minutes, then pour milk mixture into a bowl. Fold crabmeat mixture into milk mixture. Beat egg whites until stiff, but not dry. Fold egg whites into crabmeat mixture. Divide mixture among soufflé dishes. Bake for 20–25 minutes.

For the chive sauce: Mix all sauce ingredients together.

Serve immediately with chive sauce.

Inn at English Meadows
Pancetta Crustless Quiche

Yield: 6 servings

5 oz. pancetta, diced
½ cup crème fraîche
½ cup sour cream
2 large eggs
salt
freshly ground pepper to taste
½ cup Parmesan cheese, grated or shredded

Preheat oven to 375°F. Lightly spray jumbo muffin tin (6 cups) with vegetable spray and set aside. In a medium skillet, cook the pancetta until crisp and drain on a paper towel. Beat together crème fraîche, sour cream, and eggs—do not over beat. Season with salt and freshly ground pepper. Blend in the cheese and pancetta. Fill muffin tins ²/3 full. Bake in center of oven for 20 minutes or until golden. Remove from oven and let sit for 5 minutes before removing from muffin tin. The quiches can be served hot or at room temperature.

Although quiche is known as a classic French dish, it originated in Germany. The word quiche means "cake," translated from the German word Kuchen. Many variations of quiche exist with a wide variety of ingredients.

PRYOR HOUSE B&B
Sausage Quiche
Yield: 6–8 servings

For the crust:
- 3 cups all-purpose flour
- 1 cup plus 1½ Tbsp shortening
- 1½ tsp salt
- 1 egg
- ⅓ cup ice water
- 1 tsp cider vinegar

For the filling:
- 1½ tsp butter
- ¼ cup onion, chopped
- 8 oz. bulk pork sausage, cooked
- 1 cup grated Swiss cheese, grated
- 1 cup grated cheddar cheese, grated
- 3 eggs, beaten
- 1¼ cups light cream or milk
- ¾ tsp salt
- ⅛ tsp pepper

Preheat oven to 350°F. In a large bowl, cut together flour, shortening, and salt. In a small bowl, beat together egg, water, and vinegar; add to flour mixture and stir until a ball forms. Roll out dough and fit in a 9-inch pie pan; flute edges (do not prick crust). Bake for 7 minutes.

For the filling: Melt butter in a small skillet over medium heat. Add onions and cook until soft; cool slightly. Layer sausage, onion, and cheeses in crust. In a separate bowl, combine eggs, cream, salt, and pepper; pour over ingredients in crust. Bake for 30–35 minutes, or until set. Let stand for 10 minutes; slice and serve.

Tip: For a vegetarian alternative, substitute chopped tomatoes and oregano for the pork, or any other vegetable to your liking.

BROOK FARM INN
Breakfast Egg & Vegetable Puff

Yield: 4 servings

- 6 eggs, beaten
- 1 cup Bisquick®
- 2 cups milk
- 1 onion, chopped
- 1–2 cups vegetables, your choice (sundried tomatoes, mushrooms, asparagus, or other vegetables, cut in bite-sized pieces)
- 1 (8-oz.) pkg. Colby or cheddar cheese, shredded

Preheat oven to 350°F. Grease a 9x13-inch casserole dish. In a bowl, whisk eggs with Bisquick. Add milk. Sauté vegetables and stir into egg mixture. Add cheese. Pour into casserole dish. Bake 40–50 minutes.

INN AT SOUTHWEST

Eggs Boursin

Yield: 4 servings

1 small (4-6 oz.) pkg. sliced mushrooms
1 box Boursin cheese
6 eggs
6–8 teaspoons half & half
     salt and pepper, to taste

Preheat oven to 350°F. Grease 4 individual ramekins.

Sauté mushrooms in butter until tender. Place layer of mushrooms into prepared ramekins. Cover mushrooms with dabs of Boursin cheese. Beat eggs with large dash of half & half, salt, and pepper. Pour eggs over mushrooms and cheese. Bake until nicely puffed, about 15–20 minutes.

Gateways Inn
Layered Stuffed Morning Mushrooms

Yield: 8 servings

For the roasted red bell peppers:
- 4 red bell peppers, deveined, seeded, and cut into strips
- ½ head of garlic
- ⅓ cup extra virgin olive oil
- juice of 2 lemons

- 8 large Portabello mushroom caps, stems removed
- olive oil
- 12 oz. fresh spinach, wilted
- 8 jumbo eggs
- ½ cup half & half
- 2 Tbsp fresh chives, chopped
- salt and pepper, to taste
- 4 tsp butter
- 1½ cups sharp cheddar, shredded
- ½ cup Parmesan cheese, grated

For the red peppers: Preheat oven to 350°F. Place peppers in glass baking dish. Sprinkle thinly sliced cloves of garlic from ½ a head of garlic over the peppers. Drizzle about ⅓ cup of good quality extra virgin olive oil over the mixture, along with the juice of 2 large lemons. Roast, stirring occasionally, until the peppers are soft, but not browning. Can be stored in the refrigerator for up to 10 days.

Preheat oven to 350°F. Brush the outside of the mushroom caps with a little olive oil and roast about 15 minutes. Line the inside of the mushroom cap with a layer of the wilted spinach, then a layer of the roasted red peppers and set aside.

For the eggs: Beat together the eggs, half & half, chives, salt, and pepper. Melt the butter in a large skillet and scramble the egg mixture, adding in ¾ of the shredded cheddar. Scoop a nice mound of egg onto each mushroom cap over the other layers. Sprinkle with remaining cheddar and sprinkle with Parmesan. Return to oven just to melt cheese and serve.

Golden Slipper
Bacon 'n' Egg Lasagna
Yield: 6–8 servings

1 lb. sliced bacon, diced
1 large onion, chopped
1/3 cup all-purpose flour
½ tsp salt
½ tsp pepper
4 cups milk
12 lasagna noodles, cooked and drained
12 hard cooked eggs, sliced
2 cups Swiss cheese, shredded
1/3 cup grated Parmesan cheese
2 Tbsp fresh parsley

Preheat oven to 350°F.

Cook bacon, drain, and sauté onion until tender in bacon drippings. Stir in flour, salt, and pepper until blended. Gradually stir in milk, bring to a boil, cook and stir for 2 minutes. Remove from heat.

Spread ½ cup sauce in the bottom of a 9x13-inch baking dish. Layer with noodles, a third of the eggs, bacon, Swiss cheese, and white sauce. Repeat layers twice, sprinkle top with Parmesan cheese. Bake for 35–40 minutes, or until bubbly. Sprinkle with parsley. Let stand 15 minutes before cutting.

Honeysuckle Hill Inn
Apple, Sage Derby & Chive Frittata

Yield: 8 servings

4	Tbsp unsalted butter
4	tart apples, peeled, cored, and sliced thinly
14	large eggs
½	cup chopped chives or green onions
	freshly ground pepper
8–12	oz. sage derby cheese, crumbled

Preheat oven to 350°F. Lightly oil a large casserole dish (at least 2 inches deep).

Melt the butter in a heavy, medium-sized skillet. Sauté the apple slices for 2–3 minutes, until slightly softened. Transfer apples to the prepared casserole dish. Beat the eggs with the chives and pepper. Pour over the apples in the casserole dish. Stir in the crumbled sage derby cheese.

Bake for about 30–40 minutes, or until a knife inserted into the center comes out clean.

Sage Derby is a type of mild cheese that is semi-hard, mottled green with a sage flavor. The green coloring comes from mixing sage leaves, green corn, or spinach juice into the curd before it is pressed. It was first produced in seventeenth-century England for festive occasions, but it is now available all year.

Inn at Cape Cod

Bacon Frittata

Yield: 8 servings

16 oz. diced potatoes (about ¼-inch cubes), fried until light brown
16 slices bacon, cut into small pieces, and crisply cooked
½ red bell pepper, diced
12 extra large eggs
1 cup 2% milk
    salt and pepper, to taste
    Mexican-blend cheese, grated
    chives, chopped

Preheat oven to 350°F. Spray eight 5-inch ramekins with nonstick spray.

Divide fried potatoes equally into ramekins. Divide chopped bacon equally on top of potatoes. Sprinkle with diced red pepper. In a bowl, whisk together eggs, milk, and seasoning. Pour egg mix into dishes, filling almost to top. Sprinkle a handful of grated cheese and chopped chives onto each one. Bake for 25–30 minutes until cheese is golden brown and eggs are set.

Tip: Try serving this with fresh asparagus or homemade relish, garnished with a sprig of parsley.

ADAIR COUNTRY INN
& RESTAURANT
Apple Clafouti

Yield: 6 servings

*"This is one of the most popular breakfast offerings at Adair. Why?
It's pure comfort food—soft, egg-y, sweet, and cinnamon-y. It is
wonderful served with a sprinkle of powdered sugar, but keep a
jug of real New Hampshire maple syrup nearby!"*

1	cup all-purpose flour	5	Tbsp butter, melted and divided
3	Tbsp sugar	2	Tbsp brown sugar
¼	tsp salt	½	tsp cinnamon
4	eggs	2–3	apples, thinly sliced
1	cup heavy cream		powdered sugar, for garnish
1	tsp vanilla extract		maple syrup, for serving

Preheat oven to 400°F.

In a large bowl, combine flour, sugar, and salt. Whisk in eggs, cream, and vanilla. Add 3 tablespoons of melted butter and stir until smooth.

Heat a 9- or 10-inch ovenproof skillet over medium-low heat. Grease skillet. Add batter to skillet and cook until it begins to set.

Combine brown sugar and cinnamon. Add apple slices and toss to coat. Layer apple slices in a decorative pattern on batter in skillet. Drizzle remaining 2 tablespoons of melted butter over apples. Put skillet in oven and bake for 15–20 minutes, until center is firm. Slice and serve.

Clafouti is a baked French dessert consisting of flan-like batter filled with cherries and dusted with sugar. Clafouti popularity spread throughout France in the 19th century. When other fruit is substituted for cherries, the dish is properly called a flaugnarde.

Colby Hill Inn
Potato Pancakes with Poached Eggs & Cheddar
Yield: 8 servings

"For variety, try topping the potato pancakes with chopped tomato, roasted red bell pepper, spinach, or broccoli before adding the poached eggs and cheese."

- 6 large potatoes, peeled and grated
- 1 large onion, grated
- ¾ cup all-purpose flour
- 2–3 large eggs, beaten, plus 8 eggs, poached
  salt and pepper, to taste
- ¾ cup cheddar cheese (or Swiss, crumbled feta, etc.), grated

Combine potatoes, onion, flour, and beaten eggs (start with 2 eggs and add a third, if needed, to achieve desired consistency). Form potato mixture into cakes and cook on an oiled or buttered griddle or skillet over medium-high heat until golden brown on both sides. Top pancakes with a poached egg and a little cheese.

If desired, serve on ovenproof plates and place plates in a 350°F oven until cheese is melted.

MARSHALL SLOCUM GUEST HOUSE

Eggs Atlantic with Fresh Dill Hollandaise

Yield: 2 servings

4 eggs
2 Tbsp distilled white vinegar
2 English muffins
2 pieces fresh Atlantic lox
   capers

For Dill Hollandaise sauce:
6 egg yolks
1 oz. cold water
2 oz. lemon juice, divided
1¼ lbs. clarified butter
2 Tbsp fresh ground dill
   salt and pepper, to taste

Poach eggs in boiling water and distilled white vinegar. Split and toast English muffins. Slice each piece of lox in two and place on toasted English muffin. With a slotted spoon, remove poached eggs from water and let excess water drain. Place on top of salmon and English muffin. Coat with fresh dill hollandaise. Top with capers.

For the sauce: Beat egg yolks and water in a metal bowl. Add a few drops of lemon juice and mix. Place bowl in another bowl of hot water, stir mixture until thick and smooth. Remove from hot water bath. Gradually add the clarified butter. Add remaining lemon juice and dill; combine. Add salt and pepper to taste.

WHITE ROCKS INN B&B

Eggs Dijon

Yield: 8 servings

- 2 cups sour cream
- 1 Tbsp Dijon mustard
- ¼ cup dry white wine
  salt and pepper, to taste
- 16 eggs
- ½ cup sharp cheddar cheese, grated (I use Vermont white cheddar).
  plain breadcrumbs

Preheat oven to 350°F. Spray 8 individual baking dishes with cooking spray.

In a bowl, mix sour cream, mustard, wine, salt, and pepper with a wire whisk until well blended. Break 2 eggs into each dish. Cover with grated cheese; dividing cheese between the individual baking dishes. Add sour cream mixture and top with breadcrumbs. Bake about 15 minutes until eggs are desired consistency.

Appetizers, Soups, Salads & Side Dishes

"Only the pure of heart can make a good soup."

— Ludwig van Beethoven

Recipes in this Section:

Recipes in the Signature Recipes Section:

Butternut Farm

Bongo Bongo Soup

Yield: 8 servings

"Adapted from a Plaza Hotel recipe."

2 Tbsp butter
4 shallots, minced
½ cup dry white wine
2 pints chucked raw oysters, coarsely chopped, with liquid
1 tsp salt
½ tsp freshly ground pepper
1 (10-oz.) pkg. frozen chopped spinach, defrosted and squeezed dry
6 cups chicken stock, homemade or canned
2 cups whipping cream
1 tsp Worcestershire sauce
dash of cayenne pepper

In a medium saucepan, melt butter. Add the shallots; sauté until soft. Add the wine and bring to a boil. Simmer until liquid is reduced by half. Add the oysters and their liquid, salt, and pepper; heat just until the mixture is warm. Remove from heat and set aside. In a large, heavy pot, combine the spinach and stock. Bring to a boil. Add the oyster mixture; cool slightly. Pour mixture into a blender or the work bowl of a food processor and purée. Return to large pot; add the cream, Worcestershire sauce, and cayenne pepper. Adjust seasonings to taste. Heat to steaming; serve hot.

Butternut Farm
Battle of Lexington Soup

Yield: 8 servings

¾	cup onion, finely chopped
4	Tbsp butter
2	cups pumpkin purée, fresh or canned
1	cup chicken, cooked and diced
5–6	cups chicken stock, homemade or canned
2	cups whipping cream
	salt and freshly ground pepper, to taste
	pinch of nutmeg

In large skillet or soup pot, sauté onion in butter until golden. Add the pumpkin, diced chicken, and stock; bring to a boil. Reduce heat and simmer for 5 minutes. Add the cream and seasonings. Stir just until heated through. Serve immediately.

The Battle of Lexington marked the beginning of the Revolutionary War in Lexington, MA in 1775. It was important to the early American government to show British fault and American innocence in this first battle. The story of the battle became more important than truth for the Americans.

INN AT ENGLISH MEADOWS
Roasted Tomato Soup

Yield: 6–8 servings

2½	pounds fresh tomatoes (mix of fresh heirlooms, cherry, vine, and plum)
6	cloves garlic, peeled
2	small yellow onions, sliced
½	cup extra-virgin olive oil
	salt and freshly ground black pepper
1	quart chicken stock, divided
2	bay leaves
4	Tbsp butter
½	cup basil leaves, chopped (optional)
	vine cherry tomatoes for garnish (optional)
¾	cup heavy cream

Preheat oven to 450°F.

Wash, core, and cut the tomatoes into halves. Spread the tomatoes, garlic, and onions onto a baking tray. If using vine cherry tomatoes for garnish, add them as well, leaving them whole and on the vine. Drizzle with ½ cup of olive oil and season with salt and pepper. Roast for 20–30 minutes or until caramelized.

Remove roasted tomatoes, garlic, and onion from the oven and transfer to a large stockpot. Set aside the roasted vine tomatoes for later. Add ¾ of the chicken stock and bay leaves and butter. Bring to a boil, reduce heat and simmer for 15–20 minutes or until liquid has reduced by a third.

Wash and dry basil leaves, if using, and add to the pot. Use an immersion blender to purée the soup until smooth. Return soup to low heat, add cream and adjust consistency with remaining chicken stock, if necessary. Season to taste with salt and pepper. Garnish in bowl with 3–4 roasted vine cherry tomatoes and a splash of heavy cream (optional).

Colby Hill Inn

Cream of Onion Soup with Caramelized Onions & Truffle Oil

Yield: about 1 gallon (10–12 servings)

- 2 oz. butter
- 3 Spanish onions, diced small
- 2 garlic cloves
- 1 tsp fresh thyme, chopped
- 1 bay leaf
- 2 oz. all-purpose flour
- 1 cup white wine
- ½ gallon heavy cream
- 4 cups chicken stock
- salt and pepper, to taste

In a large soup pot, melt butter. Add onions and cook until translucent. Add garlic, thyme, and bay leaf. Cook 1 minute. Add flour and cook for 2 minutes. Deglaze with white wine. Add cream and stock. Bring to a boil, whisking occasionally, then simmer, 30–45 minutes. Remove bay leaf. Purée in a blender until smooth. Pass through a chinois, or fine mesh strainer. Adjust seasoning with salt and pepper. Add more stock to adjust consistency if the soup is too thick for your liking.

Tip: Serve with caramelized onions, and garnish with truffle oil and crispy shallots.

COMBES FAMILY INN
Joe's Basil & Broccoli Soup

Yield: 4 servings

"The inn's refrigeration repair man, Joe, gave us this recipe."

    5 cups broccoli, coarsely chopped
    2 cups chicken stock
    3 Tbsp butter or olive oil, or combination of both
    ¼ cup fresh basil, chopped
    3 cloves garlic, chopped
       salt and pepper, to taste
       a squeeze of lemon juice
       Parmesan cheese, for serving (optional)

In a saucepan, bring broccoli and stock to a boil. Lower heat and simmer until broccoli is tender. Purée broccoli and stock with an immersion blender, food processor, or blender until smooth. Heat oil or melted butter in a small saucepan and sauté garlic and basil briefly until garlic turns soft. Add basil and garlic to broccoli purée. Process until smooth. Season with salt, pepper, and a squeeze of lemon. To serve, sprinkle with Parmesan cheese, if desired.

Echo Lake Inn
Curried Vermont Apple Soup

Yield: 4 servings

"This recipe has been published in both Gourmet *and* Bon Appetit.*"*

½ stick butter
1 medium onion, chopped
3 medium apples, peeled and sliced
1 Tbsp curry powder, plus extra for garnish
2 cups chicken stock or broth
1 cup heavy cream
   salt and pepper, to taste
   sour cream, for garnish (optional)

Melt butter in a large, heavy saucepan over medium heat. Add onion; cook until translucent. Add apples; cook until they start to soften. Stir in curry powder. Raise heat to medium-high and, while stirring, slowly add stock. Stir in cream. Bring to a boil, lower heat and simmer for 30 minutes, stirring occasionally. Season with salt, pepper, and more curry powder, as needed. Dust rims of serving bowls with a little curry powder. Serve soup with a dollop of sour cream, if desired.

Rabbit Hill Inn

Vermont Cheddar Cheese Soup with Sundried Tomatoes

Yield: 10 servings

"Of course, we make our soup with Vermont's Cabot Cheddar Cheese."

6	Tbsp unsalted butter
1	cup onion, diced
¾	cup celery, diced
½	cup carrots, diced
2	tsp garlic, minced
	flour
4	cups chicken stock
1	lb. cheddar cheese, grated
1	tsp dry mustard
1	cup heavy cream
1	cup sundried tomatoes, chopped
1	tsp Worcestershire sauce
	salt and pepper, to taste

Melt butter in a soup pot. When hot, add onions, celery, carrots, and garlic. Sauté for 5 minutes over medium heat. Sprinkle flour on top and stir constantly for another 5 minutes. Add chicken stock, one cup at a time. Whip to incorporate each time. Bring to a boil, then reduce heat and simmer for 45 minutes. Strain soup through a mesh strainer into another soup pot, pushing through as much liquid and vegetable as possible. Place soup on a very low heat and add cheese, mustard, cream, sundried tomatoes, Worchestershire sauce, salt, and pepper. Do not return the soup to a boil.

Tip: Bacon, pancetta, or smoked chicken may be substituted for the sundried tomatoes if you prefer.

West Mountain Inn
Asparagus and Chèvre Soup

Yield: 4 servings

butter or olive oil for sautéing
1 small onion, diced
2 stalks celery, diced
3 bunches asparagus, diced
2 potatoes, peeled and diced
4 cups chicken or vegetable stock
8 oz. Vermont goat cheese
salt and pepper, to taste

In a large skillet or soup pot, sauté onion, celery, and asparagus over medium heat for about 10 minutes. Add potatoes and stock. Cook until potatoes are soft. Add goat cheese and purée in a blender. Strain. Season with salt and pepper.

Marshall Slocum Inn

Lobster Bisque

Yield: 6–8 servings

"What's better than warming up with a warm bowl of soup on a cloudy, rainy, chilly evening? This will keep you warm on those cool New England nights."

- 6 Tbsp butter
- 6 Tbsp all-purpose flour
- 1 tsp salt
- ¼ tsp ground black pepper
- ½ tsp celery salt
- 4½ cups milk
- 1½ cups chicken stock
- 3 Tbsp onions, minced
- 3 cups cooked lobster meat, shredded
- 1 Tbsp paprika
- ½ cup light cream

Melt butter in a large pot over medium heat. Stir in the flour, salt, pepper, and celery salt until it is well blended. Gradually stir in milk so that no lumps form. Stir in chicken stock. Cook over low heat, stirring constantly, until the soup thickens. Add onion and lobster. Season with paprika. Cook and continue stirring for 10 minutes. Add the cream, heat through, and serve.

Marshall Slocum Inn
Newport Clam Chowder

Yield: 6–8 servings

"This recipe is sure to remind anyone of the great times they had in Newport, and will make them feel they're back at the wharf watching the sailboats come in and out."

½ cup butter
1½ large onion, chopped
¾ cup all-purpose flour
1 quart shucked clams, with liquid
6 (8-oz.) jars clam juice
1 lb. boiling potatoes, peeled and chopped
3 cups half & half
salt and pepper, to taste
½ tsp fresh dill weed, chopped

Melt butter in a large kettle or stockpot over medium heat. Add onions and sauté until clear. Add flour and cook over low heat, stirring frequently for 2–4 minutes. Set aside to cool. In a separate pot, bring clams and clam juice to a boil. Reduce heat and simmer for 15 minutes. In a small saucepan, cover peeled potatoes with water. Bring to a boil and cook until potatoes are tender, about 15 minutes. Drain and set aside.

Slowly pour hot clam stock into butter/flour mixture while stirring constantly. Continue stirring and slowly bring to a boil. Reduce heat and add cooked potatoes. Mix in the half & half, salt, pepper, and chopped dill. Heat through. Do not boil.

Blue Hill Inn
Savory Cheddar & Sage Crackers

Yield: 6 dozen crackers

"This recipe is adapted from the Boston Globe Magazine."

1¾ cups all-purpose flour
1 tsp salt (or less) to taste
½ tsp pepper
3 Tbsp fresh sage, minced
6 Tbsp unsalted butter, very cold, cut or grated into small pieces

1½ cups extra sharp cheddar cheese, finely grated (up to ½ cup could be another cheese)
⅓ cup milk

In the bowl of a food processor, pulse the flour, salt, pepper, and sage to combine. Scatter the butter pieces over the flour mixture in the food processor, and pulse to cut the butter into the flour until it takes on the texture of fine sand, about 12 3-second pulses.

Add the cheese and pulse to combine. With the motor running, add the milk and process just until the dough comes together (about 30 seconds.) Do not over process. Transfer the dough to a work surface. To create square crackers, divide the dough in half and form each half into a long rectangle measuring about 6 inches long and 2 inches wide; for round crackers roll into a 6-inch log. Wrap each half of the roll in plastic wrap and refrigerate until very firm, at least 2 hours, and up to 3 days.

To bake the crackers: Preheat oven to 350°F. and set the oven rack in the middle position. Line a large baking sheet with parchment paper or a nonstick mat. Working with one-half at a time, rest the dough at room temperature for about 3 minutes. Working quickly, slice the dough into ¼-inch-thick crackers, arrange them about ½ inch apart on the baking sheet, and bake until the edges are just golden and the center is firm, at least 14 minutes. Rotate the baking sheet halfway through baking. Transfer the crackers to a wire rack, cool completely.

Hartwell House Inn
Vermont Cheddar Wafers

Yield: 18 wafers

"With just a hint of spice, these wafers are the perfect snack any time of day."

1	lb. Vermont sharp cheddar cheese, grated
2	sticks butter, softened
2¼	cups all-purpose flour
½	tsp salt
½	tsp white pepper
¼	tsp cayenne pepper

Preheat oven to 350°F. Combine all ingredients with a stand mixer using the dough hook attachment, or use a wooden spoon. Roll dough into 1-inch-thick round logs. Chill dough for at least 30 minutes. Slice dough into ⅛-inch-thick slices. Bake on a cookie sheet for about 12 minutes until golden brown.

BLUE HILL INN

Crispy Bacon Wrapped Stuffed Dates

Yield: 8 servings

"These are magic on the hors d'oeuvres table!"

16 large Medjool dates, pitted
16 almonds, roasted and slivered
¼ scant cup mild goat cheese, crumbled
8 slices of bacon (about 7 ounces), halved crosswise

Preheat oven to 400°F. Cut a lengthwise slit in each date. Stuff with one slivered almond and about ½ teaspoon of cheese. Pinch closed. Wrap each date securely in a slice of bacon and arrange, seam side down, on a wire rack set on a baking sheet. Bake, turning once after 10 minutes, for about 20 minutes or until the bacon is browned and crisp. Serve warm or at room temperature.

Medjool dates are large, sweet, succulent fruit originating from the date palm trees of the Middle East. They are also cultivated in southern California, Arizona, and southern Florida. Pitted dates can also be called "stoned dates." They provide a wide range of nutrients and are a good source of potassium.

Combes Family Inn
Onion Sage Pie

Yield: 8 servings

*"This pie can be served as an appetizer, an accompaniment to a meat
entrée, or brunch. It can be served hot or at room temperature. Sage is
very abundant in our inn's garden, but you can also use dried leaf sage."*

Pie crust:

1   uncooked pie shell, cook at 350°F for about 25 minutes

Pie filling:

2 Tbsp butter
2   cups onion, thinly sliced
2 Tbsp fresh sage, minced or 1 Tbsp dried
½ tsp fresh thyme, minced or ¼ tsp dried
1 cooked pie shell, see above
4 eggs
1 cup Vermont cheddar cheese, shredded
1 can evaporated milk or half & half
½ tsp salt
1/8 tsp ground nutmeg
1/8 tsp black pepper
   Sage leaves for garnish

Preheat oven to 375°F.

Melt butter in saucepan. Add onions and sauté about 5–9 minutes until
tender. Remove from heat and sprinkle with sage and thyme. Put onion
mixture into cooked pie shell. In a separate bowl, blend eggs, cheese,
milk, and spices. Pour over onion mixture in shell.

Bake the pie for about 45 minutes or so until pie sets and knife inserted
comes out clean. Let stand for 10 minutes before cutting and serving.
Garnish with sage leaves.

COLBY HILL INN
Apple Braised Cabbage

Yield: 4–6 servings

*"This fall-inspired accompaniment is great with grilled or roasted pork.
Use local apples for the best flavor. Tart apples like Granny Smith are better
to use as they compliment the sweet flavor of the cabbage and apple cider."*

- 1 Tbsp oil
- ½ onion, thinly sliced
- 2 garlic cloves, minced
- ½ head green cabbage, shredded
- 1 cup apple cider
- 3 Granny Smith apples, peeled and diced
- ½ tsp thyme leaves
- salt and pepper, to taste

In a large sauté pan, add 1 tablespoon oil over medium heat; add the
onions and cook until soft with no color, about 3 minutes. Add garlic
and cook for 1 minute. Add the cabbage and cook until soft. Add the
apple cider and cook until the liquid is reduced by half. Add the apples
and the thyme leaves. Cook until the apples are soft, but not mushy.
Season to taste with salt and pepper.

Rabbit Hill Inn
Soba Noodle Salad

Yield: 2 servings

"You are going to love this delicious (and very healthy) summer salad. This recipe is perfect for a dinner for two, leaving ample leftovers for the next day. Also, it's very easy to prepare a larger amount for a backyard summer party.
"

3 oz. soba noodles, blanched and cooled
Set aside in large bowl

Grill and add to soba noodles after cooled to room temperature:

½ cup shiitake mushrooms, sliced, tossed in 1 tsp peanut oil and grilled
2 Tbsp scallions, grilled and diced

Add the remaining ingredients to the soba noodles:

½ cup Asian pears, diced small
2 tsp toasted sesame seeds

Toss gently to combine all ingredients.

Dressing:
1½ Tbsp soy sauce
1 tsp fresh ginger, minced
1 tsp fresh garlic, minced
½ tsp sesame seed oil
1 tsp rice wine vinegar
½ tsp chili oil

Combine these ingredients and mix well. Pour over salad mixture and toss well.

1785 INN & RESTAURANT

Caesar Salad

Yield: 1 serving

pepper, to taste
¼ tsp garlic, crushed
3 anchovies
1 egg, coddled*
1 lemon
dash of Tabasco
dash of Worcestershire
dash of dry mustard
5 Tbsp Parmesan cheese, grated, divided
¼ cup olive oil
5 Tbsp Parmesan cheese, grated, divided
romaine lettuce, 1 individual plate-sized serving
croutons, 6–8 pieces, or personal preference

Pepper a large wooden bowl. Add the garlic and anchovies. Blend with a fork. Add the egg, lemon, Tabasco, Worcestershire, mustard, and 2 tablespoons of Parmesan cheese. Mix well, while adding olive oil. Add the romaine lettuce, croutons, and the rest of the cheese. Mix ingredients together. Sprinkle with extra pepper, if desired. Turn out onto an individual serving dish.

*To coddle egg: put egg in small bowl, cover with boiling water, and let sit for 4–5 minutes.

1785 Inn & Restaurant
Maple Walnut Dressing
Yield: 3 pints

    3   cups mayonnaise
    1   cup walnut oil
    ¾   cup maple syrup
    2   tsp celery seed
    2   tsp Dijon mustard
    2   tsp dry mustard
    4   scallions, chopped
    1   cup English walnuts (more, if desired)
        whipping cream, used to thin to desired consistency

Blend all ingredients together, adding cream to achieve desired consistency.

Sunset Hill House
Balsamic Maple Vinaigrette
Yield: about 1 quart

    1   cup balsamic vinegar (good quality)
    ¼   cup maple syrup (We recommend New Hampshire Grade B
        maple syrup)
    1   Tbsp Dijon mustard
    1   Tbsp whole grain mustard
    2   tsp dry mustard powder
    1   quart extra virgin olive oil (at least 25% evoo)

In a blender, mix together all ingredients, except the oil. With blender running, add oil in slow stream.

YORK HARBOR INN
Elegant Artichoke Dip

Yield: 6–8 Servings

*"This dip can be made as much as three days
ahead of time and refrigerated until ready to use."*

1½ (8-oz.) pkgs. cream cheese, softened
2 Tbsp onion, finely diced
2 Tbsp Chablis wine
1½ tsp Dijon mustard
¾ tsp salt
¾ tsp paprika
½ tsp garlic, minced
½ tsp white pepper
1 Tbsp fresh lemon juice
1 (15-oz.) can artichoke hearts, drained and cut into large
diced pieces
¼ cup red bell pepper, finely diced
½ cup breadcrumbs
2 Tbsp butter, melted
French bread, warmed, for serving

Preheat oven to 350°F. Combine cream cheese, onions, wine, mustard,
salt, paprika, garlic, white pepper, and lemon juice in a food processor;
process until well mixed. Add artichoke hearts and bell peppers; pulse
just to blend. Place artichoke mixture in a 1-quart casserole dish.

Combine breadcrumbs and butter; sprinkle over artichoke mixture.
Bake for about 20 minutes, or until top is lightly browned and dip is
bubbling around the edges. Serve immediately with warm French bread.

Marshall Slocum Inn
Three Late Afternoon Dips

Yield: about 2 cups each

"Every afternoon we put out nibbles and wine and soft drinks for everyone to enjoy in the parlor in the winter or on the back deck in the summer. These are our guests' favorites."

Boursin cheese:

- 2 (8-oz.) pkgs. cream cheese, softened
- 1 stick butter, softened
- 2 cloves garlic
- 1 tsp oregano
- ¼ tsp thyme
- ¼ tsp black pepper
- ¼ tsp dill
- ¼ tsp basil

Process all ingredients in a food processor until smooth.

Blue cheese pecan spread:

- 1⅓ cups pecans
- ½ cup blue cheese, crumbled
- 1½ (8-oz.) pkgs. cream cheese, softened

Process pecans in a food processor for 10 seconds. Add blue cheese and cream cheese. Process for 30 seconds.

Hummus:

- 1 (19-oz.) can Goya chickpeas (garbanzo beans)
- ¼ cup tahini
- ½ cup olive oil
- ½ cup hot water
- juice of 2 lemons
- ¾ tsp salt
- 1 tsp cumin
- pepper, to taste

Process all ingredients in a food processor until smooth.

Lunch & Dinner Entrees

"After a good dinner
one can forgive anybody,
even one's own relations."

— Oscar Wilde
A Woman of No Importance

Recipes in this Section:

Recipes in the Signature Recipes Section:

Butternut Farm
Chicken Breasts with Artichokes

Yield: 6 servings

- 6 chicken breast halves, boned and skinned
- 1 (8-oz.) can artichoke bottoms, drained
- 1½ cups homemade or canned chicken stock
- 1 tsp tarragon
  freshly ground pepper
  parsley as garnish

Duxelle:

- ½ stick butter
- 10 oz. mushrooms, minced
- 6–8 shallots, finely minced
  salt
  freshly ground pepper
  pinch of nutmeg

Béarnaise Sauce:

- 2 shallots, minced
- 1 Tbsp tarragon
  salt
  freshly ground pepper
- ¼ cup white wine or tarragon vinegar
- ¼ cup dry vermouth
- 3 egg yolks
- 1 stick unsalted butter, cut into small pieces and softened at
  room temperature

Remove the tenderloin from each breast and reserve for another use. Pound each breast between two sheets of plastic wrap or waxed paper until about ½-inch thick. Rinse the artichoke bottoms. Pat dry and fill with about 1 tablespoon of the mushroom duxelle mixture. Wrap a chicken breast around each and shape into neat half-rounds. Set in a shallow pan that holds the chicken rounds snugly. Add enough chicken stock to nearly cover the chicken. Sprinkle with tarragon and pepper. Cover the pan and bring to a simmer on top of the stove. Cook 10–15 minutes, or just until firm. Do not overcook. Remove to a serving platter. Serve with the Béarnaise sauce, and garnish with parsley.

For the duxelle: In a medium skillet, melt the butter. When foamy, add the mushrooms and shallots. Sauté until all the liquid has evaporated and the mixture somewhat holds together (about 10 minutes). Add spices. This may be done 1–2 days ahead and refrigerated until ready for use.

For the Béarnaise sauce: In a small skillet, simmer the shallots, tarragon, salt and pepper in the wine (or vinegar) and vermouth until only a few spoonfuls of the liquid remain. Remove from heat. Quickly whisk in the yolks. Set over a double boiler of water that's barely simmering. Whisk continuously until mixture is thick and creamy. Add the softened butter, a few pieces at a time. Continue whisking over the warm water until all the butter has been incorporated. Remove from heat. Serve immediately or allow to sit at room temperature until ready to serve (up to 45 minutes).

Rabbit Hill Inn

Roasted Lemon-Herb Chicken Breast in a Golden Lentil Coulis with Shrimp & Spinach Risotto

Yield: 5 servings

From the recipe files of Russell Stannard, Executive Chef

Chicken:

- 5 Tbsp butter
- 5 slices of lemon
- 5 chicken breasts, boneless, skin on
- 1/3 cup fresh parsley, minced
- 1/3 cup fresh chive, minced
- 1/3 cup fresh thyme, minced
- 3 oz. olive oil
- 2 oz. vegetable oil
- 3 Tbsp fresh lemon juice
  freshly milled black pepper
- 5 Tbsp salad oil
  salt, to taste

Preheat oven to 275°F.

Stuff 1 tablespoon of butter and 1 slice of lemon underneath the skin of each breast and place in baking dish. In a small bowl, combine fresh herbs, olive oil, vegetable oil, and lemon juice. Pour over chicken breasts. Season with pepper. Marinate chicken for 2–3 hours in the refrigerator.

Heat salad oil in a sauté pan until very hot. Add chicken, skin side down. Season with salt. Cook for 1 minute or until golden brown. Turn and cook for 1 minute more. Remove from the pan and place on a wire rack in the oven for 25 minutes.

To serve, pour a few tablespoons of the Golden Lentil Coulis over the chicken with a side accompaniment of Shrimp and Spinach Risotto.

Golden Lentil Coulis: (Yield: 2 cups)

1	Tbsp butter	3	oz. white wine
½	cup onions, diced	6	oz. golden lentils
½	cup celery, diced	1½	cups chicken stock
1½	tsp garlic, diced		salt, white pepper, fresh lemon
2	Tbsp parsley, minced		juice, to taste

Heat butter in a sauté pan until hot. Add onions, celery, garlic, and parsley and sauté for 7–10 minutes. Add white wine. Bring to a boil and reduce by half. Add lentils and chicken stock. Bring to a boil; then simmer for 15 minutes. Remove from heat. Purée in a food processor. If sauce is too thick, add a little more chicken stock to reach desired consistency.

Shrimp & Spinach Risotto: (Yield: 5 servings)

3	Tbsp butter	5	cups chicken stock
¾	cup onion, diced small	1	cup spinach, chopped
⅓	cup celery, diced small	4	oz. raw shrimp, diced small
1	red bell pepper, diced small	⅓	cup Parmesan cheese, grated
1	Tbsp garlic		salt & pepper, to taste
1¼	cups risotto		

Heat butter in a pan. Add onions, celery, red pepper, and garlic. Sauté for 8–10 minutes. Add risotto, coating the pan evenly with the rice. Reduce heat to low, add 1 cup of stock, and cook until the stock has been absorbed. Repeat this process 4 times. With the last cup, add the spinach and shrimp. When the last cup has been absorbed, stir in Parmesan cheese; season to taste with salt and pepper.

> *Coulis is a form of thick sauce made from puréed and strained vegetables or fruit. Vegetable coulis is often poured over meats and vegetable dishes, or used as a base for soups and sauces. Fruit coulis are commonly used on desserts.*

Golden Slipper
Hardy Meat Pies

Yield: 6–8 servings

- ¾ lb. ground beef
- ¾ lb. ground pork
- 1 onion, chopped
- ⅓ cup green onions, chopped
- 1 garlic clove, minced
- 2 Tbsp parsley
- 1 Tbsp water
- 2 tsp all-purpose flour
- ½ tsp baking powder
- ½ tsp salt
- ½ tsp pepper
- hot sauce to taste
- 2 (12-oz.) tubes buttermilk biscuits

Preheat oven to 350°F.

Brown beef and pork, drain, add onion and garlic. Stir in parsley, water, flour, baking powder, salt, pepper, and hot sauce. On a floured surface, pat 10 biscuits into 4-inch circles. Top each with about ⅓ cup meat mixture. Pat remaining biscuits into 5-inch circles and place over filling. Seal edges with water. Press edges together with a fork dipped in flour, pierce the top. Place on an ungreased baking sheet. Bake for 12–14 minutes until golden brown and filling is hot.

Meat pies popular in Europe, Australia, New Zealand, Canada, and South Africa are usually the size of a fruit pie, but made with savory ingredients. These hardy meat pies resemble the on-the-go pasties more typical of British culture. The residents of the Upper Peninsula of Michigan used pasties for portable lunches in the copper mines, using recipes adapted from Finnish immigrants.

Rabbit Hill Inn
Hungarian Goulash

Yield: 4–6 servings (or 1.5 quarts)

"Hungarian Goulash on Super Bowl Sunday? You bet! We have served this delicious rustic hearty stew recipe from the hearth on many a winter Saturday afternoon. We got this recipe from our dear friend, Paula. It always gets rave reviews."

- ¼ cup salad oil
- 2 lbs. stew meat (You may use any kind of meat … venison, beef, pork, moose, lamb, or a combination)
- 1 cup onions, sliced
- 1 clove garlic, minced
- ½ cup bell peppers, chopped
- ½ cup carrots, chopped
- 2 tsp paprika
- ½ tsp thyme
- ½ tsp rosemary
- ½ cup tomato paste
- ½ cup cider vinegar
- ¼ cup brown sugar
- 2½ cups water or beef stock

In a stockpot, heat oil and brown the meat. Remove meat from the pan when done and set aside. In the same pot, sauté onions, garlic, peppers, and carrots just until partially cooked. Add the meat back into the pot along with the remaining ingredients. Bring to a boil. Turn down to a simmer and cook for 2 hours. The liquid will reduce and the stew will thicken as it cools. Season with salt and pepper, to taste.

Tip: If you want it make it sweeter, add more brown sugar.

Butternut Farm
Mousseline of Salmon

Yield: 8–10 servings

"This recipe works nicely with several types of fish including flounder or sole, bluefish, or salmon. All go well with a shrimp sauce or the mustard sauce below."

1½ pounds salmon	**Mustard sauce:**
2 eggs	1 cup sour cream
¾ cup whipping cream	2 Tbsp prepared horseradish
salt and pepper to taste	1 tsp prepared mustard
½ tsp tarragon leaves	
4 Tbsp unsalted butter, chilled and cut into small pieces	
lemon slices or peel, as garnish	

Preheat the oven to 325°F. Butter 8–10 small timbales.

Clean the fish to remove any skin and bones. Purée in food processor. Add the eggs, cream, and seasonings; blend. With the machine running, add the butter in small pieces. Divide the fish mixture among the timbales. Cover each with a piece of buttered wax paper and set in baking pan, or mound the fish mixture slightly higher than each timbale and omit the wax paper to create a brown edging over the tops. Pour enough hot water into the pan to fill ⅓ of the way up the sides of the timbales. Bake 30–40 minutes, until a sharp knife inserted in the timbales comes out clean. Unmold immediately; they should slip out easily.

Prepare the mustard sauce by thoroughly combining all ingredients. Spoon the sauce over the unmolded timbales. Garnish with lemon slices or peel.

West Mountain Inn

Sautéed Sea Scallops in a Smoked Bacon & Maple Cream Sauce

Yield: 4–6 servings

"This can be served as an appetizer or an entrée."

12 oz. sea scallops
   salt and pepper, to taste
1 Tbsp oil
3 oz. bacon, cooked and chopped
½ cup maple syrup
¼ cup heavy cream

Heat oil in large skillet. Season the scallops with salt and pepper. Sauté in the oil, browning on both sides. Drain the oil. Add bacon and cook 1 minute. Add syrup and heat for 1 minute. Add cream and cook for an additional one minute. Serve hot.

CASA BELLA INN & RESTAURANT
Shrimp Fra Diavolo

Yield: 2 servings

15–16 jumbo shrimp (16–20 count)
   2 Tbsp olive oil
  1/3 cup chopped onion
   2 cloves garlic, chopped
      pinch of red pepper flakes
      pinch of oregano
   1 cup white wine
   2 cups tomato sauce
   2 Tbsp butter
      pinch of basil

Sauté shrimp in olive oil with onions, garlic, red pepper flakes, and oregano. When onion is translucent, deglaze with white wine. Let wine evaporate. Add tomato sauce and butter. Cook for 3–4 minutes on medium heat. Spoon on plate and sprinkle with basil. Serve with rice or mashed potatoes.

Wauwinet

Caramelized Nantucket Bay Scallops with Upland Cress, Cucumbers & Sesame Vinaigrette

Yield: 6 servings

Sesame Vinaigrette:
- ½ cup rice wine vinegar
- ¼ cup lime juice
- 2 Tbsp sesame oil
- 2 tsp orange zest, minced
- 1 Tbsp chives, chopped
- ½ tsp red pepper flakes, crushed
  dash of Tabasco
  freshly cracked black pepper, to taste

Salad:
- 3 cucumbers
- ½ lb. upland cress or watercress, washed
- 12 radishes, thinly sliced
- 2 tsp black sesame seeds, toasted

Scallops:
- 1 Tbsp extra-virgin olive oil
- 36 Nantucket bay scallops

For the vinaigrette: Combine all ingredients and let stand for 30 minutes to let flavors marry.

For the salad: Peel cucumbers, then peel cucumber flesh with a vegetable peeler to make long strips, peeling until reaching seeds. Add cucumber strips to vinaigrette; toss to coat. Put some cucumbers in the center of each plate. Arrange the upland cress in three bunches around the cucumber. Sprinkle radish slices over the cress. Garnish with sesame seeds. Drizzle vinaigrette around the plate.

Add olive oil to a very hot skillet. Add scallops and cook no more than 1 minute, tossing frequently. Arrange scallops around the salad; serve.

1785 Inn & Restaurant

Blackened Scallops with Ginger-Pineapple Salsa

Yield: 6—8 servings

Blackened seasonings and scallops:

- 1 Tbsp salt
- 1 Tbsp paprika
- ½ tsp basil
- 2 tsp white pepper
- 1½ tsp onion powder
- 1 tsp cayenne pepper
- 1 tsp black pepper
- 2 tsp thyme
- 3–4 Tbsp melted butter
- 24–36 scallops

Blend spices together until evenly mixed. Heat a cast iron skillet over a high flame for 5 minutes. Lightly touch top and bottom of scallops to the seasoning, then touch one side in the butter. Carefully place on hot skillet and sear for one minute. Flip the scallops and sear the other side for another minute. Place the scallops over the salsa.

Ginger-Pineapple Salsa:

- 3 Tbsp olive oil
- 1 chipotle, in vinegar, minced (optional)
- 1 tsp garlic, minced
- 2 tsp gingerroot, minced
- ½ tsp saffron
- ½ large red bell pepper, chopped
- ½ medium red onion, chopped
- 1 pineapple, ripe, cut into ½ -inch triangles
- 3 Tbsp lime juice
- ¼ cup pineapple juice

Mix all ingredients in a large bowl. Let sit for an hour or more before serving. This will last in the refrigerator for 3–4 days.

Inn at Crystal Lake
The Best Crab Cakes Ever

Yield: 10–12 servings

¼ lb. red onion, finely chopped
¼ lb. red pepper, finely chopped
2 oz. shallots, finely chopped
1 lb. crabmeat, shredded
2¼ cups panko breadcrumbs
1 cup mayonnaise
½ tsp salt, to taste
½ tsp pepper, to taste

Aioli:

2 cloves garlic
1 cup mayonnaise
2–3 tsp fresh lemon juice
2 Tbsp white wine
2 cloves garlic
4 tsp fresh parsley, finely chopped
salt and pepper, to taste

For the crab cakes: Mix all ingredients in a large bowl; incorporate thoroughly.

Form into small cakes. The size is up to you, but should be no more than ¾-inch thick.

Sauté in a frying pan with olive oil until each side is golden brown. Serve topped with aioli.

For the aioli: Using a food processor, chop garlic. Add all remaining ingredients and process until smooth. Store in the refrigerator until ready to use.

Rabbit Hill Inn
Shrimp, Crab & Asparagus Crêpes with Orange Sauce

Yield: 8 small crêpes

"This amazing crêpe recipe has it all!"

Crêpes:
- ½ cup flour
- 1 Tbsp sugar
- salt
- 1 cup cold milk
- 2 eggs, slightly scrambled
- 9 Tbsp butter, melted

Filling:
- 2 cups water
- 2 star anise
- ½ shallot, chopped
- 12 shrimp
- 8 asparagus spears
- 1 cup crabmeat, shredded
- 2 Tbsp tarragon, chopped
- dash of Olive oil
- 1 cup orange juice, for garnish

For the crêpes: In a bowl, combine flour, sugar, and salt. Blend with a fork. Add milk slowly, then eggs, then butter, and beat with a whisk to obtain a smooth consistency. Cook crêpes as you normally would, keeping them warm in the oven (200–225°F), until ready to fill.

For the filling: In a saucepan, combine water, anise, and shallot. Heat to a simmer. Add shrimp and half cook. Strain liquid and set shrimp aside on a separate plate to cool. Grill asparagus until tender. Set aside. In a bowl, mix shrimp, asparagus, crabmeat, and tarragon with olive oil. Open crêpes flat. Fill with shrimp mixture in the center of the crêpe. Fold sides toward middle to close. Place crêpes in slightly warm oven (200–225°F.) to heat through and stay warm until ready to serve.

Reduce 1 cup of orange juice on medium heart to a syrup-like consistency. Drizzle over crêpes and serve.

From the creative recipe files of Chef John Corliss.

Windward House B&B
Jesse's Greek Pizza

Yield: 4–6 Servings

Sauce:

1–1 ½ Tbsp extra virgin olive oil
     sea salt, to taste
     pepper, to taste
  2 cloves garlic, chopped fine
  ½ cup white wine
  1 large can Pastene kitchen-
     ready ground peeled
     tomatoes
  1 tsp basil
  1 tsp parsley

  1 tsp thyme
     fresh herbs or
     McCormack's Italian Herbs
     Grinder

Pizza:

     homemade or prepackaged pizza
        dough
     baby spinach
     marinated artichoke hearts (Goya
        or imported Italian in glass jars)

Preheat oven to 450°F. Apply a sheen of olive oil to the pizza pan.

Cover the bottom of a small saucepan/pot with the olive oil. Add salt, pepper, and garlic, and heat to medium. Once the garlic starts to sizzle, add white wine. Let the wine reduce a short while, then pour in tomatoes. Stir, adding remaining herbs. I like to use fresh herbs when I have them. If not, dried are okay, just don't use too much. Use a hand blender to make sure all the herbs and the garlic are chopped up very small. Cook about 10 minutes longer on a simmer. Cook uncovered, as you want it to be a little bit thick.

Blanch the baby spinach in hot water. Remove and pat dry. Drain the artichokes.

Roll the dough out very flat and thin. Place on pizza pan. Cover the dough with a layer of sauce. Cover with spinach and artichokes. Bake for 15–20 minutes.

Brook Farm Inn
Easy Veggie Quiche

Yield: 8 servings

3 egg whites (or whole eggs)
   bit of milk
1 (8-oz.) container cottage cheese
8 oz. cheese, cheddar or pizza blend, grated
1 (10-oz.) pkg. frozen spinach, broccoli, or other vegetables of
   your choosing
1 uncooked deep-dish pie shell

Preheat oven to 375°F.

Beat eggs, and mix with milk, cottage cheese, and grated cheese. Blend in any vegetables of your choosing. Be sure to remove as much water from all the vegetables, especially the spinach, before adding to the egg and cheese mixture. Pour mixture into pie shell. Bake for about 1 hour. Allow to settle for about 15 minutes before cutting and serving.

BIRCHWOOD INN
Tomato Basil Tart

Yield: 6 Servings

3 large tomatoes
½ tsp kosher salt, plus more to taste
¼ tsp freshly ground black pepper, plus more to taste
1 cup fresh basil

¾ cup ricotta cheese
4 large eggs, lightly beaten
2 cups Parmesan cheese, grated
1 (9-inch) prepared pie shell
nonstick cooking spray

The Day Before Serving:

Slice the tomatoes about ¼-inch thick, saving the ends and pieces as well as the slices. Place the cut tomatoes on a cookie sheet lined with a double layer of paper towels. Sprinkle the tomatoes with a pinch of salt and pepper, cover with a double-layer of paper towels. Cover the tomatoes with plastic wrap and refrigerator overnight. In a food processor, purée the basil and ricotta. Add the eggs and blend. Add the cheese, salt, pepper, and combine. Cover and refrigerate overnight.

The Day You are Serving:

Preheat oven to 400°F. Remove the pie crust from the refrigerator. Prick the crust several times with a fork. Line the bottom of the pie crust with the leftover pieces of tomato. Pour the ricotta mixture over the tomatoes. Arrange the tomato slices on top of the ricotta mixture in one, overlapping layer. Sprinkle a bit more cheese on the tomatoes. Spray the pie lightly with nonstick spray. Protect the edges of the pie with piecrust saver or aluminum foil.

Bake for 1 hour or until set and lightly browned. Remove from the oven and let sit for 5–10 minutes before slicing into individual servings. Serve hot or at room temperature.

West Mountain Inn
Asparagus & Leek Risotto

Yield: 4 servings

- 1 cup leeks, cleaned and sliced
- 1 Tbsp butter
- 1 Tbsp olive oil
- 1¼ cup Arborio rice
- ½ cup white wine
- 2 cups chicken or vegetable broth
- 1 lb. asparagus spears, cut diagonally in ½-inch pieces, blanched
- 3 Tbsp Parmesan cheese
- 2 Tbsp fresh parsley, chopped
- 2 oz. prosciutto, minced (if desired)
- salt
- pepper

In a large skillet, sauté leeks in butter and oil. Add rice and cook for 2 minutes. Add wine and simmer until all liquid is absorbed, stirring constantly. Add ¼ of the broth. Reduce heat and simmer until absorbed. Add remaining broth a little at a time, allowing it to be absorbed before adding more. Stir frequently until rice is just tender and mixture is creamy. Add asparagus and stir until heated through. Stir in Parmesan, parsley, and prosciutto, if using. Season with salt and pepper.

ONE CENTRE STREET INN B&B
Asparagus & Boursin Cheese Strata

Yield: 4–6 servings

1	lb. asparagus, tough ends snapped off, spears cut diagonally into 1-inch pieces
6	large eggs
1½	cups milk
¼	tsp ground black pepper
4	Tbsp unsalted butter
1	small onion, minced
½	tsp table salt
4	slices hearty white bread, cut into 1-inch squares
¾	cup boursin cheese, crumbled

Preheat oven to 400°F and adjust oven rack to middle position.

Toss asparagus with 2 tablespoons water in a microwave-safe bowl. Cover with plastic wrap and microwave on high power until crisp-tender, about 2 minutes. Drain.

Whisk eggs, milk, and pepper together in a large bowl. Melt butter in a large nonstick oven safe skillet over medium-high heat. When butter foams, swirl to coat skillet and add onion and salt. Cook until onion is soft, about 3 minutes. Toast the bread so that it can better absorb the egg mixture and to deepen the bread's flavor. Add bread, and cook, stirring frequently, until bread and onion are lightly browned, about 3 minutes. Be careful not to brown the onions too quickly. They will continue to brown as they cook with the bread. Remove from heat, and stir in asparagus and egg mixture until well incorporated. Scatter cheese on top and bake until top is puffed and edges have pulled away from sides of pan, 15–20 minutes.

LAKE HOUSE AT FERRY POINT
Summer Squash Frittata

Yield: 8–10 servings

olive oil for sautéing

3 cups summer squash, sliced

3 cups zucchini, sliced

2 shallots, diced

salt and pepper, to taste

thyme

$^1/_8$ lb. prosciutto, sliced very thin and diced

2 cups mozzarella cheese, shredded

8 large eggs

2½ cups whole milk

Preheat oven to 350°F. Grease a 9x13-inch glass baking dish.

Heat a large nonstick skillet over medium-high heat. Add oil to pan; swirl to coat. Add squash, zucchini, shallots, salt, pepper, and thyme; sauté for 5 minutes or until squash and zucchini are tender, stirring frequently. You may need to sauté the ingredients in smaller batches. Pour cooked vegetables into glass baking dish and spread evenly. Scatter diced prosciutto evenly over squash. Sprinkle shredded mozzarella evenly over squash and prosciutto. In a separate bowl, combine eggs and milk and beat with a whisk until well mixed. Pour the egg mixture over the cheese layer. Bake for 45 minutes or until filling is set. Cool a few minutes before serving.

Tip: substitute egg white for up to half of the eggs. Bacon can be substituted for the prosciutto.

INN AT ORMSBY HILL

Herb Cherry Tomato Strata

Yield: 6–8 servings

6	eggs		freshly ground pepper, to taste
2	cups whole milk	1	loaf challah bread (peel off
1	cup heavy cream		outer crust if it is tough), cut
½	cup Parmesan cheese, freshly		into 1-inch cubes
	grated	1	tsp dried herbs de Provence
1	Tbsp fresh thyme, minced	2	cups cherry tomatoes, cut
1	Tbsp fresh parsley, minced		in half
1	small bunch of chives, minced	8	oz. fresh mozzarella, diced
1	tsp salt		

Preheat oven to 350°F. Butter or grease a 9x13-inch glass baking dish.

In a large bowl, whisk together the eggs, milk, cream, Parmesan cheese, thyme, parsley, chives, salt, and pepper. Arrange bread cubes in the baking dish and sprinkle with the herbs de Provence. Pour the egg mixture evenly over the bread. Press down the bread cubes with a spatula to submerge in the liquid. Distribute half the cherry tomatoes over the bread, and top with the diced mozzarella. Sprinkle the other half of the tomatoes over the top. Let the strata sit for 30 minutes before baking, or cover and refrigerate overnight. Take the strata out of the refrigerator one hour before baking.

Bake uncovered for one hour, until puffed and golden. Let sit for 10 minutes before serving.

Herbs de Provence is a mixture of dried herbs from the region of Provence, France. The mixture typically contains savory, fennel, basil, thyme, and lavender leaves. The mixtures started formulating in the 1970s by spice wholesalers and are commonly sold in larger bags than other herbs.

INN AT ORMSBY HILL
Polenta Soufflé

Yield: 6 servings

1 lb. Swiss or rainbow chard, washed with tough stems removed	¾ cups polenta (corn grits)
	1 bunch of chives, minced
	2 tsp fresh thyme leaves, minced
2 Tbsp olive oil	salt and freshly ground
1 Vidalia onion, medium diced	pepper, to taste
¼ cup chicken broth or water	½ cup Cabot cheddar cheese
2 cups whole milk	3 large eggs, separated
½ cup heavy cream	½ cup Parmesan cheese, grated

Preheat oven to 350°F. Butter or oil a 9x13-inch baking dish. Stack and roll up 5 or 6 chard leaves like a cigar. Slice across the rolls into thin ribbons. After slicing all the greens, heat a large frying pan on medium-high heat and add the olive oil. Add the onion and the chard and cook until the greens are wilted. Add the chicken broth or water, cover and reduce heat to low. Cook, stirring occasionally, until greens are tender and the liquid is absorbed, about 20 minutes. Put greens in a colander to drain any remaining liquid. Transfer to a large bowl.

While chard is cooking, bring milk and cream to a simmer in a heavy saucepan. Add polenta, whisking to prevent lumps. Add the chives, thyme, salt, and pepper. Cover and cook over low heat, stirring frequently, until the polenta is tender and the liquid is absorbed, about 20 minutes. If the polenta gets too thick before it is tender, add more milk and reduce the heat. Remove from heat and stir in the cheddar cheese. Add to the bowl of greens and stir to combine.

In a small bowl, lightly beat the egg yolks and stir into the polenta mixture. Put egg whites into a large bowl and beat with an electric mixer until stiff peaks form. Use a spatula to carefully fold the egg whites into the warm polenta mixture. Pour into the prepared pan. Sprinkle with Parmesan cheese. Bake for abut 40 minutes, or until top is golden brown. Serve hot.

Desserts & Fruit Specialties

"You'll never convince me
there's more to life
than chocolate chip cookies."

— Charles Schulz

Snoopy

Recipes in this Section:

Recipes in the Signature Recipes Section:

Scranton Seahorse Inn
Molasses Sugar Cookies
Yield: about 42 cookies

"We try to keep the cookie jar in the coffee bar stocked. There are a lot of midnight cookie monsters out there so this is a difficult task at times! We had a group of guests from Germany recently that begged me for my molasses cookie recipe. I wish I could say it was mine! This was passed on to me from my friend Liza who in turn got it from Jillifer's Emporium, Great Barrington, MA. Enjoy!"

1	lb. butter
¾	cup dark molasses
¼	cup water
½	Tbsp salt
3	cups brown sugar
3	large eggs
6½	cups unsifted flour
1	Tbsp baking soda
1	Tbsp cinnamon
2	tsp ground cloves
2¼	tsp ground ginger
	granulated sugar

In a large bowl, cream butter, molasses, water, salt, and brown sugar together. Beat in the eggs. In a separate bowl, sift dry ingredients together, then add to creamed mixture. Mix well. Refrigerate for 24 hours.

Preheat oven to 350°F. Roll dough into 1-inch balls, then roll in granulated sugar. Bake for 15–18 minutes. Adjust time for convection ovens.

Windward House B&B

Vegan Sugar Cookies

Yield: about 2 dozen small cookies

2¾ cups all-purpose flour
1 tsp baking soda
½ tsp baking powder
1 cup vegan butter, softened (Earth Balance)
1½ cups organic (vegan) sugar, plus ¼ cup to roll the dough in before cooking
1 banana
1 tsp vanilla extract

Preheat oven to 375°degrees F. In a small bowl, stir together flour, baking soda, and baking powder. Set aside. In a large bowl, cream together the vegan butter and organic sugar until smooth. Beat in banana and vanilla. Gradually blend in the dry ingredients. Roll rounded teaspoonfuls of dough into balls, roll in sugar, and place onto ungreased cookie sheets.

Bake 12 minutes in the preheated oven, or until golden. Let stand on cookie sheet two minutes before removing to cool on wire racks.

Distinctions are sometimes made between different categories of veganism. Dietary vegans (or strict vegetarians) refrain from consuming animal products, not only meat and fish but, in contrast to ovo-lacto vegetarians, also eggs, dairy products and other animal-derived substances. The term ethical vegan is often applied to those who not only follow a vegan diet, but extend the vegan philosophy into other areas of their lives, and oppose the use of animals or animal products for any purpose. Another term used is environmental veganism, which refers to the rejection of animal products on the premise that the harvesting or industrial farming of animals is environmentally damaging and unsustainable. Taken from Wikipedia

BREWSTER BY THE SEA
Coconut Chocolate Chip Cookies

Yield: 36 cookies

*"A new rendition of the traditional chocolate chip cookie.
These never last long in the cookie jar!"*

1½	cups crushed graham crackers
½	cup all-purpose flour
2	tsp baking powder
1	stick butter, softened
1	(14-oz.) can sweetened condensed milk
1⅓	cups shredded coconut
1½	cups chocolate chips
1	cup walnuts, chopped

Preheat oven to 375°F. Lightly grease a cookie sheet.

In a medium bowl, combine graham crackers, flour, and baking powder. In a large bowl, beat butter and sweetened condensed milk with a mixer until smooth; add to flour mixture, and mix well. Stir in coconut, chocolate chips, and walnuts. Drop dough by rounded teaspoonfuls onto cookie sheet. Bake cookies for 9–10 minutes, until lightly browned.

Inn at Cape Cod
Choc-chip Peanut Butter Pretzel Cookies

Yield: about 3 dozen cookies

2½	cups all-purpose flour
1	tsp baking soda
1	tsp salt
2	sticks unsalted butter, softened
1¾	cups sugar
2	eggs
1	tsp pure vanilla extract
4	Tbsp peanut butter
1	cup peanut butter/chocolate chips
1	cup pretzels, roughly crushed

In a large bowl, whisk together flour, baking soda, and salt. In a separate bowl, cream butter and sugar together, then add eggs one at a time. Add vanilla extract and peanut butter; mix again until smooth.

Stir flour mixture into butter mixture; beat gently. Stir in chips and pretzels, and mix by hand. Chill overnight if possible.

Preheat oven to 350°F. Use melon scoop to place dough on cookie trays lined with parchment paper. Bake for 9–11 minutes until cookies are golden brown at edges and raised in center, reversing trays halfway through baking time.

Cool for a few minutes, then transfer to wire racks to cool completely.

Inn at Crystal Lake
Tim's Double Chocolate Chip Cookies

Yield: 50–55 cookies

"Add raisins or dried cranberries for a truly 'loaded' cookie."

2½ cups old-fashioned rolled oats
2 sticks butter, softened
1 cup white sugar
1 cup packed brown sugar
2 eggs
1 tsp vanilla extract
2 cups all-purpose flour
½ tsp salt
1 tsp baking powder
1 tsp baking soda
1 (4-oz.) Hershey bar, melted
12 oz. semi-sweet chocolate chips
1½ cups walnuts, chopped
1½ cups raisins or dried cranberries (optional)

Preheat oven to 350°F. Blend oats in a blender or food processor to a fine powder. In a large bowl, cream together butter, white sugar, and brown sugar. Mix in eggs and vanilla. In a medium bowl, combine oats, flour, salt, baking powder, and baking soda; add to butter mixture and mix well. Add melted Hershey bar and mix until well combined. Stir in chocolate chips, nuts, and raisins or dried cranberries, if desired. Roll dough into balls and place 2 inches apart on a cookie sheet. Bake for 10 minutes.

LAKE HOUSE AT FERRY POINT
Cranberry, White Chocolate & Pecan Cookies

Yield: about 3 dozen cookies

*"These cookies are among the favorite cookie recipes at the
Lake House at Ferry Point. I make them frequently.
Guests rave about them, and so do the kids."*

1²/₃ cups all-purpose flour
1 tsp cinnamon
1 tsp baking powder
¼ tsp baking soda
¼ tsp salt
1 cup butter, slightly softened
(or use ½ C butter and ½ C margarine for softer cookies)

1 cup packed brown sugar
1 Tbsp orange marmalade
1 egg
2½ tsp vanilla extract
1½ cups pecans, chopped
2 cups dried cranberries
1¹/₃ cups white chocolate morsels

Preheat oven to 350°F. Cover a cookie sheet with parchment paper. In a large bowl, stir together thoroughly the flour, cinnamon, baking powder, baking soda, and salt.

With a mixer, beat butter on medium until soft and fluffy. Add brown sugar and marmalade and beat until well mixed. Add the egg and vanilla; beat again until very fluffy. Slowly beat in the flour mix until evenly blended. Stir in the pecans, cranberries, and white chocolate until evenly spread. Drop dough onto cookie sheet. Bake 8–10 minutes, turning the cookie sheet halfway through for even browning.

Allow cookies to cool a couple of minutes before transferring to wire racks to cool.

Variations: Try with dried blueberries or dried cherries, walnuts or almonds.

STRONG HOUSE INN
Coconut Melt-Away Cookies

Yield: 36 cookies

"Melt-away cookies are very elegant and they WILL melt in your mouth! If you want to make the cookies without the coconut, use almond extract instead of coconut. These cookies freeze well."

1	cup butter, room temperature
1/3	cup confectioners' sugar
3/4	cup cornstarch
1	cup flour
1/8	tsp salt

Frosting:

2	Tbsp butter, melted
1	cup confectioners' sugar
1	tsp coconut extract
2	tsp half & half
1–2	drops of red food coloring to make a soft pink icing

sweetened coconut for topping

In a mixing bowl, combine butter, sugar, cornstarch, flour, and salt. Form dough into 1-inch balls. Lightly dust your hands with flour to make the dough easier to form. Indent the cookie with a thumbprint in the center to make a nest for the frosting. Refrigerate for 1 hour.

Preheat oven to 350°F. Bake on lightly greased cookie sheet for 15–17 minutes. Let cool.

In a small bowl, mix all frosting ingredients until very creamy. Ice each cookie to fill the thumbprint and top with sweetened coconut.

INN AT ENGLISH MEADOWS
Black Bottom Cups

Yield: 12 muffins

"Cream cheese keeps these cupcakes moist and delicious for several weeks."

1½ cups all-purpose flour
1 cup sugar
¼ cup unsweetened cocoa
1 tsp baking soda
½ tsp salt
1 cup water
¹/₃ cup vegetable oil
1 Tbsp white vinegar
1 tsp vanilla

Cream Cheese Filling:
8 oz. cream cheese, room temperature
1 egg
¹/₃ cup sugar
¼ tsp salt
1 cup semisweet chocolate chips

Preheat oven to 375°F. Line mini muffin pan with cupcake papers.

In a large bowl, combine flour, sugar, cocoa, soda, and salt, and mix well. Add water, vegetable oil, vinegar and vanilla. Blend well.

For the filling: In a small bowl, blend cream cheese, egg, sugar, and salt. Fold in chocolate chips.

Fill cupcake papers about ¾-full with batter mix. Drop a heaping tablespoon of the cream cheese mixture into the center of each. Bake until golden on top, about 30 minutes.

Windward House B&B
Pecan Pie Cupcakes

Yield: 24 miniature cupcakes

1	cup chopped pecans
½	cup all-purpose flour
1	cup packed brown sugar
⅔	cup butter, melted
2	eggs

Preheat oven to 350°F. Spray a miniature muffin tin with nonstick cooking spray.

Combine all ingredients and mix well. Fill each muffin tin ¾-full. Bake for approximately 18 minutes.

Golden Slipper
Cream Cheese Cupcakes

Yield: 12 cupcakes

1	(3-oz.) pkg. cream cheese, softened
1	pkg. yellow cake mix
1¼	cups water
½	cup butter, melted
3	eggs
	Frosting of your choice

Preheat oven to 350°F.

In a large bowl, beat cream cheese until smooth. Add remaining ingredients, and beat until smooth. Fill paper-lined muffin cups with ¼ cup batter. Bake for 25 minutes or until golden brown. Remove to wire rack to cool completely, then frost.

Francis Malbone House
Butter Cake

Yield: 1 Bundt cake

2 cups sugar
2 sticks butter, softened
2 tsp rum extract or rum
4 large eggs
3 cups all-purpose flour
1 tsp baking powder
½ tsp baking soda
1 cup buttermilk or sour milk*
   powdered sugar, for garnish

Rum sauce:
¾ cup sugar
5⅓ Tbsp butter
3 Tbsp water
1–2 tsp rum extract or 2 Tbsp
   dark rum

For the cake: Preheat oven to 325°F. Generously grease and lightly flour a 12-cup Bundt pan.

In a bowl, cream together sugar and butter. Add rum extract and eggs; mix well. Add remaining ingredients, except powdered sugar. Beat with a mixer on low speed until moistened, then beat on medium speed for 3 minutes. Pour batter into pan. Bake for 55–70 minutes, or until a toothpick inserted in center comes out clean.

With a long-tined fork or a long toothpick, pierce cake 10–12 times. Slowly pour hot rum sauce over warm cake. Let stand for 5–10 minutes, or until sauce is absorbed. Invert cake onto a serving plate. Cool for 90 minutes, or until a toothpick inserted in center comes out clean. Just before serving, sprinkle with powdered sugar.

For the sauce: Combine sauce ingredients in a saucepan over low heat. Cook, stirring occasionally, until butter is melted and combined (do not boil).

*To make 1 cup of sour milk, stir 1½ tablespoons of white vinegar into 1 cup of milk. Let stand in a warm place for 20 minutes.

Morrison House B&B
Date Cake (Gluten Free)

Yield: 8–9 servings

8–10 oz. pitted dates, chopped
1½ cups boiling water
1 tsp baking soda
½ cup butter, softened
1 cup sugar, plus ½ cup sugar for topping
2 eggs
¼ tsp salt
½ cup white rice flour
¼ cup potato starch
¾ cup sorgum flour
1 tsp xanthan gum
½ cup finely chopped nuts of your choice

Preheat oven to 325°F. Spray a 8x11-inch baking pan with cooking spray.

Pour boiling water over dates, add soda (it will foam up a bit), and set aside to cool. Leave it long enough to cool and absorb most of the water.

With a mixer, beat butter and 1 cup sugar together. Beat in eggs, one at a time. Beat in salt, white rice flour, potato starch, sorgum flour, and xanthan gun. Then, with the mixer on slow, add cooled date mix, pouring slowly so as not to splash. Pour into the prepared baking pan. Cake rises about 1 inch, so make sure pan is deep enough. Sprinkle sugar, then nuts on top. Bake for 50–60 minutes, until a toothpick comes out clean. Let cool in the pan.

MARSHALL SLOCUM INN
Lemon Sugar Cake

Yield: 10–12 slices

1   cup butter, softened
3   cups sugar
5   eggs
1   Tbsp vanilla extract
3   cups all-purpose flour
1   tsp baking soda
1/8 tsp salt
1   cup vanilla yogurt
¼   cup lemon juice

Topping:
1   cup powdered sugar
1   egg white
    strawberries, chopped, for garnish

Preheat oven to 350°F. Grease and flour a standard Bundt pan.

In a mixing bowl, cream together butter and sugar. Add eggs one at a time and blend well. Add vanilla extract, and mix well, scraping sides of the bowl. In a separate bowl, combine flour, baking soda, and salt. Add the dry mixture to the wet mixture, alternating with the yogurt and lemon juice. Pour batter into the prepared Bundt pan, and bake for 45 minutes, or until a cake tester comes out clean. Cool the cake and remove from the pan. Drizzle icing over the cake and top with strawberries.

For the topping: mix powdered sugar and egg white to form an icing.

LIBERTY HILL FARM INN
Strawberry Pie

Yield: 6–8 servings

1 pie crust, uncooked
½ cup chocolate chips
   fresh strawberries, sliced

Glaze:
   ½ cup water
   1 cup sugar
   3 Tbsp cornstarch
   1 cup strawberries, mashed

   fresh whipped cream, for garnish

Bake the pre-made pie crust. Once it comes out of the oven, spread the chocolate chips in the hot crust, and let it cool. Once it has cooled, fill with fresh sliced strawberries.

Cook together water, sugar, and cornstarch; boil until clear. Then put in mashed strawberries, cook again until clear red. Let cool until luke-warm, pour over top of uncooked berries. Let set. Serve with fresh whipped cream.

LIBERTY HILL FARM INN
Alberta's Apple Pie

Yield: 6–8 servings

1 unbaked pie shell
  apples, peeled and sliced thin to fill pie shell (I use Cortlands or a mix of apple varieties)
½ cup sugar
1 tsp cinnamon

Batter crust:
½ cup Cabot butter, melted
1 egg
1 cup flour
½ cup chopped nuts
  pinch of salt

Preheat oven to 375°F.

Fill the pie shell with peeled and sliced apples. Mix sugar and cinnamon together and sprinkle over the apples. In a mixer, beat together ingredients for batter crust and pour over top of apples. Bake for 45 minutes. Serve with ice cream and Cabot cheddar cheese!

1785 INN & RESTAURANT
Fresh Blueberry Pie

Yield: 6–8 servings per pie

Crust (yields 3 pies– you may freeze 2 portions)

- 4 cups all-purpose flour
- 2 tsp salt
- ¾ stick butter
- ½ cup water
- 1 Tbsp vinegar
- 1 large egg

Blueberry sauce (for 1 pie):

- 1 cup fresh or frozen blueberries
- 1 cup sugar
- 1 cup water, divided
- ¼ cup all-purpose flour

Filling (for 1 pie):

- 1 (8-oz) pkg. cream cheese, softened
- 3 cups fresh or frozen blueberries

  sweetened whipped cream, for garnish
  vanilla extract

For the crust: Preheat oven to 425°F. Butter a pie pan. In a large bowl, combine flour, salt, and butter. In a medium bowl, combine water, vinegar, and egg. Add egg mixture to flour mixture; combine well. Divide dough into 3 equal parts. Roll out 1 part and place in pie pan (extra dough can be frozen). Bake for 10 minutes, or until done.

For the sauce: Combine blueberries, sugar, and ¾ cup water in a saucepan over medium heat. Bring to a boil, lower heat, and simmer until blueberries burst. In a small bowl, combine flour and remaining ¼ cup of water; add to blueberry mixture. Cook, stirring, for 2–3 minutes, until sauce thickens.

For the filling and to serve: Spread a thin layer of cream cheese over bottom of crust. Sprinkle 1½ cups of blueberries over cream cheese. Top with ⅓–½ of blueberry sauce. Top with remaining 1½ cups of blueberries. Top with remaining sauce. Chill for at least 1 hour. Serve topped with a dollop of sweetened whipped cream flavored with a little vanilla.

BIRCHWOOD INN

MacArthur Park's San Francisco Mud Pie

Yield: 8 servings

Crust:
- ½ lb. chocolate chip cookies (homemade or store-bought)
- 5 Tbsp unsalted butter, softened

Filling:
- 1½ pints chocolate ice cream
- 1½ pints coffee ice cream
- 2 Tbsp espresso coffee, very black and very strong
- ¼ cup coffee liqueur

Fudge Sauce:
- 2 oz. unsweetened baking chocolate, grated
- 1 Tbsp unsalted butter
- ½ cup boiling water
- 1 cup granulated sugar
- 1/8 cup light corn syrup
- 1 tsp pure vanilla extract sweetened whipped cream for garnish

Chill a 10-inch pie plate in the freezer.

Break the cookies into coarse chunks and place the cookies in a food processor. Add the softened butter. Use the "pulse" option in 1-second bursts, checking between each burst until the cookies and butter have formed a coarse and crumbly paste (not smooth), about 10–15 seconds. Remove the pie plate from the freezer and line it with the butter-chocolate crust, using your fingers to pat it down evenly. Return the pie plate to the freezer.

Soften both ice creams at room temperature until just soft enough to handle. Spoon the ice creams into a bowl of an electric mixer. Run the mixer at slow speed, gradually increasing the speed to medium, and continue mixing until the ice creams are thoroughly mixed, creamy, and frothy. Stop the mixer and add the liquid espresso and the coffee

(continued on next page)

liqueur. Run the mixer again just long enough to completely mix in the new ingredients. Immediately spoon the filling into the ice-cold pie shell, filling the shell to the brim. Cover the pie loosely with aluminum foil and return the pie to the freezer, making sure that the pie is absolutely level. Freeze the pie long enough to freeze, not necessarily rock-hard but firm enough so that the pie can be cut in wedges without running, usually 2–3 hours.

You can use any fudge topping, but if you have time, this is the ultimate.

Set up a double boiler with the water gently bubbling and actually touching the bottom of the top saucepan. Melt the grated chocolate with the butter in the top saucepan, stirring continuously. At the same time, in a separate pan or kettle, quickly heat the water to boiling. As soon as the chocolate is melted, add the boiling water, sugar, and corn syrup, vigorously working them together.

Lift the pan out of the double boiler, quickly dry its bottom, and place it on direct heat, gently bringing the contents up to the boiling point, still stirring continuously. Let the fudge gently bubble, still stirring it fairly often, uncovered for 6 minutes, until the sugar has completely dissolved.

Take the saucepan off the heat and let the fudge cool for 5 minutes. Stir in the vanilla extract. The fudge at this point should be fairly thick but still thin enough to be spreadable with a lightly buttered rubber spatula. If it is too thick, you can thin it with a dash or two more of corn syrup. Hold the fudge, covered, in the saucepan to be reheated later.

Put the serving plates in the freezer for 10 minutes until they are ice-cold. Gently reheat the fudge in the double boiler. When the fudge is quite hot and thin enough to be spoonable, this is the time to serve your pie. Cut the pie into wedges. Place each wedge on an ice-cold plate. Spoon a generous amount of the hot fudge on top of each wedge. Garnish with whipped cream.

CRAIGNAIR INN
New York Style Cheesecake—
Craignair Style

Yield: 6–8 servings

Crust:

- 12 chocolate graham crackers
- 6 Tbsp melted butter
- 1 stick butter for greasing a 10-inch springform pan

Filling:

- 7 (8-oz.) pkgs. of cream cheese (room temperature)
- 8 oz. sour cream
- 5 eggs
- 2¼ cups white sugar
- ½ cup flour
- 1 tsp vanilla

Preheat oven to 400°F. Grind crackers in food processor until super fine. Pour into separate bowl; add about ¾ of the melted butter and mix with fingers. When mix is pinched between fingers, it should hold its integrity. If not, slowly add butter until it does.

Grease the springform pan (bottom and sides) overzealously with the stick of butter. For easier removal of slices, invert the bottom of the pan so that the lip is pointing down. Pour the cracker mixture into the pan, and sift around to make even. Then take something round (try a ¼ measuring cup with no handle) and pack the crust down fairly firmly so that it seems an even thickness all around (it should not climb the side of the pan). Place in the oven for about 11 minutes for toasting. Remove and put in refrigerator.

Get a large pot of water boiling for the water bath that is needed for baking.

In a mixer, cream the sour cream. Use a spatula to pull cheese from bottom of bowl and bring chunks to top. Cream for another 2–3 minutes (it should be fluffy).

In the separate bowls: Crack open eggs in one bowl; blend flour and sugar with whisk in another, and in a third bowl, blend the sour cream and vanilla with a spoon. While cream cheese is blending, alternately add eggs (one at a time), sour cream and vanilla mixture and then flour and sugar. Mix each addition fairly well. When all is added, mix until all are super blended (maybe another 2–3 minutes). Line the springform pan with tinfoil, double the foil for extra coverage and crimp just to the top edge making a uniform look and making sure that the cake won't attach itself to the foil while baking (trust me on this one). Now, pour the mix into the pan until it is about ⅛-inch from the top edge. Set the springform in the middle of a large hotel pan and add the boiling water until it reaches the halfway mark of the springform. Slowly place the entire thing into the oven. With a shallow pan (upside down), cover the entire thing and twist so that the corners vent a little. If you don't, the cake will "suffle" on you and scare the customers. Bake for 40 minutes. Drop temp to 320°F and bake for another 40 minutes. Turn oven off and let rest in oven for 20-25 minutes. Pull out, unwrap the foil, and let stand until it reaches room temperature. Put into refrigerator, and cool overnight.

Tip: Between each temp change, sneak a peek and jiggle the hotel pan gently. As it finishes it will more than likely crack but should be fairly firm in the center. Too much jiggle equals—not quite done. That is why the last 20 minutes may need to go a bit longer.

West Mountain Inn
Vermont Apple Crisp

Yield: 12 servings

Filling:

12	Macintosh apples, peeled and sliced
1	cup sugar
½	cup all-purpose flour
1	tsp salt
1½	tsp cinnamon
1	tsp nutmeg
2	Tbsp lemon juice

Topping:

2	cups flour
1	cup quick oats
1	cup brown sugar
1	cup butter

Preheat oven to 350°F.

In a large bowl, combine all filling ingredients and pour into a 9x13-inch cake pan. In a separate bowl, combine flour, oats, and brown sugar. Cut in butter. Sprinkle on top of filling and bake until golden brown, approximately 45 minutes.

BLUE HILL INN
Blueberry Buckle

Yield: 8 servings

½ cup white sugar
¼ cup butter
1 egg
2 cups all-purpose flour
2 tsp baking powder
½ tsp salt
½ cup milk
2 tsp vanilla (optional)
2 cups blueberries

Topping:
¼ cup white sugar
¼ cup dark brown sugar
⅓ cup all-purpose flour
½ tsp freshly ground cinnamon
¼ cup butter, softened

Preheat oven to 350°F. Grease one 8x8-inch pan or one large pie plate.

In a large bowl, cream sugar, butter, and egg. In a separate bowl, mix together flour, baking powder, and salt. Stir into sugar mixture, alternating with milk and vanilla. Fold in blueberries. Use a spatula to scrape batter into the prepared pan.

For the topping: In a small bowl, combine white and brown sugars, flour, cinnamon, and butter. Spread evenly over the batter.

Bake 25–35 minutes, until the edges are browned and a toothpick in the center comes out clean.

Combes Family Inn
Blueberry Boy Bait

Yield: 6–8 servings

"I like to tell the tale that during Revolutionary times, the woman who made this dessert would be sure to get herself a man, hence the name 'boy bait.' I was already married when I discovered this recipe."

2	cups flour
1½	cups sugar
2	tsp baking powder
1	pinch salt
²/₃	cup vegetable oil
1	cup milk
2	eggs
2–3	cups blueberries (or blackberries, raspberries, canned peaches, or fresh plums)
1	cup sugar
1	tsp cinnamon
	fresh cream or half & half

Preheat oven to 350°F. Grease and flour a 9x13-inch baking pan.

Mix together flour, sugar, baking powder, salt, vegetable oil, milk, and eggs in electric mixer for 3 minutes. Pour into prepared baking pan. Arrange fruit on top. Mix sugar and cinnamon together and sprinkle over the fruit. Bake for 50 minutes. Serve with fresh cream or half & half. Can be served warm or cold. Leftovers are great for breakfast.

INN AT ORMSBY HILL

Peach Streusel with Cinnamon Rum Whipped Cream

Yield: about 12 servings

1½ loaves challah bread (peel off outer crust if it is tough)
10 peaches, peeled and sliced
8 large eggs
3 cups half & half
⅓ cup light brown sugar
1 tsp vanilla
1 Tbsp ground cinnamon

Topping:
1 stick unsalted butter, softened

1 cup packed light brown sugar
3 Tbsp agave nectar (or dark corn syrup)
1 cup chopped pecans
1 cup old-fashioned rolled oats (not quick cooking)

Cinnamon rum whipped cream:
1 cup whipping cream
1 Tbsp spiced rum
¼ tsp ground cinnamon

Coat a 9x13-inch baking dish with butter or cooking spray. Cut the bread into 1-inch cubes. Layer in baking dish. Scatter the peaches over the bread. Combine eggs, half & half, sugar, vanilla, and cinnamon in a blender until frothy (about 10 seconds). Pour the mixture evenly over the bread.

For the topping: In a bowl, beat the butter, sugar, agave nectar or corn syrup until creamy. Fold in the pecans and oats, mixing just until combined. Spread the topping over the peaches and bread. Cover with foil and refrigerate overnight.

Preheat oven to 375°F. Bring the dish to room temperature (about an hour). Place the dish on a baking sheet to catch any drips, and cook with the foil on for 40 minutes. Remove the foil and bake for another 20 minutes. Let the streusel sit for 10 minutes before cutting.

For the whipped cream: Whip the cream, rum, and cinnamon together with a hand or stand mixer. Dollop on top of the warm streusel.

BEACH PLUM INN & RESTAURANT
Chocolate Chambord Soufflé

Yield: 6 servings

Soufflé base:
- 1 cup milk
- 2 tsp vanilla extract
- ¹/₃ cup plus 1 Tbsp all-purpose flour
- ¹/₃ cup plus 1 Tbsp sugar
- 4 egg yolks

Bring milk and vanilla just to a boil in a small saucepan; remove from heat. In a bowl, whisk together flour, sugar, and eggs. Whisking constantly, slowly stream hot milk mixture into flour mixture. Return mixture to saucepan and cook over low heat for 5 minutes, stirring constantly. Strain and chill.

Soufflé:
- butter, melted
- ½ cup sugar, plus more
- ½ cup soufflé base
- 1 Tbsp Kahlúa
- 3 Tbsp Chambord or other raspberry liqueur
- ¼ cup melted semi-sweet chocolate
- 6 Tbsp raspberry purée, divided
- 8 egg yolks
- 6 egg whites
- powdered sugar, for garnish
- whipped cream, for serving

Preheat oven to 350°F. Brush 6 (6-oz.) ramekins with melted butter, then dust with sugar. In a stainless steel bowl, whisk together soufflé base, Kahlúa, Chambord, melted chocolate, 3 tablespoons of raspberry purée, and egg yolks. Beat egg whites with a mixer on medium-high speed. As whites begin to thicken, add ½ cup of sugar and beat until soft peaks form. Gently fold egg whites into Kahlua mixture; divide among ramekins. Immediately place ramekins in a baking pan filled half-full with hot water. Bake for about 20 minutes. Dust with powdered sugar. Serve immediately, topped with whipped cream and drizzled with remaining 3 tablespoons of raspberry purée.

Brook Farm Inn

Apricot Squares

Yield: 12 squares

¾ cup butter or margarine
1 cup brown sugar
1½ cups flour
1 tsp salt
½ tsp baking soda
1½ cups quick rolled oats
1 (10-oz.) jar apricot jam

Preheat oven to 400°F. Grease and flour a 9x13-inch pan.

In a bowl, mix butter and sugar together, then mix in all other ingredients except jam. Spread half of mixture in pan. Top with jam, then sprinkle remaining mixture on top and pat lightly. Bake for 20–25 minutes.

Maine Stay Inn & Cottages
Baked Apple Walnut Blintzes

Yield: 14 crêpes, 2 per person

"The apple walnut filling can be made up to 3 days ahead. If you make the filling with a sweet apple, such as Golden Delicious, reduce sugar to ½ cup."

Crêpes:

- 1¼ cups milk
- 1 cup all-purpose flour
- 3 large eggs
- 2 Tbsp unsalted butter, melted
- ½ tsp granulated sugar
- pinch of salt
- oil for cooking crêpes in skillet
- 2 Tbsp unsalted butter for greasing pans and brushing crêpes before baking

Filling:

- 1¼-1½ lbs. (2 large) tart apples, such as Granny Smith, Jonathan, Greening, or Braeburn
- 2 Tbsp frozen apple juice concentrate or unsalted butter
- ½ cup Zante currants or raisins
- ⅓ cup granulated sugar
- ½ tsp ground cinnamon
- ¾ cup walnuts, coarsely chopped

Preheat oven to 425°F. You will need a crêpe pan or nonstick skillet, 6½ –7 inches across the bottom, and a baking dish 11x7-inch or larger.

For the crêpes: In a food processor or blender, combine milk, flour, eggs, melted butter, sugar, and salt. Process to make a smooth batter. Put a clean dishtowel on the counter beside the range. Heat the crêpe pan or skillet over moderate heat. Lightly grease the pan. Lift the pan off the heat. Pour 3 tablespoons of batter into the middle of the pan and rotate the pan clockwise until the batter covers the bottom. Fill any holes by spreading on a little extra batter with a spatula. Put the pan back on the heat. As soon as the crêpe is cooked around the edges

(continued on next page)

and just curling back from the pan, loosen the edge with a thin-bladed spatula, and turn the skillet upside down over the dishtowel so that the crêpe falls out. These crêpes are cooked on one side only. Continue making the crêpes with the remaining batter, for a total of 14, stacking one of top of the other.

For the filling: Peel, quarter, and core the apples, then dice. Heat the apple juice concentrate, or melt the butter over moderate heat in a 10-inch skillet that has a lid. Add the apples, currants or raisins, sugar, and cinnamon to the pan. Toss gently to mix. Cover and cook 3 minutes, until apples are tender but still hold their shape. Remove from the heat. Stir in the walnuts and cool for 5–10 minutes before using.

When you're ready to fill the crêpes, melt the 2 tablespoons of butter. Brush some on the bottom and sides of the baking dish. Turn over the entire stack of crêpes so that the unbrowned sides are up. Lay 4 or more crêpes out on the counter top (brown sides down.) Put a heaping tablespoon of apple walnut filling on each crêpe close to the edge nearest you. Fold the bottom of the crêpe over the filling. Fold the sides in, and then roll the crêpe up. Put seam down in the prepared baking dish. Continue with remaining crêpes and filling. Brush the filled crêpes with the remaining butter. If you wish, you may cover and refrigerate up to 3 days or freeze for up to one month.

Bake the blintzes uncovered for 20–25 minutes until browned, slightly crisp, and very hot.

PRIMROSE INN
Coconut Joys

Yield: about 36 candy pieces

*"For a less sweet candy, use half unsweetened coconut.
Also, use half semi-sweet chocolate chips for a richer flavor."*

1 (14-oz.) pkg. sweetened coconut
²/₃ cup sugar
6 Tbsp all-purpose flour
¼ tsp salt
4 egg whites
1 tsp almond extract (optional)
36 whole almonds (about)
1¹/₃ cups milk chocolate chips

Preheat oven to 325°F. Combine coconut, sugar, flour, and salt. Stir in egg whites and almond extract. Cover and chill for 20–30 minutes. Encase each almond in enough coconut mixture to form 1-inch balls. Rinse hands in cold water, if necessary, to keep coconut mixture from sticking to fingers. Put coconut balls on a parchment paper-lined baking sheet. Bake for about 20 minutes, until lightly browned. Cool completely on a wire rack.

Melt chocolate chips for 1–2 minutes in a microwave and stir until smooth. Dip tops of coconut balls in melted chocolate. Chill for about 20 minutes, until chocolate is set. Store in an airtight container with wax paper between layers.

SUNSET HILL HOUSE
Chocolate BonBons

Yield: 16 cookies

Filling:

- 2 cups powdered sugar
- 2 cups flaked coconut
- 3 Tbsp evaporated milk
- 2 Tbsp unsalted butter, melted
- 1 tsp vanilla

Coating:

- 2 Tbsp butter
- ¼ cup heavy cream
- 1 cup (8 oz.) semi-sweet chocolate chips

Line baking pan with wax paper, set aside.

In a small bowl, combine sugar, coconut, evaporated milk, melted butter, and vanilla. To make bonbons, shape ½-teaspoons of filling mixture into balls. Place on lined baking sheet and place in refrigerator until firm.

Melt butter in saucepan. Add heavy cream. Add chocolate chips, and stir continuously with rubber spatula over low heat until smooth.

Dip bonbon filling in chocolate mixture and place back on lined baking sheet. Refrigerate until firm. Store in refrigerator.

Inn on Golden Pond
Cranberry-Pecan Bark

Yield: 12–16 pieces

1 cup pecan halves
1 (20-24 oz.) pkg. white candy coating
¾ cup dried cranberries
¼ tsp nutmeg

Preheat the oven to 325°F. Line a cookie sheet with parchment paper or nonstick aluminum foil, nonstick (dull) side facing up. Spread the pecan halves in a single layer on the cookie sheet. Bake for 10–15 minutes, stirring once during toasting.

Transfer the cookie sheet to a wire rack and let the pecans cool. In microwave, melt the white candy chips. Stir in cooled nuts, cranberries, and nutmeg. Spread mixture on aluminum foil-lined cookie sheet so that it is ¼-inch thick. Refrigerate for several hours. Break into 1½-inch pieces when cool.

GOLDEN SLIPPER
Chocolate Raspberry Fondue

Yield: about 6 cups

1 (14-oz.) pkg. caramels
2 cups semi-sweet chocolate chips
1 (12-oz.) can evaporated milk
½ cup butter
½ cup seedless raspberry jam
   pound cake and assorted fruit

In a large saucepan, combine the first 5 ingredients. Cook about 15 minutes, until all is melted, stirring until smooth. Transfer to fondue pot and serve warm with cake and fruit for dipping.

The extension of the name 'fondue' to dips other than those made with cheese first appeared in the 1950s in New York. Konrad Egli, a Swiss restaurateur, introduced a beef burgundy sauce at his Chalet Suisse restaurant in 1956. Then in the mid 1960s, he invented chocolate fondue as part of a promotion for Toblerone chocolate.

Birchwood Inn
Mango Tango

Yield: 8 servings

¼	seedless watermelon	lime zest
2	mangoes, ripe but not mushy	mint sprigs, for garnish
2	limes, juiced	

Cut the watermelon into bite-sized chunks, or use a melon baller to make watermelon balls. Transfer the watermelon pieces to a medium bowl. Cut off the bottom of the mangoes so they will stand up straight. Use a sharp paring knife to remove the peel. Cut the mangoes into bite-sized pieces. Add to the watermelon. Add the lime juice to the fruit and toss. Cover and refrigerate. Remove the fruit from the refrigerator 15 minutes before serving. Sprinkle lightly with the lime zest. Add a sprig of mint and serve in a martini glass or parfait dish.

Birchwood Inn
Grilled Peaches/Nectarines

Yield: 2 servings

2	ripe but firm peaches or nectarines	sorbet
	berries	mint leaf for garnish

Preheat your barbecue or grill to medium-high. Slice the fruit in half and remove the pit. Grease a barbecue basket with cooking spray and add the fruit, pit side down. Grill the fruit for 5–8 minutes with lid closed, until the fruit is warm and there are grill marks on the top. Turn the basket over, close the barbecue lid, and cook for another minute or two. Serve filled with berries or a berry syrup and top with a tangy sorbet and a mint leaf.

BIRCHWOOD INN
Poached Pears with
Candied Orange Zest Glaze

Yield: 8 servings

*"Making candied orange peel is easy but time-consuming, and
at the end of the process, the syrup gets thrown away. What a waste!
The marriage of pears—great brain food!—and the
candied orange zest glaze is made in heaven!"*

Candied Orange Zest Glaze:
- 6 navel oranges
- 4 cups water
- 3 cups sugar
- ½ tsp salt

**Syrup (you may substitute white wine for this simple syrup recipe,
however do not eliminate the lemon juice):**
- 4 cups sugar
- 4 cups water
- ¼ cup lemon juice, freshly squeezed
- 4 Bosc pears
  mint, for garnish

Remove zest from the oranges in long wide strips using a vegetable
peeler. Be sure to remove any white pith from the zest with a paring
knife. Cut the zest into julienne strips. Fill a saucepan ¾-full with cold
water, add the zest and bring to a boil. Boil for 1 minute, then drain in
a sieve. Return the zest to the saucepan and fill ¾-full with cold water.
Bring to a boil, reduce heat, and simmer uncovered for 10 minutes.
Drain the zest. Once again, return the zest to the saucepan and fill
¾-full with cold water. Bring to a boil, reduce the heat, and simmer
uncovered for another 10 minutes. Drain the zest.

Add 4 cups of water, 3 cups of sugar, and ½ teaspoon salt to the sauce-pan. Bring to a boil, stirring until the sugar is dissolved. Add the zest and gently simmer, uncovered, stirring occasionally, until the zest is completely translucent and the syrup has thickened (about 15–20 minutes). Pour the syrup and zest into a plastic container. Cover and refrigerate until ready to use. The glaze will keep for at least two weeks in the refrigerator or a month in the freezer.

Make a simple syrup, using equal parts water and sugar. Bring to nearly a boil and simmer for 10 minutes. Add the lemon juice (this helps prevent the pears from turning brown). You can also use white wine instead of the simple syrup. Peel the pears with a vegetable peeler. Cut the pears in half, and, using a melon baller, scoop out the seeds from each half. With a slotted spoon, place the pear halves in the simple syrup, cut side up. Simmer the pears in the simple syrup or white wine until the pears are still somewhat firm but can be pierced with a tester (about 20–30 minutes, depending on how ripe the pears are).

Place each pear half on a plate. Spoon a teaspoon of the syrup and several zest strips over the pear. Add a sprig of mint at the top of the pear. The pears can be served hot, room temperature, or cold. Store the leftover glaze in the refrigerator or freezer. Try it on ice cream!

CAPTAIN FREEMAN INN

Cranberry Apricot Chutney

Yield: 12–16 servings

- 4 cups fresh whole cranberries
- 2 cups dried apricots, cut into cranberry size pieces
- 1 cup orange juice
- ¼ cup wine vinegar
- 2½ cups sugar
- 2 tsp Tabasco, or your favorite hot sauce
- ¼ tsp ground cloves
- ½ tsp ground cinnamon

Combine all ingredients in a non-reactive saucepan. Heat slowly to a simmer, stirring occasionally. Simmer for an hour, cool and store in the refrigerator for up to two weeks.

Variation: Peach and Mango Chutney—substitute peaches for cranberries and mango for apricots.

> *A chutney is a type of condiment used in South Asian and Indian cuisine that usually has some combination of spices, vegetables, and/or fruits. They can be wet or dry, and the texture may vary. The former method for making chutney involved grinding with a stone mortar and pestle. Currently, the popular way to make chutney involves the use of a food processor or blender.*

COLBY HILL INN
Dried Fruit Chutney

Yield: 12–16 servings

"An excellent accompaniment to duck."

2 Tbsp shallot, minced
   oil for sautéing
1 cup vinegar
½ cup honey
4 cups water
¼ cup lemon juice
¼ tsp crushed red pepper
1 star anise pod
½ cinnamon stick
¼ tsp ground allspice
8 oz. dried figs, diced
8 oz. dried apricots, diced
8 oz. dried cranberries
8 oz. dried cherries
   (2 lbs. total of dried fruit, any combination will work)

In a medium saucepan, sweat shallots in a small amount of oil. Add remaining ingredients, bring to boil, and then simmer for 20 minutes. Serve with spiced breast of duck or a duck confit hash with sweet potatoes and cipollini.

The cippolini onions are specific to Italian cooking and cuisine and they are represented by smaller onions, which are relished for roasting and Kabobs. The onion can vary in color but the most common one is the yellow cippolini in a flatter shape. Other cippolini onions are golden or bronzed and they have a very intense flavor, but less hotness (from RecipesWiki).

GRÜNBERG HAUS
Maple Poached Pears

Yield: 1 pear per serving

*"Who knew that something so simple could be such a hit?
Grünberg Haus inn guests are delighted to be introduced to the
idea of poached fruit. And the aroma of the warmed nutmeg
makes them irresistible."*

pears, peeled and cut into halves
Vermont maple syrup
water
French vanilla yogurt, for serving
nutmeg, for garnish

Peel and halve pears. Core. Place in pot so that pears are covered by water mixed with Vermont maple syrup. Approximately ¼ cup syrup to a pint of water. Bring to a boil then turn off heat. Cover and let poach overnight.

In the morning reheat and check with fork for tenderness. Pears should still be crisp but not hard.

Serve on a dollop of French vanilla yogurt swirled on a small plate and sprinkle with nutmeg.

(Pears should be poached cut-side up and served cut-side down.)

Rosewood Country Inn
Chilled Peach & Cantaloupe Soup

Yield: 10 servings

1   fresh ripe cantaloupe, cubed
3   ripe peaches, peeled and cut into chunks
1   tsp almond extract
¼   cup amaretto liqueur
2   tsp lemon juice
2   cups whipping cream
   sliced strawberries
   dash nutmeg

In a blender or food processor, mix small amounts of the fruits and liquids at a time. Chill. Serve in stemmed glasses with a dollop of whipped cream, sliced strawberry, and a dash of nutmeg.

An Innkeeper's Place
Breakfast Soup

Yield: 4–6 servings

1   (12-oz.) bag of frozen strawberries
2   cups whipping cream
1   cup heavy cream
¾   cup sugar
½   cup sour cream
   mint leaf or strawberry slice, for garnish

Place strawberries in a blender and let sit for about 10 minutes to thaw a bit. Add the remaining ingredients. Blend on chop (about 1 minute). Then blend on liquefy until thick and smooth. Place in the refrigerator overnight. Garnish with a mint leaf or a slice of strawberry.

GRÜNBERG HAUS
Glazed Bananas

Yield: 4 servings, generally 1 banana per serving

For every 2 to 3 bananas combine the following:

- ¼ cup brown sugar
- 1/8 tsp cinnamon
- 2 Tbsp butter
- ¼ tsp lemon juice

Mix the brown sugar and cinnamon in a saucepan large enough to accommodate the number of bananas you will be preparing. Melt the butter in a microwave. Slice the bananas into the hot sauce and stir gently until banana slices are coated. Place in scalloped bowls. Reheat 45 seconds in microwave before serving.

MAINE STAY INN & COTTAGES
Gingered Fruit Salad

Yield: 4–6 servings

- 1/3 cup sugar
- 1/3 cup water
- 1/3 cup lime juice
- whole pineapple, cut into cubes
- blueberries
- Granny Smith apples, cut into bite-sized pieces
- ¼ cup crystallized ginger, finely chopped

In a small saucepan, bring sugar, water, and lime juice to a boil. Stir until sugar is dissolved. Remove from heat and cool to room temperature. Toss fruit in lime sauce and sprinkle with chopped ginger.

SUGAR HILL INN
Cherry Brandy Sauce

Yield: 12–16 servings

"Goes great over ice cream or with pancakes."

¼ cup red wine
2 cups sugar
2 cinnamon sticks
3 whole black peppercorns
2 cups water
10 pitted cherries, cut in half

Place all ingredients into a saucepan and bring to a boil. Be careful, since the ingredients will expand and get very hot. Reduce by half, then let cool. If the sauce is too thick, add more water, bring to a boil again, then cool. Remove the cinnamon sticks and peppercorns.

AN INNKEEPER'S PLACE
Smoothie Workout Shake!

Yield: 1–2 Servings

"Enjoy on your way to the gym or as a replenishment drink afterward."

1 small banana
½ cup orange juice
1 cup plain yogurt
½ cup frozen blueberries

Add all ingredients to blender and blend until smooth.

ALPHABETICAL LISTING OF INNS

RECIPE INDEX